About Amalia

Amalia's love affair with cooking started where so many others do: in her grandmother's kitchen. Hers was in Guatemala. "I still remember the flavors I grew to love as a girl," Amalia says. "I remember the banana leaves, Guatemalan chiles, the cinnamon, loroco, chipilín, and all those native spices and flowers." As an adult, Amalia immigrated to the United States for college and had a first career in international banking. After earning an executive master's degree in international business from St. Louis University, she graduated from Le Cordon Bleu. Later she founded Amalia Latin Gourmet (AmaliaLLC. com), a business designed to help others develop a broader understanding and appreciation of Latin cultural nuances through gourmet cuisine. Since then, she has been delivering a cultural and culinary experience to many Fortune 100 and 500 companies, nonprofits, historical societies, universities and schools, and others through custom events. Worldwide traveling has further enhanced Amalia's culinary and cultural perspective. During her second career, Amalia has supported many community-driven organizations through charitable donations of her time and skills and also co-founded Women Entrepreneurs of Minnesota (wemn. org), a nonprofit organization that fosters women entrepreneurship. Amalia is a consultant, keynote speaker, teacher, and is a familiar face in the local media. She lives in the Twin Cities with her husband, Kenn (whose Danish origins add another cultural influence to Amalia's kitchen), and their son Jens.

Amalia's
Guatemalan Kitchen

*GOURMET CUISINE
WITH A CULTURAL FLAIR*

Amalia Moreno-Damgaard

ISBN 13: 978-1-59298-553-1

Library of Congress Catalog Number: 2012948666

Printed in the USA

Third Printing: 2022

26 25 24 23 22   7 6 5 4 3

Cover and interior design by James Monroe Design, LLC.
Photography by Todd Buchanan.
Guatemalan map. © Copyright 2007 by World Trade Press. All Rights Reserved.

BEAVER'S
POND
PRESS

Beaver's Pond Press, Inc.
939 Seventh St. W.
Saint Paul, MN 55102
(952) 829-8818
www.BeaversPondPress.com

To order, visit www.ItascaBooks.com
or call (800) 901-3480. Reseller discounts available.

To Jesusito, my rock and the center of my universe.

To my husband and best friend, Kenn, for his love and his support of everything I do. To my son, Jens Tulio, my pride and joy and sous-chef, who has always demonstrated much interest and skill in the kitchen. I love you both so much.

To my father, Doctor Marco Tulio Moreno Iriarte, and to my maternal grandmother, Mélida Guerra Jiménez, for their wise teachings and unconditional love.

To my beloved country, Guatemala—you have always been very near and dear to my heart.

Contents

Calle del Arco, La Antigua Guatemala

Preface

Ancient Traditions | Modern Infusions

*A*malia's Guatemalan Kitchen is my modern take on an ancient cuisine that is not well known outside Guatemala. I was inspired to write this book by a demand for it, by my passion for cooking, and by the opportunity to bring attention to a cuisine that hasn't yet won the respect it deserves. This work is my gift to my beloved country and family. I am committed to building appreciation for Guatemalan cuisine. It is a vital element of Guatemalan culture. It is an important legacy of the great Mayan civilization. The Maya are as distinct from the Aztecs of Mexico and the Incas of Peru as the Italians are from the French. So are the cuisines that have grown from these cultures.

Amalia's Guatemalan Kitchen is for Guatemalans living in the United States who want to reconnect with their home culture. It is for U.S. adoptive parents and their Guatemalan children. It is for all supporters and friends of Guatemala. It is for foodies and families. It is for anyone interested in exploring Guatemalan culture through the nation's simple, fresh, and delicious cuisine.

In Guatemala, as in many cultures, recipes have passed from generation to generation and have evolved alongside the culture. And like the cuisines of other countries, Guatemalan cuisine is undergoing a renaissance and a fusion with other cuisines. The change is propelled by a new sense of awareness, more skilled chefs, quicker access to information, and a desire to refresh the cuisine.

Amalia's Guatemalan Kitchen draws not only on my homeland's traditional cuisine, but also on my personal experiences. Growing up in and traveling through Guatemala, cooking with my grandmother and shopping for fresh ingredients at the Mayan markets, spending time at my great-grandfather's dairy farm and coffee plantation, and cooking with family and friends have all informed my cooking and eating philosophy.

My food philosophy is practical and healthy. I grew up eating lots of fresh fruits and vegetables, legumes, lean proteins, unprocessed foods, and healthy oils such as olive and canola oil. Some Guatemalan cooking uses lard, but my grandmother avoided it because she needed a special diet, so I didn't develop a taste for it. I learned at a young age that foods in their natural state, free of chemicals, are the best. I grew up as an organic-eating locavore—although back then, these terms didn't exist.

Amalia's Guatemalan Kitchen offers many suggestions for making traditional dishes in healthy ways without compromising flavor and quality. Guatemalan cooking can easily accommodate a plant-based diet with low-fat proteins, a gluten-free diet, or a vegetarian diet. Throughout this book, you will find many recipes that are already vegetarian or gluten-free, or that can be converted easily with few substitutions.

The book contains 170 of my favorite recipes. It includes not only traditional recipes, but also recipes of my own creation. My original recipes fuse Guatemalan flavors with techniques that I learned at Le Cordon Bleu and perfected through years of cooking professionally. I have adapted all the recipes to home cooking, reflecting my personal experiences and preferences. The recipes take advantage of modern kitchen conveniences. Practical cooking techniques replace rustic ones that require hours—or even days. Modern infusions add layers of flavor without compromising authenticity. Throughout the book, you will find substitution recommendations for hard-to-find ingredients. Using *Amalia's Guatemalan Kitchen,* you can make healthy, quick, and easy gourmet Guatemalan dishes. Your efforts will produce a feast for the eyes as well as the palate. Guatemalans say, *"La cocina entra por los ojos"* ("Food enters through the eyes")." If food looks good, people want to eat it.

I have worked diligently and traveled constantly—to Guatemala and around the world—to cook with friends and family and to create a book that Guatemalans and I are proud of. Thank you for your interest in my homeland and my book. I encourage you to discover Guatemala through the recipes and cultural tidbits in this book as a prelude visiting the country. *Amalia's Guatemalan Kitchen* is a fun and easy way to get a grasp of the culture while enjoying new, fresh, simple, healthy, and delicious foods.

¡Buen provecho! Happy eating!

Amalia

Cultural Snapshot of Guatemala

Country's Nickname: Chapinlandia (land of *chapines*). Guatemalans call themselves *chapines* or *chapinas*.

Motto: *El País de la Eterna Primavera* (land of the eternal spring).

Climate: Average temperatures range throughout the year from about 55°F to 72°F in Guatemala City. The climate is tropical on the coasts and temperate in the valleys. It can be chilly (and sometimes even freezing) in the highlands. Guatemala has two seasons: dry and rainy.

Location and Size: Guatemala is located in Central America. It is about the size of the U.S. state of Tennessee. It is divided into twenty-two *departmentos* (states).

Independence: September 15, 1821.

Capital: Guatemala City (the largest city in Central America). This is the fourth capital location; the first three were Tecpán, Ciudad Vieja, and Antigua. The capital was relocated so many times due to conflict and natural disasters.

Government: Constitutional democratic republic.

Population: 14.7 million in Guatemala, 3 million in Guatemala City.

Literacy: 82 percent and improving.

Languages: Spanish (official) plus twenty-two Mayan languages, Xinca, and Garifuna.

Currency: Quetzal. (The U.S. dollar is also widely accepted throughout Guatemala.) Guatemala's currency takes its name from the quetzal, Guatemala's national bird.

Religion: Predominantly (50 to 60 percent) Roman Catholic. The ancient Mayas were polytheistic (believed in many gods). Their descendants blend Mayan and Catholic beliefs and rituals. About 40 percent of Guatemalans practice Protestantism and other religions.

Ethnic Groups: Guatemala's four main ethnic groups are the Ladino or mestizo (mix of Spanish or other European with Mayan ethnicity), the Maya (twenty-two subgroups), the Xinca (Amerindian non-Maya), and the Garifuna (Afro-Caribbean). Guatemala is also home to other European (especially German), U.S., and Chinese minorities.

Buenos Aires • Desempeno • Xculculche • Yacalobispo • Corozal •

Candelaria • Concepcion • Chichanha • Orange Walk •

San Miguel • Maskalls •

San Filipe • Water Bank •

Paixban • Dos Lagunas • Hill Bank •

Carmelita • Sierra de Agua • Belize •

Recreo • Uaxactun Yaloch • El Cayo • **BELIZE**

Progreso • Paso Caballos • Tikal • Benqueviejo •

Champa • La Pava Nueva • **BELMOPAN** Dangriga •

MEXICO Flores • La Libertad Mountain Cow •

Santa Teresa • *PETEN* Rancho Grande •

Chanal • La Florida El Ceibal • Dolores • Palmar Camp •

La Independencia • Santa Marta Poptun • Monkey River •

Las Margaritas • La Union Pico De Oro • El Prado San Luis • Spring •

Comitan de Dominguez • Punta Gorda •

Zompopero • Chacalte • *Gulf of Honduras*

El Palmar San Juan •

HUEHUETENANGO *QUICHE* *ALTA VERAPAZ* Secocbol Caqui Creek • **Puerto Barrios**

Nenton • San Antonio Chicuxub Sesajal *IZABAL* La Ensenada • Cayo Piedra •

Yula San Juan • El Baldio Cahabon El Estor Morales • Cacao •

Soloma • **G U A T E M A L A**

Todos Chajul Coban Senahu Los Amates • Macuelizo •

Santos Uspantan San Cristobal Papalja **HONDURAS**

Huehuetenango Verapaz Gualan Laentrada •

San Miguel Cubulco **Salama** La Union Elparaiso •

Ixtahuacan **Santa Cruz** *ZACAPA* Santa Barbara •

SAN MARCOS **Del Quiche** *BAJA VERAPAZ* **Zacapa** San Francisco •

6 Joyabaj **El Progreso** Huite Santa Rosa • de Ojuera •

San Marcos 3 Guastatoya La Encarnacion • Gracias •

Totonicapan Comalapa *GUATEMALA* **Chiquimula**

Quezaltenango **Solola** **Chimaltenango** *CHIQUIMULA* Nueva Ocotepeque •

Tecun Uman **Antigua** 4 **GUATEMALA** **Jalapa** Laesperanza •

SOLOLA Santiago **Guatemala** *JALAPA* Esquipulas • Valladolid •

Seccion Atitlan Petapa Metapan • Concepcion •

Pacaya **Retalhuleu** **Cuilapa** Ayarza Asuncion Chalatenango •

Mazatenango 5 Santa Lucia Mita Suchitoto •

RETALHULEU Cotzumalguapa **Jutiapa** Santa Ana • Ilobasco •

Champerico • Bracitos **Escuintla** *SANTA ROSA* Ciudadarce •

Obero Taxisco *JUTIAPA* Ahuachapan • **SAN SALVADOR**

Nueva Venecia • *ESCUINTLA* Los Cerritos **EL SALVADOR**

Tecojate • San Jose Sonsonate • Zacatecoluca

Sipacate Acajutla • Usulutan •

Laliberlad • Jiquilisco •

PACIFIC OCEAN

Culture: Collectivist. Guatemalans are a "we" society, rather than an "I" society like the United States. Family and religion play central roles in daily life and in decision making. Guatemalans value elders highly for their wisdom and address them using *Don* (esteemed or distinguished man) or *Doña* (esteemed or distinguished woman) as a sign of respect. Similarly, Guatemalans call professionals by their titles of specialty, such as *Doctor*, *Licenciado* (lawyer or other business professional), *Arquitecto*, or *Ingeniero*, followed by their last name. Guatemalans kiss a lot. A quick kiss on the cheek is the common way to say hello and good-bye, good morning and good night. Guatemalans are very friendly and hospitable people. They will invite you to their home even if they have just met you. They are also very caring and kind. They hurry to help those in need without expecting anything in return.

National Bird: The quetzal is a beautiful and rare bird with a small green body, a red chest, and, in males, an unusually long tail. It inhabits the Guatemalan tropical rain forests. It is a symbol of freedom because it cannot live in captivity. It is also a key element of the Guatemalan flag and the name of the currency.

National Instrument: The marimba is a musical instrument that resembles a large xylophone with wooden keys. Usually, a group of people plays it together harmoniously. Marimba music is the traditional music of choice for very special celebrations.

National Flower and Tree: *La monja blanca* (the white nun) is an orchid that resembles a nun's habit. The ceiba is the national tree.

Amalia's Top Sites: Antigua Guatemala (a UNESCO World Heritage Site) | Mercado Central (central market, Guatemala City) | Lake Amatitlán | Panajachel and Lake Atitlán | Chichicastenango's Mayan open markets | Archaeological sites in Petén (Tikal, a UNESCO World Heritage Site), Huehuetenango (Zaculeu), and Izabal (Quiriguá) | Quetzaltenango (Xelajú) and Huehuetenango (Cuchumatanes Mountains) | Quezaltepeque (where I learned to read) | Esquipulas (Shrine of the Black Christ) | Ipala volcanic lagoon | Izabal (Puerto Barrios, Lake Izabal, and Livingston Garifuna country) | Black sand beaches on the Pacific Ocean

Country Highlights: Delicious cuisine. *Dulces típicos* (artisanal candies). World-class chocolate and coffee. Bounty of tropical fruits and vegetables. Mayan culture. Colonial and modern cities. Ancient Mayan pyramids. Awesome historical landmarks and sightseeing. Rain forests and other ecosystems. Stunning volcanoes and mountain chains. Colorful hand-woven textiles. Wrought iron and other metalwork. Leather artistry. Pottery and ceramics. Wood carvings, including religious statues.

Volcán de Agua, view from La Antigua Guatemala

Amalia's Guatemalan Kitchen

Guatemalan-isms

Anyone interested in Guatemala can gain insight into the culture by learning a few words in Spanish and some Guatemalan expressions. Colloquial and regional figures of speech reveal nuances of culture.

Guatemalans use many words and expressions that are unique to Guatemala. Some words use letters and sounds that are common in Mayan dialects, such as *ch* and *x* (sh). Others end in *-ito* or *-ita*, denoting friendliness and closeness. Here are a few examples:

Salutations

Con mucho gusto: "With much pleasure."

¿Mucho gusto?: "How do you do?"

¿Hola vos? "How you doin'?"

Que le vaya bien: "Good-bye" or "Farewell."

Social Settings

Cafecito: Term of endearment literally meaning "little coffee" that refers to spending time with a friend, relative, or sweetheart chatting over a cup of coffee.

Un minuto, por favor or *Ya voy:* Literally, "one minute, please," but can mean several minutes or longer.

Food and Dining

¡Buen provecho! "Bon appétit!" or "Happy eating!" Guatemalans use this phrase at the beginning and end of a meal.

¡Salúd! "Cheers!" or "God bless you!" or "Gesundheit!"

Comamos: "Let's eat."

Desayunemos: "Let's have breakfast."

Almorcemos: "Let's have lunch."

Cenemos: "Let's have dinner."

Mesero, la cuenta por favor: "Waiter, the check please."

Vino tinto/vino blanco: "Red wine/white wine."

Churrasco: "Barbecue."

Ron: "Rum."

Cerveza cruda de barril: "Barrel raw beer."

Cerveza morena/oscura: "Dark beer."

Cubiertos: "Silverware."

Trastos: "Dishes."

Estoy lleno(a): "I am full."

¡Qué delicia! "Delicious!"

Comida típica: "Guatemalan traditional food."

Comida casera: "Home cooking."

Tarjeta de crédito: "Credit card."

Shuco(a): "Dirty" or "Street hot dog."

Common Expressions

¡A la gran! "Wow!" or "Incredible!"

Vos: "You" in very friendly terms.

Usted: "You" in formal terms, used with elders and as a sign of respect.

¡Púchis! or *¡Púchica!* "What the heck!"

A pués: "Well?" or "Go on!"

¡Ba! ¡Vaya! "OK" or "I told you so."

Vaya pues: "OK, go on."

¡Fíjese! or *Es que fijese:* "Watch out" or an excuse for failing to do something.

¿Qué onda? "What's going on?"

¡Qué clavo! "How embarrassing!"

Coche: "Dirty" or "Pig" or "Fat."

Chilero, chilazo, echando chile: Pretty, fast, showing off.

In Amalia's kitchen with her son Jens

JOSE

ZACAPA   QUESO ESPECIAL
FRESCO   CREMA ESPECIAL

*Indoor mercado (market) in
Guatemala City*

What Is Guatemalan Cuisine?

*g*uatemala's landscape, climate, history, and culture all influence the local cuisine. Guatemala is a land where the Old World and New World mingle. Its history and culture span thousands of years. Its terrain and climate can change within minutes of travel.

The land is alive with active volcanoes and natural springs, fertile and arid areas, mountain chains, tropical rain forests, natural reserves, and major rivers and lakes. Guatemala's Atlantic and Pacific shores boast paradisiacal white- and black-sand beaches. Snow tops the highest volcanoes and mountains.

The land is alive with history and culture, too. Guatemala is the cradle of the Mayan civilization. Within this civilization are twenty-two subgroups, or tribes, each with distinctive customs, traditions, dialects, and diets. The predominant tribes today live in the highlands, but other Mayan groups once had a larger presence and left plenty of evidence behind in the form of pyramids and descendants. From the majestic north with its impressive Mayan pyramids to the tropical northeast and south, from the western and central highlands to the mystical east with its famous Shrine of the Black Christ, from ancient ruins to colonial influences, Guatemala's culture and history are colorful and exciting.

Terrain and climate determine what grows naturally from region to region. Guatemala produces wide varieties of native fruits and vegetables, chile peppers, roots and tubers, edible buds and flowers, vines and sprouts, and many wild greens that are safe to eat, such as *chatate* (a plant with thick, dark green leaves), *chipilín* (aromatic leaves

A TYPICAL GUATEMALAN DAY

DESAYUNO | Breakfast: One of the heaviest meals of the day, and the most important one.

REFACCIÓN | Midmorning Snack: A very small meal consisting of bread and coffee or other very light food.

ALMUERZO | Lunch: A well-balanced medium-size meal.

SIESTA | Midday nap: A traditional break practiced mostly by elder Guatemalans after lunch.

REFACCIÓN | Midafternoon snack: A very small meal consisting of very light food.

CENA | Dinner: A light meal often consisting of lunch leftovers, black beans, and fried plantains.

for soups and tamales), and more. A bounty of ingredients add flavor, texture, and color to Guatemala's cuisine, including native herbs and spices, seeds and pods like achiote (seeds from the achiote, or annatto, tree), and wild herbs like *zamat* (which tastes—but doesn't look—like cilantro). Guatemalan cacao seeds (cocoa beans) are deeply rooted in Mayan culture, and Guatemalan coffee is among the best in the world.

Geography combines with culture to produce a local diet. Because Guatemala is home to so many cultures and such geographic variation, its cuisine varies from region to region. It includes four main cuisines: native (Mayan), traditional (Mayan-Spanish), home cooking (Spanish-Mayan), and Garifuna (Afro-Caribbean). Guatemalan cuisine also includes a lively street food scene.

Native cuisine is rustic, ancient, and based on the customs and traditions of very early native peoples and of Mayan tribes of hunters, gatherers, and farmers. Prior to Guatemala's discovery, conquest, and colonization by the Spanish, native cuisine consisted of local staples such as corn, beans, squash, chile peppers, tomatoes, tomatillos, achiote, chocolate, seeds, wild herbs, insects, reptiles, monkeys, turtles, turkeys, deer, fish, and shellfish. Some Mayas in the highlands continue to practice the food traditions of their ancestors.

NEW WORLD?

The so-called New World wasn't really new when the Europeans arrived. It was simply new to them. The Mayas and other Native-American peoples had been living in this territory for thousands of years. Native foods of the Americas, such as corn, beans, squash, and others (staples then and now), were already cultivated. Many of these native foods came to enrich the Old World, both financially and gastronomically. Perhaps a more appropriate name for the New World would have been the Ancient Americas.

Traditional cuisine is a blend of native and Spanish cuisines, including all of Spain's ancient cultural influences (Phoenician, Greek, Carthaginian, Roman, Arab, and Jewish). Some dishes, ingredients, and techniques have traces of ancient and Old World traditions. The exchange of cultures, animals, plants, and foods that occurred during the early days of European exploration enriched and modified the local diet. New techniques and tools made food preparation easier. Pork, chicken, beef, and their by-products entered the scene. These and many other new ingredients merged with native ingredients. Traditional Spanish recipes were adapted to local tastes in Guatemala.

Home cooking is closer to Spanish cuisine with Mayan touches. Home cooking is simpler than native or traditional cuisine. Spicy sauces are served on the side. Predominant spices, herbs, and oils in home cooking are thyme, oregano, bay leaves, parsley, cilantro, achiote, chile peppers, and olive, canola, and corn oil. Traditional Mayan dishes (stews and soups) play a part in special celebrations but are not everyday food for urban Guatemalans.

The Garifuna are a group of Afro-Caribbean people descended from Arawaks, Caribs, and West Africans. The Garifuna live mainly on the Caribbean coast of Central America, in Guatemala, Belize, Honduras, and Nicaragua. A small population lives in the United States. Garifuna cuisine fuses native ingredients with Garifuna flavors and techniques to create Afro-Caribbean–influenced dishes. Popular dishes include rice and beans; *tapado*, a chowder of seafood, yuca (cassava), bananas, plantains, and coconut; spiced grilled seafood; and green banana fritters.

The street food scene is very lively in the cities and the countryside. An abundance of stands, shacks, carts, sidewalk shops, and even pickup trucks sell delicious foods. Vendors with baskets full of food swarm buses and cars when they make stops during their travels through the countryside. Hungry pedestrians and travelers can choose from a wide variety of options. The street menu includes just about all the foods Guatemala has to offer.

After the Spanish conquest and colonization, other European and non-European peoples immigrated to Guatemala. These immigrants brought their customs with them. Their foods have been "Guatemalized" and are now part of a hybrid cuisine. For example, many hot dog restaurants sell Guatemalan-style hot dogs. These hot dogs are open-faced sandwiches consisting of a sausage, herbed pickled cabbage slaw, guacamole, and ketchup atop a corn soft corn tortilla. European-style pastry houses and delicatessens sell European-Guatemalan fusion pastries and other tasty treats.

A very popular dish—and cultural experience—in Guatemala is ceviche. Ceviche in Guatemala is made of raw or cooked seafood with lime juice, tomatoes, onions, mint and/or cilantro, and condiments such as Worcestershire sauce and hot sauce. It's typically accompanied by soda crackers and paired with a local beer. A *cevichería* (ceviche restaurant) serves Guatemalan-style ceviche and seafood dishes exclusively. Many *cevicherías* are mom-and-pop restaurants that let patrons make their own ceviche right at their tables. Waiters deliver freshly prepped ingredients, and eager regulars assemble their ceviche to suit their taste.

Because Guatemalan cuisine uses a variety of chile peppers, many people expect it to be spicy. In fact, Guatemalan cuisine is not spicy, but rather very flavorful, fresh, and colorful. Some stews, soups, and sauces may have some kick, but spicy sauces are generally served on the side. This custom allows everyone to spice their food according to their taste.

Loroco Flower Buds

Chamborote Chile

Chipilín

Picamás Guatemalan Chile Sauce

Hibiscus Flower (Rosa de Jamaica)

Zambo Chile

Ancho (top), Guajillo (bottom),
and Pasilla (forefront) chiles

Crema

Chiltepe Chile

Güicoyitos (Squash)

Mashán Leaves

Achiote (seed and powder)

Amalia's Guatemalan Pantry

The key to creating great Guatemalan dishes is to start with the right ingredients. Your Guatemalan *despensa* (pantry) need not be large to create the recipes in this book. My list is long simply so I can highlight important ingredients and explain all the ingredients thoroughly.

You may have noticed that in the past few years, Latin culture has become more visible in the United States. Latinos are now the number one U.S. minority, and the Latin-American population continues to grow. Grocery stores are stocking more Latino items, and the number of Latino grocery stores in major cities has increased. You'll find that many of the items on this list are available at your local grocery store in the Latino or ethnic section, at Latino stores in your area, or online. (See Ingredient Sources listing on page 395.) For less-common items that may be challenging to find, I have listed close substitutes.

Achiote (also called achote or annatto): Achiote is the seed of the pod of the achiote or annatto tree, which is native to the tropical Americas. It is available whole, ground, or in liquid or paste form. Achiote is used for coloring, not for aroma or flavor. (In large quantities, it can taste earthy or bitter.) Its orange hue adds visual appeal to dishes. You must immerse whole achiote seeds in medium-hot oil to extract the color. You can use ground achiote as a rub or dissolve it in water and add it to soups, sauces, and rice dishes. Achiote that comes as a seasoning liquid is ready to use as is. You must dissolve achiote paste in liquid before adding it to food; a little goes a long way. The best options for Guatemalan cooking are using pure whole and ground achiote.

Capers (*alcaparras*): Spanish capers are about the size of a raisin or larger and may be packed in salt, brine, or vinegar. Capers packed in salt are a bit bitter and taste stronger than capers packed in brine or vinegar. If Spanish capers are unavailable at your store, use nonpareil capers instead. Nonpareil capers are hand-harvested small capers in vinegar. They are top-quality capers from the Mediterranean.

Chepil (*chipilín*): Chepil is a plant native to Guatemala. It produces small, delicate, aromatic, and flavorful leaves. Use them in tamales, soups, rice, and beans. Chepil is available frozen.

Chile peppers: Chile peppers add not only heat, but also much flavor and texture to stews, soups, and sauces. The following list describes several chiles in the approximate order of intensity, from hottest to mildest. Guatemalan chiles are not yet widely available in the U.S. and substituting chiles is a challenging task because of *terroir*, however, these substitutes have given me good results in my kitchen. If you have access to Guatemalan chiles, use those indeed.

- Seven Soups (*siete caldos*): This fresh chile (yellow or red) resembles a manzano chile and can be used for soups, sauces, and salsas. Substitute with manzano or rocoto.

- Cobán (*cobanero*): This chile is named after the town of Cobán in Guatemala's Alta Verapaz region. It is a small, hot pepper used both fresh and dried. The powder has a smoky flavor and is used widely with foods from fruit to soups. Substitutes are smoked piquín or árbol chile powder.

- Dog's tooth (*diente de perro*): Dog's tooth is a small red pepper resembling a dog's canine tooth. Use it fresh or dried. Substitute with piquín or árbol.

- Chocolate or green (*chocolate or verde*): This chile is long and skinny (about 3 inches long). It's used mostly for garnishing *paches* (spicy potato and pork tamales) when green, but it's also available dried. For garnish, if chocolate chile is unavailable, substitute with Serrano chile.

- Chiltepe (*chiltepín*): Chiltepe is the most widely used chile pepper in Guatemala. It is round, smaller than a pea, very spicy, and flavorful. Its color varies according to ripeness. Guatemalans commonly use the chiltepe in its fresh form for sauces and salsas. Although it is best fresh, it is also available dried and pickled at some Latin stores. If chiltepe is unavailable, substitute with fresh bird's eye chile (Thai chile).

- Chamborote: Chamborote is a fresh spicy pepper that resembles the habanero in looks, but it is larger and less spicy. It's used fresh to garnish *fiambre* (marinated vegetables, meats, cold cuts, seafood, and cheeses), but it is also pickled and used in fresh sauces. For garnish, substitute with manzano chile or cut a Fresno chile into a flower.

- Guaque: Guaque is a chile 5 inches long and about 2 inches wide, and it is used mostly dried and sometimes fresh. Its maroon hue gives great color and flavor to stews. It is one of the most popular chiles in Guatemalan cooking. Substitute with guajillo.

- Pasa: The pasa is 4 to 5 inches long and 2 to 3 inches wide. It is a very flavorful dark brown chile often used dried along with guaque in *recados* (sauces) and stews. Substitute with primarily ancho or secondarily with pasilla.

- Zambo: This reddish brown dried chile is about 2 inches long and 2-3 inches wide. Use in sauces and stews. Substitute with mulato or new Mexico chile.

- Pimiento: This mildly spicy fresh pepper (red or green) is used for chiles *rellenos*, soups, stews, and rice dishes. Substitute with poblano or Anaheim.

- Morrón: This is a multicolored fresh sweet pepper resembling a bell pepper. Substitute with any colored bell pepper.

Chocolate: Guatemalan chocolate (regular and dark) has great depth of flavor. It's meant for drinking and cooking, not for eating right out of the package. Do not substitute with cocoa. Guatemalan chocolate comes in different shapes and sizes (thin rounds, long thick tablets, and short thick tablets), depending on the brand. The chocolate is very hard and must be broken for measuring. To break the chocolate, put it in double ziplock bags, wrap it twice in a kitchen towel, and pound it with the smooth side of a metal meat mallet until the chocolate is almost powdery. Then transfer it to a measuring cup and measure the desired amount.

Coffee (*café de Guatemala*): Guatemalan coffee is among the best in the world. The finest varieties come from the highlands.

Corn flour:

- Masa is dough made from ground nixtamalized corn (see page 21.) It is used as a thickener and for tortillas, pupusas, tamales, and other dishes. Some Latin stores carry fresh masa made from scratch. Use fresh masa if you can find it in your area; it offers a world of diference in taste and texture compared to the dried, powdered form.

- Masa harina, or instant corn masa flour, is masa that has been dried and further ground into a powder.

- *Harina de salpor* is lighter than instant corn masa flour. It's used mostly for baking, but it also works great in pancakes and other recipes. Bob's Red Mill stone-ground corn flour is a good substitute.

Cornstarch (*maizena*): Cornstarch is used as a thickener for sauces, *atol*, or desserts.

Crema (Latino table cream): *Crema* is the Latino version of American sour cream although a bit runnier. *Crema* is available in *agria* (sour) and table cream (mild). I favor the mild *crema* because it is closer to Guatemalan *crema*.

Ducal juices (*jugos Ducal*): Ducal juices are canned juices from Guatemala made of common and exotic fruits. These are available at some Latino stores and online.

Flowers and buds:

- Ayote: Squash blossoms are stuffed, sautéed with *crema*, or added to soups. These are available online.

- Izote: Izote is the flower of the spiky-leaved yucca plant. Guatemalans prepare izote steamed with lime, add it to stews, make it into fritters, and use it as a stuffing. Izote is available frozen.

- Pito: Pito is a slim, 1-inch-long edible flower bud that resembles a skinny whistle or a tiny machete in its sheath. Pito is a plant native to Guatemala and Central America. The bud is bright red and encased in a bright green stem. (Both are edible.) Pito buds taste similar to green beans but are more tender. They are used in bean dishes and other dishes. Pito is available frozen.

- Loroco: This is a delicate, flavorful, and aromatic flower bud native to Guatemala and the surrounding region. It is used in tamales, stews, empanadas (baked or fried pockets made with a variety of doughs and fillings), and many other dishes. Loroco is available frozen or pickled. Fresh is always best, but for cooking, you can use frozen loroco.

- *Manzanilla: Manzanilla* is chamomile. Chamomile is used to make tea infusions, and the tea can be used to flavor desserts. *Manzanilla* is available at Latin stores in blundles or in tea packages.

Herbs and spices: Guatemalan spices have a deep flavor and aroma. You can find all of these spices at Latino stores. If you must, substitute with local spices.

- Allspice (*pimienta gorda*): Allspice is used in sauces, *recados*, moles, desserts, and drinks.

- Anise (*anís*): In Guatemala anise is used mostly in seed form in *buñuelos*, desserts, and dessert sauces and syrups, and hot drinks. Use either anise seed or substitute with star anise.

- Bay leaves (*laurel*): Bay leaves are used fresh or dried—usually whole.

- Cinnamon (*canela en raja*): Guatemalan cinnamon is also known as Ceylon cinnamon. It is softer, more aromatic, and more flavorful than the cinnamon found in most supermarkes (cassia cinnamon). *Canela en raja* has a barky texture, breaks easily, and quickly infuses deep flavor. *Canela* is available in *raja* (stick) and *molida* (ground). If it's unavailable at your store, substitute with other Latin *canela*.

- Cloves (*clavo*): Cloves are used whole or ground.

- Cumin (*comino*): Cumin is used whole or ground.

- Oregano (*orégano*): Oregano is used whole, fresh, or dried.

- Pepper (*pimienta de castilla*): This refers to black peppercorns.

- Spanish paprika (*pimentón*): Spanish paprika is sweet and smoky.

- Thyme (*tomillo*): Thyme is used whole, not ground. It may be fresh or dried.

Guaque Chile

Habanero Chile

Pacaya Palm Flowers

Tamarind

Guatemalan Beer

Chocolate Chile

Allspice (forefront), Black Pepper (upper
ft), Canela (top), Star anise (bottom right)

Pimiento Chile

Guatemalan Chocolate and
Cocoa Beans

Güisquil (Squash)

Cobán Chile

Dried Corn Husks

Hibiscus flower (*rosa de Jamaica*): You can steep dried hibiscus calyses of the hibiscus *sabdariffa* flower in hot water to make an infusion that tastes like cranberry juice. Hibiscus tea is also available as a sweetened concentrate.

Incaparina: This is a fortified nutritious drink mix used to make *atol* (a hot drink) combined with cinnamon, water, and milk. Incaparina is a common offering at public schools in Guatemala. Many people make it for breakfast. Incaparina is available at Latino stores.

Leaves (fresh and dried): Guatemalans use leaves for steaming tamales, baking meats, wrapping cheeses and other foods, as a vessel for serving foods, and more. *Hojas de elote* are fresh corn husks. *Tusas* are dried corn husks. *Hojas de plátano* are banana leaves. In Guatemala it is common practice to use *hojas de mashán* in conjuction with banana leaves when making tamales. *Hojas de mashán or maxán* are the leaves of a plant native to Guatemala called *Calathea lutea*. Dried corn husks are available in plastic bags at most grocery and Latino stores. You can collect fresh corn husks during the summer, when sweet corn is in season. Banana leaves are available frozen and sometimes fresh. No close substitutes exist for any of these leaves. In my kitchen I use a combination of aluminum foil and banana leaves as a liner. Foil accelerates the cooking process.

Legumes (*legumbres*):

- *Frijoles negros* are black beans. You can use them dried or canned.

- *Blancos* are white beans. Substitute *blancos* with dried navy beans or great northern white beans.

- *Colorados* are red beans. Substitute *colorados* with dried or canned red kidney beans.

- *Piloyes* are large round red beans native to Guatemala. They're used in *Piloyada Antigüeña*, a bean salad from Antigua containing meats, cheese, and other fresh ingredients. Substitute *piloyes* with dried or canned red kidney beans.

- *Habas* are fava beans. You can use fresh, dried, or canned fava beans for soups and atols.

- *Lentejas* are lentils. Use dried or canned lentils for soups and stews.

- *Garbanzos* are chickpeas or garbanzo beans. Use dried or canned garbanzo beans for soups and stews.

- *Frijoles Volteados Enlatados Ducal or Malher* are canned bean brands from Guatemala. Fresh beans are always best, but when you're short on time, these are the next-best thing. They're so tasty that you can eat them right out of the can. Kick up the flavor a notch by adding fried onions.

Oats (*avena*): Use oats to make *mosh*, a porridge of soaked raw oats, milk, cinnamon, salt, and sugar.

Oils (*aceites*):

- *Aceite de maíz* is corn oil.
- *Aceite de canola* is canola oil.
- *Oliva* is Spanish extra-virgin olive oil.
- *Mantequilla* is butter. Use butter sparingly in place of lard.

Olives (*aceitunas*): These are Spanish olives stuffed with pimentos.

Pacaya palm flowers or fronds: These are the edible flowers of the pacaya palm tree. The flower is bitter and a bit rubbery and crunchy. It is best when fresh. It is also available pickled in Latino stores. If you can find frozen pacaya flowers, you can make them into salad or into fritters with tomato sauce. Pacaya flowers are a key ingredient in *fiambre*, a one-dish meal of marinated vegetables, meats, cold cuts, seafood, and cheeses. The flowers must be cooked in water to remove some of the bitter taste.

Raisins and prunes (*pasas y ciruelas*): Raisins and prunes are used in desserts, tamales, and hot drinks.

Raw cane sugar (*panela* or *piloncillo*): Raw cane sugar is used for drinks, desserts, and sauces. Brown sugar is a close substitute. *Panela* is very hard and must be broken for measuring. To break it, put it in double ziplock bags, wrap it twice in a kitchen towel, and pound it with the smooth side of a metal meat mallet until the *panela* is almost powdery. Then measure the desired amount.

Rice (*arroz*) and rice flour: Use any long-grain white rice of high quality. Rice flour is used for tamales and for baking.

Rums: *Ron Botrán y Zacapa Centenario*: These are two different kinds of rum made by the same distillery in Guatemala City. *Botrán* is the name of the distillery's well-established line of rums. *Zacapa Centenario* is the distillery's newer line of rums. This newer line was introduced to commemorate the one-hundredth anniversary of the foundation of the department of Zacapa in eastern Guatemala. Both are great-quality rums. They're used in cold and hot drinks and in desserts. I use them for flaming, too. If necessary, you can substitute with Bacardi Puerto Rican rums.

Saffron (*azafrán*): Use Spanish saffron or any other good-quality saffron.

Salts: Chefs prefer kosher salt (*sal kosher*) because it's flaky, dissolves easily, has a clean taste, and contains very few additives. Sea salt (*sal de mar*) is more healthful and flavorful than other salts because it's natural and contains traces of minerals. Some recipes in this book use coarse sea salt as a garnish, rather than as a main ingredient.

Sauces and condiments (salsas and *condimentos*): Chiltepe sauces come from the chiltepe chile and are spicy and very flavorful. Guatemalan ketchup is sweeter than American ketchup. Maggi sauce is a concentrated sauce resembling soy sauce in looks and salt content—but not in flavor, and it doesn't contain soy. (It does contain wheat gluten.) Picamás is a creamy and flavorful red or green chile sauce.

Seeds (*semillas*): Poppy seeds (*chan*), pumpkin seeds (*pepitas*), and sesame seeds (*ajonjolí*) are available raw, roasted, and ground at most U.S. grocery stores.

Sugarcane unrefined alcohol (*aguardiente Venado* or *Indita*): Venado and Indita are two Guatemalan brands of a high-alcohol sugarcane brandylike spirit. Use Bacardi white rum as a substitute.

Tamarind (*tamarindo*): Tamarind is available at most Latino markets in fresh (pod) form, in frozen pulp form, or in sweetened concentrate (purée) form. It is used to make drinks and as a base for sauces.

Tortillas, corn (tortillas *de maíz*): Guatemalan fresh corn tortillas are thicker than commercially made tortillas in the United States. Substitute with good-quality packaged corn tortillas, or make your own with instant corn masa flour. See Tortillas *de Maíz* (corn tortillas, page 25.).

Vinegar (*vinagre*): Guatemalan Sharp vinegar is lightly flavored vinegar used in *fiambre*, salads, and *escabeches*. (*Escabeche* is a technique that consists of sautéing onions, garlic, fresh herbs, and spices in olive oil and finished with good quality vinegar. The term also refers to a quick, chunky pan sauce used to top fried fish or other seafood.) Substitute with champagne vinegar, white wine vinegar, or white vinegar. Red wine vinegar is also used in salads.

Wheat farina (*corazón de trigo*): *Corazón de trigo* literally means "heart of wheat." It is ground wheat germ used to make *atol*. Fortified *corazón de trigo* is a great source of thiamine (vitamin B1), riboflavin (vitamin B2), niacin (vitamin B3), folic acid, iron, and zinc. Substitute with American Cream of Wheat.

Yuca (yucca, cassava or manioc): Yuca is a delicious tuber popular in Guatemala and throughout Latin America. People add yuca to soups, eat it as a snack, and mash it and make it into patties. Yuca is a good alternative to potatoes. Because of its high starch content, it is also processed into flour and made into tapioca. Yuca can be a bit gummy, and it has a stringy core that should be removed after cooking.

Easy, Healthy Cooking Techniques and Tips

*G*uatemalan cuisine, like other cuisines, has its own distinct cooking techniques. When you use these techniques with certain key ingredients, you get the right results. Many Guatemalan cooking techniques are rustic and have been practiced since ancient times. As Guatemalan chefs refresh their cuisine and fuse it with other cuisines, they blend traditional and professional cooking techniques. Savvy cooks are realizing that a new approach can produce faster and healthier cuisine that's as delicious as ever. My professional background is in classic French cuisine, so I tend to blend that with Guatemalan cuisine. The following pages describe some of the most common blended techniques and cooking tips that I use in my kitchen.

Mise en Place

Mise en place is a French culinary expression that means, roughly, "put everything in place," or "organize all ingredients for a recipe before you start cooking." Organization is essential in any kitchen. It makes the cooking process easier, smoother, and more fun. Reading and understanding the steps of a recipe are as important as having the right ingredients and equipment.

Sazón and Tasting

In Guatemalan cooking, *sazón* refers to the proper seasoning of foods. An outstanding recipe can produce poor results without proper seasoning. Basic seasonings such as salt and freshly ground black pepper can make the difference between a bland dish and a delicious one. Tasting goes hand in hand with seasoning. You cannot possibly know how much seasoning you need without tasting.

Carryover Heat

Carryover heat is an important element of the cooking process. It refers to the fact that food retains heat and continues to cook after you remove it from the heat source. The temperature will continue to rise by about 10°F while sitting on your kitchen counter. So it's best to slightly undercook vegetables, meats, and seafood (by about 8 to 10°F). Planning for carryover heat can make the difference between a properly cooked food and an overcooked one.

Escabechar and Marinar

Escabechar is an ancient technique that came to Latin America from the Middle East through Spain. It consists of making a quick, chunky sauce (*escabeche*) in a skillet by sautéing onion, peppers, garlic, herbs, and spices in oil and finishing the sauce with vinegar. In Guatemala *escabeche* is commonly used to marinate (*marinar*) chiles, carrots, and cauliflower. *Escabeche* varies from country to country in Latin America and can contain many other vegetables. This sauce can top panfried fish or other proteins, or it can stand on its own. It is the perfect complement for fried seafood, as it provides a nice break between fatty bites.

Curtir

Curtir means "to pickle." This technique consists of either steaming or blanching vegetables al dente (until tender-crisp) and then pickling them in a spiced vinegar-based sauce. Guatemalans make *curtidos* (pickled vegetables) for various purposes: to preserve vegetables for later use, to make quick condiments and toppings, and to make salads. *Curtidos* must contain a balanced mixture of vinegar, water, spices, and seasonings.

Dry Roasting, Soaking, and Grinding

Dry roasting consists of heating a dry skillet or griddle to pan roast anything from seeds to vegetables. The purpose of dry roasting is to char, toast, or brown a food, heightening flavors in the process, without adding any fat. Corn tortillas are cooked on a dry *comal*, or clay griddle. Peppers and tomatoes are charred to blacken them or to remove the skins. Pumpkin seeds and some spices are toasted to heighten their flavors. Soaking in a hot liquid is a technique used to reconstitute dry-roasted chiles or other dried ingredients for stuffing or puréeing. Grinding dried peppers or other foods in a spice mill is a technique used to pulverize ingredients for dry rubs and sauces.

Quick Soaking

A quick way to soak chiles or tortillas in stock or water is to heat them in a microwave oven for 1 to 2 minutes, then let them stand about 10 minutes.

Searing and Oven Finishing

Searing is browning meat or vegetables in a little fat on the stovetop at high heat to heighten flavors, seal in juices, and add eye appeal. Oven finishing is transferring the seared food to the oven and cooking it to the desired temperature.

Simple Grilling

Guatemalans usually grill food on grates over charcoal. This grilling technique provides the best flavor and aroma. Before grilling, meats may be marinated with onions, orange, herbs, and a little oil to prevent sticking. *Churrasco* is the Guatemalan term for "barbecue." *Churrasco* also refers to the grilled dish, such as grilled meats, or to a barbecue party.

Marinades

Wet marinades are called adobos. A dry marinade is simply a mixture of ground garlic, onion, spices, salt, and pepper.

Grills and Griddles

Grills are called *parrillas* in Guatemala, and griddles are called *planchas*. Large *parrillas* and *planchas* are more common in restaurants than in homes.

Simmering, Puréeing, and Panfrying

This combined technique consists of simmering vegetables in some liquid first, then puréeing them, and lastly panfrying them to achieve the desired texture and flavor in stews, sauces, and soups. To produce the desired results, vegetables are often dry roasted and soaked first.

Braising

Braising meat is cooking it slowly (in the oven, on the stovetop, or in a Crock-Pot) in a covered dish in liquid that covers the meat about three-quarters of the way. Guatemalan cooks often dry marinate meats and poultry prior to braising them in a clay Dutch oven. Braising is ideal for tough cuts of meat that need slow cooking to break down connective tissue and become tender. This technique works well with turkey, too.

Oven Roasting

Oven roasting is baking at a high temperature, usually 400°F or higher. Oven roasting gives the effect of frying without adding much—or any—fat. It is a delicious and healthy way of preparing potatoes, meats, and poultry. Oven roasting is a good alternative to pan roasting pumpkin seeds and sesame seeds—just keep a close eye on them, so the seeds don't burn.

Fire Roasting and Hot Oil Dipping

These techniques char or blister vegetables for easy peeling or to enhance their flavor. Hot oil dipping consists of dipping a vegetable in very hot oil for a few seconds to loosen the skin. Fire roasting is charring the skins of vegetables, such as chiles or tomatoes, directly on the flames of a burner to enhance their flavor and to make peeling easier. Sealing the charred vegetables in a plastic bag for a few minutes eases the peeling process. Use wet paper towels (not water) to remove bits of charred skin that are hard to peel. Or just leave them on to enhance the look or flavor of the dish. Fire-roasted tomatoes and chiles make delicious sauces and stews.

Quick Blackening

Blackening is a technique used on tortillas, plantain peel, and other ingredients to add flavor and color to stews. A quick way to blacken food is by toasting it in a toaster oven on the darkest setting until the food looks medium brown (4 to 6 minutes).

Baking

Moderate baking (350 to 375°F) is useful for cooking vegetables and meats and for baking cakes. You can also use baking to finish meats that you've cooked partway on a grill or seared on the stovetop.

Broiling

Broiling is grilling food in the oven from above. Cooks often use this technique for finishing foods after they are cooked. Foods are quickly heated from above to melt cheeses or to quickly brown them.

Cooking in Natural Leaves

Cooking food in corn, banana, *mashán*, or other leaves is an ancient technique. It's similar to the French method of cooking *en papillote* (inside a pouch, usually of parchment paper). Cooks enclose foods in the leaves and wrap them up like packages, then steam the food on the stovetop or bake it in a conventional oven or an outdoor oven over charcoal.

Quick Steaming

Stovetop steaming is a fast, healthy way to cook vegetables and seafood. You can combine steaming with other cooking methods, such as broiling, to add eye appeal and flavor. Start with steaming; cook vegetables al dente and slightly undercook seafood. Then brush the food with olive oil, season it, and broil it quickly.

Poaching

Poaching is gently simmering food in a flavored liquid over low heat for a relatively short time. In Guatemalan cuisine, poaching is used mostly in making desserts such as *dulces* (sweets). These sweets are poached in spiced *panela* syrup. The poaching liquid often becomes the sauce of the dessert. Poaching with wine, herbs, and lemon is a great technique for cooking delicate fish or seafood.

Quick Panfrying

Stovetop panfrying is used to make foods that cook quickly, such as plantains and *sofrito*. (*Sofrito* is a base for many Guatemalan dishes. Basic *sofrito* is a mixture of onions and tomatoes seasoned with salt. More elaborate *sofritos* can include other ingredients, such as garlic and bell peppers.) Panfrying adds flavor and eye appeal. Guatemalan cooks often combine this technique with other techniques in making stews. Some stews are simmered or braised first and then finished by panfrying them quickly with onions and garlic to heighten their flavor.

Sautéing al Dente

Sautéing is cooking quickly over medium-high heat. Sautéing vegetables al dente enhances their flavor, texture, and eye appeal. This technique is used to create vegetable side dishes such as *escabeche* in minutes.

Crock-Pot Simmering

Crock-Pot simmering is useful in many ways. You can brown foods on the stovetop first and then braise them in a Crock-Pot. You can cook dried legumes in a Crock-Pot on the high setting without having to soak them first. This is stressless cooking; once all the ingredients are in the Crock-Pot, they cook by themselves with only minor supervision.

Resting

Resting is letting freshly grilled or roasted meats rest on your kitchen counter, slightly tented with foil, to finish cooking. This technique seals in the juices and allows the meat to reach the desired temperature. Grilled or roasted meats will be juicy and properly cooked if you allow them to rest at least 10 minutes before slicing them.

MAÍZ | CORN

CORN IN GUATEMALA

Corn is one of the earliest agricultural crops in human history. It is the common denominator in Latin cuisine. Corn is the sacred food of the Maya and is closely tied to their sacred book, *Popol Vuh*.

Corn is one of the two most important foods in Guatemala. The other is black beans. Corn and beans together form a complete protein (provide all the amino acids that humans need). And because both are high in fiber, they are very satisfying.

To a Guatemalan, there's nothing more delicious than fresh corn tortillas to accompany any meal. Guatemalan cuisine includes many recipes that use corn as the main ingredient or as a thickener for sauces and stews. Virtually every part of corn plays a role in Guatemalan cuisine: the kernels, the silk, the husks, and even the cob (for cooking fuel).

When corn is young, the kernels are tender, sweet, and milky. Fresh corn on the cob is a popular street food. Vendors either boil the corn in the husks or strip off the husks and grill the corn, then rub it with lime and salt and serve it on the green husks. Tender corn kernels can also be puréed and used for *atol de elote*, a popular hot drink commonly sold at parks, plazas, and church atriums or for sweet corn tamales steamed in the green husks.

When corn is mature, the kernels are dry, hard, and starchy (*maíz*), and Guatemalans use them for other purposes. Dry kernels can be processed to produce a variety of drinks, including *chilate* and *pinol*. *Chilate* is a hot drink made with roasted, coarsely ground *maíz* and *panela*. *Pinol* is a delicious, mild drink made with *maíz*, cacao, and cinnamon. My grandmother used to drink *pinol* in place of coffee, which irritated her stomach.

Mature kernels may also undergo a process called nixtamalization. Nixtamalization is cooking and soaking *maíz* in limewater (calcium oxide), then rinsing the *maíz*. This process softens the kernel and loosens and dissolves the hull. It makes the *maíz* easier to grind and increases its nutritional value. Nixtamalized corn is called nixtamal. Nixtamal is ground to make fresh masa. Masa can be dried and further ground into a powder to make masa harina, instant corn masa flour. This makes it more accessible and increases its shelf life. Masa is used in dough to make tortillas, tamales, *atol blanco* (a white, savory, hot drink with a variety of toppings), as a thickening agent, and in other dishes.

Tamalitos de Elote (page 43)

atemalan Kitchen

ABOUT GUATEMALAN TAMALES

*F*or Guatemalans, tamales mean home, closeness, and celebration. During preparation and eating, tamales bring families together. Tamales are a cultural ritual. In Guatemala, people traditionally make and eat them twice every week of the year. Guatemalans make fancy tamales for special occasions, such as Christmas and other religious celebrations.

Tamales are at the core of the Mayan diet. They used to be more exotic and contained only ingredients native to the land. Today they marry Mayan and Old World flavors and traditions.

All tamales are tasty, hearty packages of dough and meat or vegetables and sauce steamed in natural leaves. But Guatemalan tamales come in many varieties and differ from region to region. They may be small, medium, or large. Some are steamed in banana and *mashán* leaves and others in green or dried corn husks or *güisquil* (a type of chayote squash) leaves. The smaller and simpler tamales serve as snacks or accompaniments to a spicy stew. The larger ones serve as one-dish meals.

Tamales can include a great array of ingredients. They may be savory or sweet, mild or spicy. They can be made of corn masa dough, of rice and corn masa dough, of fresh corn dough, or of corn masa and potato dough. The dough preparation and ingredients differs from tamale to tamale. The presentation, fillings, and colors vary widely.

ON NATURAL LEAVES

Steaming food in natural leaves is an ancient Mayan technique. It was already in place when the French created a similar technique called *en papillote*. The Mayan technique developed out of necessity and to infuse flavor. The French invented their technique for convenience and flair. Both methods are effective, but parchment paper is not a good substitute for natural leaves in Guatemalan cooking. Leaves add flavor, authenticity, and visual appeal at the dining table.

Banana leaves, *mashán*, and fresh and dried corn husks have endless uses in the Guatemalan kitchen. In my kitchen, I use leaves not only for steaming tamales, but also for steaming fish and other foods and for garnishing and decorating plates. Banana leaves are my signature culinary tool because they represent my culture and keep me close to it.

Tamales colorados (red tamales) and *paches* (potato tamales) are the most common and largest tamales in Guatemala. *Tamales colorados* are Guatemala's national dish. In Guatemala City, people eat them every Saturday. They eat paches every Thursday. Tamale vendors place a red light outside their casa or *tienda* (home or neighborhood store) to signal to passersby that they have tamales for sale. Guatemalan tamales are delicate treats with a velvety texture containing a saucy and meaty core.

To serve tamales at home, Guatemalans discard the outer layer of leaves. They clip the innermost layer or fold it inside out and around the edges of the plate. A lime wedge is always the garnish. Guatemalans love to sprinkle lime juice on tamales *colorados* and *paches*—and on many other foods—right before eating them. *Pan francés* (French bread, Guatemalan style) often accompanies the tamale. A cup of hot Guatemalan chocolate is the perfect drink pairing.

This chapter contains my favorite tamale recipes and the most popular tamales in Guatemala. I chose a variety of recipes containing different ingredients to suit different tastes and dietary needs. I have simplified the steps to make home preparation easier. I've also adjusted some ingredients to make the tamales tastier and healthier. For example, I've replaced lard (a traditional ingredient) with a healthier fat in smaller amounts, and I've replaced water with chicken stock to elevate the quality and flavor. I've also added some twists in preparation and presentation.

EASY STEAMING

At home I steam tamales in an 8-quart-tall stainless steel pot that has a pasta strainer insert and a short steamer basket, which I use for the tamales. It has enough room for the amount of water needed to steam the tamales in this chapter for over 1 hour without having to add any more during the entire cooking process. If you don't own one, you might want to consider purchasing one. It is reasonable in price and a good investment since it is a multipurpose tool.

You can transform tamale recipes into casseroles by making a few simple adjustments, as I did in *Cazuela de Chuchitos* (spicy red chile–chicken tamale casserole in corn husks, page 40). Making tamales can be an easy, fun family activity. The reward is a delicious one-dish meal that everyone looks forward to eating.

TORTILLAS *DE MAÍZ*
Corn Tortillas

The corn tortilla is a staple in the Guatemalan diet. It's the perfect accompaniment to any meal—breakfast, lunch, or dinner. It is a low-fat source of fiber, complex carbohydrates, and some protein. People buy freshly made tortillas daily for all meals. In some areas of Guatemala City, women run neighborhood tortilla shacks. They make tortillas by hand while standing in front of large, hot clay griddles. In rural areas, vendors carry baskets full of fresh tortillas and sell them door to door or at plazas. In Quezaltepeque they make *memelas* (thick tortillas) and *totopostes* (thin and crispy savory tortillas). Some households also eat *pan francés*, but the tortilla is king. In Guatemala corn tortillas are made from fresh masa. To make them at home in the United States, it's more practical to use masa harina, or instant corn masa flour. There's a big difference between fresh masa and masa harina, but the latter is awfully convenient. It doesn't get any easier than this!

Makes 6 tortillas

1 cup instant corn masa flour
1 cup cold water

1. Combine the flour and water to make a very moist dough. It should not stick to your hands. If the dough feels dry, add a little more water. If it's too wet, add more flour. When you form the dough into a ball, it should hold its shape and should not crack when pressed. Keep it covered with a damp cloth, as it tends to dry quickly.

2. Divide the dough into 6 equal parts and form them into balls. Line both sides of a tortilla press with plastic wrap to prevent sticking and mess. Flatten the balls to about 1/8 inch in thickness (5 to 6 inches in diameter).

3. Put each tortilla on a preheated griddle or nonstick skillet over medium heat and cook until edges loosen (about 1 minute). Flip the tortilla with a wide, heat-resistant rubber spatula and cook for another minute. Transfer to a tortilla warmer or cloth and keep covered. Tortillas should be visibly cooked and pliable. (If they are crispy, they are overcooked and can be used for tostadas.)

Common Uses of Corn Tortillas

- Tostadas *Guatemaltecas*: These are crispy corn tortillas topped with guacamole, beans, and salsa (page 111).

- Crunchies: Cut tortillas into matchsticks or other shapes and drizzle them with canola oil and a little salt. Bake the matchsticks at 350°F until crunchy (20 to 25 minutes), tossing them with tongs from time to time. Watch closely to prevent burning. Use as garnish for Guatemalan Enchiladas (page 115), salads, and soups.

- *Mixtas y Shucos*: These are Guatemalan hot dogs (page 113).

- Guatemalan Enchiladas: These are fancy lettuce cups with spiced beef, marinated vegetables, tortilla crunchies, egg, and cheese (page 115).

- Tacos *Dorados con Guacamol Chapín*: These are Guatemalan rolled crispy tacos with guacamole (page 117).

- Tortillas *con Carne, Longaniza, Pollo, ó Huevo Duro*: These are open-faced soft corn tortilla sandwiches with *carne asada* (grilled meat, usually beef), *longaniza* (a type of sausage), chicken, or hard-boiled eggs (page 121).

- *Garnachas*: These are tasty morsels topped with chicken and spicy cabbage slaw (page 120).

EMPANADAS DE LOROCO Y REQUESÓN

Loroco Flower Buds and Ricotta Cheese–Stuffed Corn Masa Cakes

A Empanadas are very popular in Guatemala and throughout Latin America. They differ from region to region and from country to country. They can be savory or sweet and filled with proteins, vegetables, fruit, or cheese. They can be made with a variety of doughs and can be baked, fried, or cooked on a hot *comal*. Empanadas are a popular street food.

Makes 6 empanadas

Masa (Dough)
- 1 cup instant corn masa flour
- 1 cup fat-free, low-sodium chicken stock

Relleno (Filling)
- 1/2 cup thawed, chopped frozen loroco
- 1/2 cup chopped yellow onions
- 1 teaspoon canola oil
- 3/4 cup *requesón* (Latino ricotta cheese)
- Kosher salt and freshly ground black pepper

Chilito (bird's eye chile, onion, lime, and olive oil sauce, page 325)

1. Combine the flour and stock to make a very moist dough. It should not stick to your hands. If the dough feels dry, add a little more stock. If it's too wet, add more flour. When you form the dough into a ball, it should hold its shape.

2. Divide the dough into 6 equal size portions and form them into balls. Line a tortilla maker with plastic wrap on both sides. Flatten the balls to about 1/8 inch thick.

3. Sauté the loroco and onions in the oil for 2 minutes. In a bowl, combine the loroco mixture with the cheese and add salt and pepper to taste. Place about 2 tablespoons of filling in the center of each tortilla and distribute evenly in the center only. Fold the tortillas into half-moons, enclosing the filling. Seal the edges by pressing them gently with your fingers.

4. Heat a nonstick griddle or skillet over medium heat. Cook the empanadas until they're medium brown (3 to 4 minutes per side). Lower the heat if empanadas get too dark too fast. Keep empanadas warm in a tortilla warmer or wrapped in kitchen towels until you're ready to eat.

5. Serve the empanadas with *chilito* sauce.

Amalia's Note

You can also fill empanadas with other fillings. Try refried black beans (page 62), roasted pork, or cheese (quesadilla, *blanco*, or *queso fresco* combined with refried beans).

PUPUSAS CON CURTIDO

Cheese-Filled Corn Masa Cakes
with Herbed Pickled Cabbage Slaw

A *Pupusas* are originally Salvadoran, but they are very popular in and around Guatemala City. *Pupuserías* (*pupusa* vendors) may be restaurants, small shops, or simply small home operations. *Pupusas* can be made with a variety of fillings, including beans, pork rind, cheese, or a combination of these ingredients. Pork rind is by far the most popular and the tastiest—although not the healthiest. *Pupusas* freeze well and can be reheated in a toaster oven or skillet. Pickled slaw keeps in the refrigerator for weeks.

Makes 6 small *pupusas*

1 batch *Curtido* (herbed pickled cabbage slaw, page 263) or 1 batch *Curtido Crudo* (spicy lime cabbage slaw, page 263)

Masa (Dough)
1 cup instant corn masa flour
1 cup fat-free, low-sodium chicken stock

Relleno (Filling)
1 cup shredded quesadilla cheese (or cheese and refried beans)

Canola oil spray

1. Combine the flour and stock and to make a very moist dough. It should not stick to your hands. If the dough feels dry, add a little more stock. If it's too wet, add more flour. When you form the dough into a ball, it should hold its shape.

2. Divide the dough into 6 equal portions and form them into balls. Line a tortilla maker with plastic wrap on both sides. Flatten the balls to about 1/8 inch thick.

3. Place about 2 teaspoons of cheese in the center of each tortilla. Work the dough with your fingers to enclose the cheese inside a ball of dough. Carefully flatten the balls again with the tortilla maker. This time make them a little thicker (about 1/4 inch thick) to hold the cheese inside.

4. Heat a nonstick griddle or skillet on the stovetop over medium-high heat. Spray a thin coating of oil on both sides of the *pupusas*. Cook the *pupusas* until they're medium brown (3 to 4 minutes per side). Keep them warm in a tortilla warmer or wrapped in kitchen towels until you're ready to eat.

5. Serve the *pupusas* topped with the slaw of your choice.

CHILAQUILAS DE QUESO FRESCO CON SALSA DE TOMATE

Fresh Cheese–Stuffed Corn Tortilla Pockets with Tomato Sauce

Chilaquilas are a delicious and easy-to-make treat. They consist of stuffed corn tortillas dipped in egg batter and then panfried and topped with tomato sauce. You can make *chilaquilas* with leftover ingredients, roasted pork, or another tasty filling of your choice. You can also make them with *güisquil* (chayote squash) in place of tortillas. (See variation following the recipe.)

Makes 6 *chilaquilas*

Salsa *de Tomate* (Tomato Sauce)
- 1 tablespoon canola oil
- 2 cups chopped Roma tomatoes
- 1 cup chopped yellow onion
- Kosher salt and freshly ground black pepper

- 1 cup crumbled *queso fresco* (fresh Latino cheese)
- 6 corn tortillas, gently heated to make them flexible

Huevo Batido (Egg Batter)
- 2 large eggs, separated
- 1/8 teaspoon kosher salt
- 1 1/2 tablespoons all-purpose flour

Canola oil

Adorno (Garnish)
- Chopped flat-leaf parsley

1. Put the oil in a hot skillet. Add the tomatoes and onion and season them. Cook until saucy (3 to 5 minutes). Taste and adjust seasonings if necessary.

2. In a bowl, combine the *queso fresco* and 3/4 cup of the tomato sauce. Divide the mixture into 6 equal portions. Stuff each tortilla with the mixture. Fold gently in half and set aside.

3. Beat the egg whites until stiff peaks form. Add the yolks, salt, and flour. Beat 1 minute to make a soft batter.

4. Heat a skillet with about 1 tablespoon of oil.

5. Dip each stuffed tortilla in the egg batter and immediately place in the skillet. Cook the *chilaquila* until it's light brown (about 1 minute per side). Transfer the cooked *chilaquila* to a platter lined with paper towels and cover it with a cloth to keep it warm. Adjust the oil if needed as you fry each *chilaquila*.

6. Serve the *chilaquilas* topped with the remaining sauce and the garnish.

Recipe Variation

Make *chilaquilas de güisquil* (fresh cheese–stuffed chayote squash in egg batter with tomato sauce). Follow the recipe above, but use thin slices of chayote squash cooked al dente in place of corn tortillas. Cook the squash in salted hot water for 2 to 3 minutes and then pat it dry.

TAMALITOS DE QUESO
Fresh Cheese Mini-Tamales in Banana Leaves

A Traditional mini-tamales are simple for a reason. They are meant to complement a spicy *guiso* (stew) or soup. They provide a delicious break between spicy bites. They can make a quick snack, too. Try them with a dollop of fresh Guatemalan *crema* (or Latino table cream).

Makes 12 rectangular mini-tamales

Masa (Dough)

2 cups instant corn masa flour

3 cups fat-free, low-sodium chicken stock

6–7 ounces (3/4–7/8 cup) all-vegetable shortening (no trans fat)

1 cup crumbled *queso fresco* (Fresh Latino cheese)

Kosher salt (optional)

12 6x11-inch pieces banana leaves, wiped on both sides with a damp cloth

12 12x11-inch pieces aluminum foil

Relleno (Filling)

24 jarred roasted red bell pepper strips (1/2 inch wide)

1. In the bowl of a mixer with a paddle attachment, combine the flour with the stock to make soft, moist dough. Add the shortening and the cheese and fluff the dough for 3 minutes at medium speed. Taste the dough and adjust the salt if needed. (Alternatively, put the dough ingredients in a deep bowl and beat vigorously with a wooden spoon for 3 to 5 minutes.) Divide the dough into 12 equal portions.

2. For each tamale, lay 1 piece of banana leaf (matte side up) on top of 1 piece of foil. Place 1 dough portion on the banana leaf and foil. Top the dough with 2 pepper strips. Wrap the tamale and seal it tightly. Bring together the edges of the 2 longer parts of the foil and make 3 small folds beginning at the top. Then press the foil and leaves flat, from the outside in, to hold the ingredients in the center. Make 3 small folds in the unsealed foil edges, folding inward toward the tamale to seal it tightly.

3. Fill a deep pot with 2 quarts of water. Place all tamales vertically in a steamer basket and put the basket in the pot. Bring the water to a boil, cover the pot, and adjust the heat to medium-low. Steam the tamales until they're cooked (about 1 hour). When the tamales are done, the dough should hold the shape of the package and should be shiny and slightly translucent, not opaque.

Amalia's Notes

When you use chicken stock or fresh cheese in any recipe, keep in mind that they already contain salt. To prevent excess saltiness, mix all the other ingredients first (except added salt), taste, and add more salt dissolved in a little stock or water at the end if needed.

If the tamales appear a bit soft or runny at the end of the cooking time, let them sit in the pot covered (with the heat off) for at least 1 hour before serving them. This resting time will bring the temperature down, and the tamales will firm up a bit.

For lighter tamales (less calories), decrease the amount of shortening and cheese according to taste. This recipe produces very moist tamales with a velvety texture. Note that reducing the amount of shortening by a significant amount will yield drier and less delicate tamales.

Tamales freeze well. To reheat them, steam them for 20 to 30 minutes. Reheat refrigerated tamales by steaming them for 15 to 20 minutes.

TAMALITOS DE CHIPILÍN
Guatemalan *Chipilín* Tamales in Corn Husks

These tasty mini-tamales are meant for snacking. Chipilín is a plant native to Guatemala. Its leaves are small, delicate, very flavorful, and aromatic. Street vendors often sell mini-tamales to bus commuters, and they're common at fairs and other major celebrations. They are delicious and very easy to make. For a flavor twist, top with a dollop of fresh Guatemalan *crema* (or Latino table cream).

Makes 12 to 14 mini-tamales

2 cups instant corn masa flour

3 cups fat-free, low-sodium chicken stock

6–7 ounces (3/4–7/8 cup) all-vegetable shortening (no trans fat)

1 cup crumbled *queso fresco* (Fresh Latino cheese)

3 to 4 ounces thawed, chopped frozen *chipilín* leaves

Kosher salt (optional)

12 to 14 dried corn husks soaked in hot water for about 20 minutes

12 to 14 ties made from additional soaked corn husks torn by hand into strips 1/2 inch wide

1. In the bowl of a mixer with a paddle attachment, combine the flour with the stock to make soft, moist dough. Add the shortening, the cheese, and the *chipilín* leaves, and fluff the dough for 3 minutes at medium speed. Taste the dough and adjust the salt if needed. (Alternatively, put the dough ingredients in a deep bowl and beat vigorously with a wooden spoon for 3 to 5 minutes.) Divide the dough into 12 to 14 equal portions.

2. For each tamale, place one portion of dough on a corn husk. Wrap the husk to overlap the edges, so the dough is completely enclosed. Lay the tamale flat. Beginning at the pointed side, press gently with your fingers to force the masa toward the center of the husk, leaving enough space on both ends for tying. Fold the husk to bring the 2 ends together for tying, or tie the tamale at both ends.

3. Fill a deep pot with with 2 quarts of water. Place all tamales vertically in a steamer basket and put the basket in the pot. Bring the water to a boil, cover the pot, and adjust the heat to medium-low. Steam the tamales until they're cooked (about 1 hour). When the tamales are done, the dough should hold the shape of the package and should be shiny and slightly translucent, not opaque.

Amalia's Notes

When you use chicken stock or fresh cheese in any recipe, keep in mind that they already contain salt. To prevent excess saltiness, mix all the other ingredients first (except added salt), taste, and add more salt dissolved in a little stock or water at the end if needed.

If the tamales appear a bit soft or runny at the end of the cooking time, let them sit in the pot covered (with the heat off) for at least 1 hour before serving them. This resting time will bring the temperature down, and the tamales will firm up a bit.

For lighter tamales (less calories), decrease the amount of shortening and cheese according to taste. This recipe produces very moist tamales with a velvety texture. Note that reducing the amount of shortening by a significant amount will yield drier and less delicate tamales.

Chipilín is available frozen at Latino markets in the United States.

Tamales freeze well. To reheat them, steam them for 20 to 30 minutes. Reheat refrigerated tamales in the microwave for 1 to 2 minutes.

TICUCOS

Spicy Black Bean Tamales

*A*icucos are also called *tamalitos de viaje*, or traveler's tamales, because in the old days rural people packed them for their travels. Because they're so nutritious and simple, they make a perfect snack for the road. My grandmother used to bring *ticucos* when we traveled to Guatemala City by bus. She lived in a small town about 4 1/2 hours away, and I always looked forward to eating these tasty morsels, which were delicious even when they were cold. This is my version of *ticucos* with a little kick.

Makes 10 to 12 rectangular mini-tamales

Masa (Dough)

- 2 cups instant corn masa flour
- 3 cups fat-free, low-sodium chicken stock
- 6–7 ounces (3/4–7/8 cup) all-vegetable shortening (no trans fat)
- 1 cup crumbled *queso fresco* (Fresh Latino cheese)

Kosher salt (optional)

Relleno (Filling)

- 1/2 cup chopped tomatoes
- 1/2 cup chopped onions
- 1 garlic clove, minced
- 2 teaspoons canola oil
- 1 teaspoon guaque chile powder (guajillo powder)
- 1/2 teaspoon cobán chile powder, or substitute with smoked piquín or árbol chile powder
- Kosher salt and freshly ground black pepper
- 1 15-ounce can *frijoles parados* (whole beans), rinsed

- 10 to 12 6x11-inch pieces banana leaves, wiped on both sides with a damp cloth
- 10 to 12 12x11-inch pieces aluminum foil

1. In the bowl of a mixer with a paddle attachment, combine the flour with the stock to make soft, moist dough. Add the shortening and the cheese and fluff the dough for 3 minutes at medium speed. Taste the dough and adjust the salt, if needed. (Alternatively, put the ingredients in a deep bowl and beat vigorously with a wooden spoon for 3 to 5 minutes.) Divide the dough into 10 to 12 equal portions.

2. Cook the tomatoes, onions, and garlic in the oil until saucy (about 3 to 5 minutes). Season with the chile powders and the salt and pepper to taste. Mash the mixture with a potato masher to make a smoother sauce. Add the beans and cook 2 to 3 minutes longer. Taste the filling and adjust seasonings, if needed.

3. For each tamale, lay 1 piece of banana leaf (matte side up) on top of 1 piece of foil. Place 1 dough portion on the banana leaf and foil. Top the dough with 1 heaping tablespoon of filling and push it gently into the dough. Wrap the tamale and seal it tightly. Bring together the edges of the 2 longer parts of the foil and make 3 small folds beginning at the top. Then press the foil and leaves flat, from the outside in, to hold the ingredients in the center. Make 3 small folds in the unsealed foil edges, folding inward toward the tamale to seal it tightly.

4. Fill a deep pot with with 2 quarts of water. Place all tamales vertically in a steamer basket and put the basket in the pot. Bring the water to a boil, cover the pot, and adjust the heat to medium-low. Steam the tamales until they're cooked (about 1 hour). When the tamales are done, the dough should hold the shape of the package and should be shiny and slightly translucent, not opaque.

Amalia's Notes

When you use chicken stock or fresh cheese in any recipe, keep in mind that they already contain salt. To prevent excess saltiness, mix all the other ingredients first (except added salt), taste, and add more salt dissolved in a little stock or water at the end if needed.

If the tamales appear a bit soft or runny at the end of the cooking time, let them sit in the pot covered (with the heat off) for at least 1 hour before serving them. This resting time will bring the temperature down, and the tamales will firm up a bit.

For lighter tamales (less calories), decrease the amount of shortening and cheese according to taste. This recipe produces very moist tamales with a velvety texture. Note that reducing the amount of shortening by a significant amount will yield drier and less delicate tamales.

Tamales freeze well. To reheat them, steam them for 20 to 30 minutes. Reheat refrigerated tamales by steaming them for 15 to 20 minutes.

CAZUELA DE CHUCHITOS

Spicy Red Chile–Chicken Tamale Casserole in Corn Husks

*C*huchito is a slang word that means "doggie." In Guatemalan cuisine, *chuchitos* are small tamales sometimes made with pork or chicken and eaten as a snack, rather than as a meal. They're a popular street food sold on weekends at parks, plazas, and church atriums. They're topped with tomato sauce and crumbled dried cheese. This is my easy version of the original recipe as a casserole, rather than as individual tamales. If you would rather make traditional chuchitos, refer to the recipe variation notes following this recipe.

Makes one loaf pan

1 batch *Recado para Chuchitos* (tomato, red bell pepper, and guajillo sauce, page 322)

Masa (Dough)

2 cups instant corn masa flour

1 teaspoon baking powder

3 cups fat-free, low-sodium chicken stock

6–7 ounces (3/4–7/8 cup) all-vegetable shortening (no trans fat)

1 cup crumbled *queso fresco* (Fresh Latino cheese) (optional)

1 9x5-inch loaf pan

Kosher salt (optional)

Relleno (Filling)

5 boneless, skinless chicken thighs, cut into 3x2-inch pieces, seasoned with salt and pepper

12 dried corn husks soaked in hot water for about 20 minutes

Aluminum foil

Adorno (Garnish)

1/2 cup of sauce

1/2 cup finely crumbled *queso fresco o seco* (fresh or dried cheese)

1. Preheat the oven (or toaster oven) to 375°F.

2. In the bowl of a mixer with a paddle attachment, combine the flour and baking powder with the stock to make soft, moist dough. Add the shortening and the cheese and fluff the masa for 3 minutes at medium speed. Taste and adjust the salt, if needed. (Alternatively, put the ingredients in a deep bowl and beat vigorously with a wooden spoon for 3 to 5 minutes.)

3. Drain the corn husks well. Line the bottom of the loaf pan with four of the husks, overlapping the leaves in the pan and using the widest part in the bottom of the pan. Put half the dough in the pan and spread it evenly over the bottom of the pan. Add the chicken and distribute it evenly. Add 1/2 cup of the sauce, and then spread the rest of the dough evenly over the sauce. Finish with 1/2 cup of sauce and top the casserole with the remaining corn husks. Cover the pan with foil, seal it tightly around the edges, and bake until cooked, about 1 hour and 15 minutes. Save the remaining sauce as a garnish.

4. Let the casserole rest 20 to 30 minutes after taking it out of the oven. Remove and discard the foil and the top corn husks first. Turn the casserole upside down on a platter or cutting board and then remove and discard the remaining husks. Transfer the casserole to a platter or serving dish and top it with the remaining sauce and cheese.

Amalia's Note

When you use chicken stock or fresh cheese in any recipe, keep in mind that they already contain salt. To prevent excess saltiness, mix all the other ingredients first (except added salt), taste, and add more salt dissolved in a little stock or water at the end if needed.

Recipe Variation

Instead of making a casserole, you could make traditional *chuchitos*. Follow the dough recipe for *Cazuela de Chuchitos* (spicy red chile–chicken tamale casserole in corn husks above), except leave out the baking powder. Divide the masa and chicken into 12 to 14 equal portions. When assembling each tamale, push the chicken gently into the dough. Top with the sauce divided equally, and make mini-tamales following the same steps as for *Tamalitos de Chipilín* (Guatemalan *chipilín* tamales in corn husks, page 3).

If the tamales appear a bit soft or runny at the end of the cooking time, let them sit in the pot covered (with the heat off) for at least 1 hour before serving them. This resting time will bring the temperature down, and the tamales will firm up a bit.

For lighter tamales (less calories), decrease the amount of shortening and cheese (if using) according to taste. This recipe produces very moist tamales with a velvety texture. Note that reducing the amount of shortening by a significant amount will yield drier and less delicate tamales.

TAMALITOS DE ELOTE
Corn and Butter Tamales

A This recipe is inspired by my grandmother's scrumptious *tamalitos de elote* (little corn tamales), which she made with *elote sazón* for special occasions. We ate them topped with fresh cream for breakfast. *Elote sazón* is corn at the stage between fresh and mature corn with the right amount of starch needed for the texture of *tamalitos de elote*. I use frozen corn in lieu of *elote sazón*, as it is practical and easily available in the United States. Because frozen corn doesn't have as much starch as *elote sazón*, I combine it with some corn masa flour to make up for the difference. You can also make *tamalitos de elote* as a casserole.

Makes about 10 tamalitos

Masa (Dough)

3 cups frozen corn, thawed

1 1/4 cups milk

6 to 7 ounces (3/4 to 7/8 cup) unsalted butter, melted

1 cup instant corn masa flour

1/2 cup sugar

1 teaspoon kosher salt

1 teaspoon ground *canela* (Ceylon cinnamon)

Dried corn husks soaked in hot water for about 20 minutes

Adorno (Garnish)

Crema (Latino table cream) or Salsa *de Chocolate Oscuro* (Guatemalan dark chocolate, ancho, and rum sauce, page 337)

1. In a food processor, purée the corn with the milk and the butter until mostly smooth yet a little chunky.

2. In the bowl of a mixer with a paddle attachment, combine the puréed corn mixture, butter, flour, sugar, salt, and cinnamon, and mix well at low speed for 1 to 2 minutes. Fluff the masa for 3 minutes at medium speed. Taste and adjust seasonings, if needed. (Alternatively, put the ingredients in a deep bowl and beat vigorously with a wooden spoon for 3 to 5 minutes.)

3. To assemble the *tamalitos*, divide the dough into 10 equal portions. Put 1 portion in the center of each corn husk. Wrap the husk around the dough, overlapping the edges so that the dough is completely enclosed. Lay the tamale flat. Beginning at the pointed side, press gently with your fingers to force the masa up and toward one side almost to the edge of the husk. Fold the husk upward toward you with the seam within the fold. Stand the *tamalitos* upright in a bowl to keep the dough inside.

4. Fill a deep pot with with 2 quarts of water. Place all tamales vertically in a steamer basket and put the basket in the pot. Bring the water to a boil, cover the pot, and adjust the heat to medium-low. Steam the tamales until they're cooked (about 1 hour). When the tamales are done, the dough should hold the shape of the package and should be shiny and slightly translucent, not opaque.

5. Serve topped with *crema*.

Amalia's Notes

If the tamales appear a bit soft or runny at the end of the cooking time, let them sit in the pot covered (with the heat off) for at least 1 hour before serving them. This resting time will bring the temperature down, and the tamales will firm up a bit.

For lighter tamales (less calories), decrease the amount of butter according to taste. This recipe produces very moist tamales with a velvety texture. Note that reducing the amount of butter by a significant amount will yield drier and less delicate tamales.

Tamales freeze well. To reheat them, steam them for 20 to 30 minutes. Reheat refrigerated tamales in the microwave for 1 to 2 minutes.

TAMALES *COLORADOS*
Red Chicken and Pork Tamales in Banana Leaves

Avery time I visit Guatemala, I look forward to eating tamales *colorados*. My sister taste-tests tamales made throughout her neighborhood's *tiendas*, tamale houses, and grocery stores to determine which ones are the best. Within Guatemala, there are variations in taste and ingredients from maker to maker. My tamales contain more meat and garnishes than most commercially made tamales in Guatemala, as this is the way my family likes them. Tamales in Guatemala are usually wrapped in just banana and *mashán* leaves and tied with *cibaque* (a natural fiber), as leaves are abundant and foil is expensive. Tamales *Navideños*, or red and black tamales (see instructions following this recipe), are a Christmas dish. My mom used to make Tamales *Navideños* with rice flour instead of corn masa, and this gave them a more delicate texture.

Makes 8 rectangular tamales

1 batch *Recado para* Tamales *Colorados*
   (roasted ancho, guajillo, mulato, tomato,
   and pumpkin seed sauce, page 317)

Masa (Dough)

2 cups instant corn masa flour

4 cups fat-free, low-sodium chicken stock

6–7 ounces (3/4–7/8 cup) all-vegetable
   shortening (no trans fat)

Kosher salt (optional)

8 8x11-inch pieces banana leaves, wiped on
   both sides with a damp cloth

8 14x11-inch pieces aluminum foil

Relleno (Filling)

8 3x2-inch pieces pork loin, seasoned with salt
   and pepper

8 3x2-inch pieces boneless, skinless chicken
   thighs, seasoned with salt and pepper

16 jarred roasted red bell pepper strips (1/2
   inch wide)

8 Spanish olives stuffed with pimentos

Adorno (Garnish)

1 to 2 limes cut in wedges or slices

1. Make the sauce and set it aside.

2. In the bowl of a mixer with a paddle attachment, combine the flour with the stock to
   make soft, moist dough. Add the shortening
   and fluff the dough for 3 minutes at medium
   speed. Taste and adjust the salt, if needed.
   (Alternatively, put the ingredients in a deep
   bowl and beat vigorously with a wooden spoon
   for 3 to 5 minutes.)

3. Transfer the dough to a skillet and cook it on
   the stovetop at low heat, stirring constantly
   with a whisk to keep it from forming lumps and
   from sticking to the skillet until the dough is
   ready. The dough is ready when the whisk starts
   leaving tracks and the dough starts lifting from
   the edges, about 15 minutes. Let the dough
   cool slightly. Divide the dough into 8 equal
   portions.

4. For each tamale, lay 1 piece of banana leaf (matte side up) on top of 1 piece of foil. Place 1 dough portion on the banana leaf and foil. Take 1 piece each of pork and chicken, 2 pepper strips, 1 olive, and push them gently into the dough. Top with the sauce divided equally. Wrap the tamale and seal it tightly. Bring together the edges of the 2 longer parts of the foil and make 3 small folds beginning at the top. Then press the foil and leaves flat, from the outside in, to hold the ingredients in the center. Make 3 small folds in the unsealed foil edges, folding inward toward the tamale to seal it tightly.

5. Fill a deep pot with 2 1/2 quarts of water. Place all tamales vertically in a steamer basket and put the basket in the pot. Bring the water to a boil, cover the pot, and adjust the heat to medium-low. Steam the tamales until they're cooked (about 1 1/2 hours). When the tamales are done, the dough should hold the shape of the package and should be shiny and slightly translucent, not opaque.

6. Serve the tamales garnished with lime wedges or slices.

Amalia's Notes

When you use chicken stock in any recipe, keep in mind that it already contains salt. To prevent excess saltiness, mix all the other ingredients first (except added salt), taste, and add more salt dissolved in a little stock or water at the end if needed.

If the tamales appear a bit soft or runny at the end of the cooking time, let them sit in the pot covered (with the heat off) for at least 1 hour before serving them. This resting time will bring the temperature down, and the tamales will firm up a bit.

For lighter tamales (less calories), decrease the amount of shortening according to taste. This recipe produces very moist tamales with a velvety texture. Note that reducing the amount of shortening by a significant amount will yield drier and less delicate tamales.

Tamales freeze well. To reheat them, steam them for 20 to 30 minutes. Reheat refrigerated tamales by steaming them for 15 to 20 minutes.

Recipe Variation

Tamales *Navideños*: Follow the dough recipe for *Tamales Negros* (Sweet Christmas Rice Tamales with Mole sauce, page 49), except omit the sugar and adjust the salt according to taste. Then follow the recipe above, plus the dough recipe for *Tamales Negros*, and steps 1, and 4 through 6, and use turkey pieces instead of pork and chicken or a combination of any of these.

TAMALES *NEGROS*
Sweet Christmas Rice Tamales with Mole Sauce

Tamales *negros* (black tamales) are sweet tamales eaten during the Christmas season. Traditionally these tamales are made using the sauce for tamales *colorados* as a base plus pureéd raisins and chocolate. Tamales *negros* can contain turkey, chicken, or pork. This is my easy version using the mole sauce that usually accompanies panfried plantains for dessert and using the traditional garnishes that give them a distinctive touch. If you prefer, use the traditional sauce found under *Recado para* Tamales *Colorados* (roasted ancho, guajillo, mulato, tomato, and pumpkin seed sauce, page 317). Guatemalans eat tamales *negros* for dinner on Christmas Eve and sometimes for breakfast on Christmas Day, too.

Makes 8 rectangular tamales

1 batch Mole (chocolate and chile sauce, page 315), or 1 recipe *Recado para* Tamales *Negros* (roasted ancho, guajillo, mulato, tomato, pumpkin seed, and chocolate sauce, page 319)

Masa (Dough)

1 cup rice flour

1 cup instant corn masa flour

4 cups fat-free, low-sodium chicken stock (plus 1/8 teaspoon kosher salt and 3 tablespoons sugar dissolved)

6–7 ounces (3/4–7/8 cup) all-vegetable shortening (no trans fat)

8 8x11-inch pieces banana leaves, wiped on both sides with a damp cloth

8 14x11-inch pieces aluminum foil

Relleno (Filling)

16 3x2-inch pieces turkey or chicken thighs or pork loin, seasoned with salt and pepper

8 prunes

24 raisins

16 blanched almonds

16 jarred roasted red bell pepper strips

Adorno (Garnish)

1 to 2 limes cut in wedges (optional)

1. Make the sauce and set it aside.

2. In the bowl of a mixer with a paddle attachment, combine the flours with the stock to make soft, moist dough. Add the shortening and fluff the masa for 3 minutes at medium speed. Taste the dough and adjust the seasonings, if needed. (Alternatively, put the ingredients in a deep bowl and beat vigorously with a wooden spoon for 3 to 5 minutes.)

3. Transfer the dough to a skillet and cook it on the stovetop at low heat, stirring constantly with a whisk to keep it from forming lumps and from sticking to the skillet until the dough is ready. The dough is ready when the whisk starts leaving tracks and the dough starts lifting from the edges (about 15 minutes). Let the dough cool slightly. Divide the dough into 8 equal portions.

4. For each tamale, lay 1 piece of banana leaf (matte side up) on top of 1 piece of foil. Place 1 dough portion on the banana leaf and foil. Take 2 pieces of meat, 1 prune, 3 raisins, 2 almonds, 2 pepper strips, and push them gently into the dough. Top with the sauce divided equally. Wrap the tamale and seal it tightly. Bring together the edges of the 2 longer parts of the foil and make 3 small folds beginning at the top. Then press the foil and leaves flat, from the outside in, to hold the ingredients in the center. Make 3 small folds in the unsealed foil edges, folding inward toward the tamale to seal it tightly.

5. Fill a deep pot with 2 quarts of water. Place all tamales vertically in a steamer basket and put the basket in the pot. Bring the water to a boil, cover the pot, and adjust the heat to medium-low. Steam the tamales until they're cooked (about 1 1/2 hours). When the tamales are done, the dough should hold the shape of the package and should be shiny and slightly translucent, not opaque.

6. Serve the tamales garnished with lime wedges.

Amalia's Notes

When you use chicken stock in any recipe, keep in mind that it already contains salt. To prevent excess saltiness, mix all the other ingredients first (except added salt), taste, and add more salt dissolved in a little stock or water at the end if needed.

If the tamales appear a bit soft or runny at the end of the cooking time, let them sit in the pot covered (with the heat off) for at least 1 hour before serving. This resting time will bring the temperature down, and the tamales will firm up a bit.

For lighter tamales (less calories), decrease the amount of shortening according to taste. This recipe produces very moist tamales with a velvety texture. Note that reducing the amount of shortening by a significant amount will yield drier and less delicate tamales.

Tamales freeze well. To reheat them, steam them for 20 to 30 minutes. Reheat refrigerated tamales by steaming them for 15 to 20 minutes.

Guatemalan artisan chocolate (page 373)

PACHES
Spicy Potato and Pork Tamales

A In and around Guatemala City, people eat *paches* every Thursday for dinner and often for breakfast on Friday. People eat them in Quetzaltenango (the Mayan highland region), too, but with a slightly different sauce. *Paches* are made with potatoes and sauce and thickened with either instant corn masa flour or French bread crumbs. *Paches* are usually spicier than other tamales. The spice comes from a tasty and slim tapered chile called chocolate chile (also known as chile verde), which is native to Guatemala.

Makes 6 rectangular *paches*

1 batch *Recado para Paches* (roasted spiced tomato and dried chiles sauce, page 320)

Masa (Dough)
2 cups cooked cubed potatoes
2/3 cup instant corn masa flour
6 ounces (3/4 cup) all-vegetable shortening (no trans fat)
1 teaspoon kosher salt
6 8x11-inch pieces banana leaves, wiped on both sides with a damp cloth
6 14x11-inch pieces aluminum foil

Relleno (Filling)
12 3x2-inch pieces pork loin, seasoned with salt and pepper
3 serrano chiles halved lengthwise or 6 whole bird's eye chiles or chocolate chiles (also known as chile verde)

Adorno (Garnish)
1 to 2 limes cut in wedges or slices

1. In the bowl of a mixer with a paddle attachment, combine the potatoes, 1 cup of the sauce, the flour, the shortening, and the salt, and fluff the dough for about 2 minutes at low speed. The dough should be pasty yet chunky. Taste and adjust the salt, if needed. (Alternatively, put the ingredients in a deep bowl and beat vigorously with a wooden spoon for 3 to 5 minutes.) Divide the dough into 6 equal portions.

2. For each *pache*, lay 1 piece of banana leaf (matte side up) on top of 1 piece of foil. Place 1 dough portion on the banana leaf and foil. Take 2 pieces of pork, and 1 piece of chile, and push them gently into the dough. Top with the remaining sauce divided equally. Wrap the *pache* and seal it tightly. Bring together the edges of the 2 longer parts of the foil and make 3 small folds beginning at the top. Then press the foil and leaves flat, from the outside in, to hold the ingredients in the center. Make 3 small folds in the unsealed foil edges, folding inward toward the *pache* to seal it tightly.

3. Fill a deep pot with 2 quarts of water. Place all *paches* vertically in a steamer basket and put the basket in the pot. Bring the water to a boil, cover the pot, and adjust the heat to medium-low. Steam the *paches* until they're cooked (about 1 1/2 hours). When the *paches* are done, the dough should hold the shape of the package and should be shiny and slightly translucent, not opaque.

4. Serve the *paches* garnished with lime wedges or slices.

Amalia's Notes

If the *paches* appear a bit soft or runny at the end of the cooking time, let them sit in the pot covered (with the heat off) for at least 1 hour before serving them. This resting time will bring the temperature down, and the *paches* will firm up a bit.

For lighter tamales (less calories), decrease the amount of shortening according to taste. This recipe produces very moist tamales with a velvety texture. Note that reducing the amount of shortening by a significant amount will yield drier and less delicate tamales.

Paches freeze well. To reheat them, steam them for 20 to 30 minutes. Reheat refrigerated *paches* by steaming them for 15 to 20 minutes.

2

FRIJOLES Y OTRAS LEGUMBRES
BEANS AND OTHER LEGUMES

A VIP DISH

Black beans are Guatemala's VIP dish. Because they are abundant and affordable, some Guatemalans unjustly call beans "the food of the poor." But in reality, beans transcend class barriers. Nationwide, most Guatemalans eat them regularly. Like corn, beans are not only nutritious, but also delicious. They are easy to prepare and make the perfect complement to any meal.

While Guatemalans eat mostly black beans, they also consume white and red beans and other legumes of many different colors, shapes, and sizes. All legumes grow in pods. Some grow on vines, while others grow as ground cover or on bushes. Some legumes are eaten fresh, while others are harvested green and then dried for storage. Legumes are high in iron, antioxidants, and fiber. Legumes plus rice, corn, or another grain eaten on the same day make a complete protein. Beans are a high-quality vegetarian and gluten-free food choice.

There's more than one way to cook beans. This chapter will show you several simple ways with a Guatemalan touch. Depending on where you are in Guatemala, you can find beans prepared with a variety of methods—as a main meal combined with pork and accompanied by corn tortillas, as a side dish with fried onions and garlic, refried, in soup, and so on. Beans are versatile and easy to work with, and they take on any flavor you add to them. Better yet, they freeze well without losing flavor or quality.

> ## PRODUCTOS LÁCTEOS CHAPINES
> ### Guatemalan Dairy Products
>
> Guatemalan milk, cream, and cheese are of very good quality and have wonderful flavor. In the rural areas, right before breakfast or dinner, homemakers rush to the neighborhood *tienda*, or store, to buy the freshest milk, cream, or cheese for their meal. Beans and cheese or cream are the complement of choice, usually for breakfast and dinner.
>
> Guatemalan *quesos*, or cheeses, are unaged. They may be dry and crumbly (*queso seco*), such as the renowned *queso de* Zacapa. (Zacapa is a department in eastern Guatemala.) Or they may be smooth and moist (similar to mozzarella), such as *queso de capas* wrapped in banana leaves (from the surrounding region). Guatemala also produces a variety of farmer cheeses. *Quesos* are often eaten with beans and in open-faced tortilla sandwiches.

Black beans are a Guatemalan tradition. They're a staple in most Guatemalan homes, eaten for breakfast, lunch, dinner, and sometimes even as a snack. Guatemalans appreciate black beans because they are delicious, nutritious, and readily available. After all, they are native to this part of the world.

Maleta de Frijoles con Arroz (page 62)

FRIJOLES CHAPINES
Basic Guatemalan Black Beans and Variations

A Black beans are high in iron, fiber, and protein. Combined with rice or corn, black beans make a nutritious, affordable, and delicious vegetarian dish. The traditional Guatemalan everyday bean recipe is cooked beans in any style combined with a *sofrito* of minced, fried onion and garlic. Traditional toppings are *crema*, *queso fresco* or *seco*, *chilito* (spicy pepper salsa), and corn tortillas. Following are my versions of this easy, tasty dish.

Makes 4 cups

2 cups dried black beans, free of debris and rinsed

1 whole medium yellow onion, peeled and t-scored

1 whole unpeeled garlic head

5 cups water

Kosher salt (added during each recipe variation below)

1. Combine all ingredients except salt in a medium Crock-Pot set on high. Cover and cook until beans are tender, about 3 1/2 hours. (Alternatively, soak the beans in the water overnight, and then cook them in the same water with the onion and garlic on the stovetop over medium-low heat until tender, about 1 1/2 hours.) Discard the onion and garlic.

2. Use the beans as a base for any of the following recipes.

Recipe Variations

Frijoles Parados con Pitos (whole beans with *sofrito* and pito buds): Panfry 1 cup of chopped yellow onions in 2 tablespoons of canola oil until medium brown. Add 1 tablespoon of minced garlic and sauté 1 minute. Add 3/4 cup of whole pito buds (page 8) and 1 cup of canned crushed tomatoes and cook for 2 to 3 minutes. Add the cooked beans to this mixture, season with salt, and taste. Simmer uncovered to thicken the broth (15 to 20 minutes). Or purée 3/4 cup of the beans and return to the pan to thicken the sauce faster. (Alternatively, panfry just the onion and garlic and omit the tomatoes and pito buds to make traditional Guatemalan black beans with *sofrito*.) Makes about 5 1/2 cups.

Frijoles Parados con Chipilín (whole beans with *sofrito* and *chipilín*): Use the recipe for *Frijoles Parados con Pitos*, but replace the pito buds with 1/2 cup *chipilín* leaves.

Frijoles Colados con Chile Pimiento (bean purée with red bell pepper *sofrito*): Use the recipe for *Frijoles Parados con Pitos*, but replace the pito buds with 1/2 cup finely diced red bell peppers. After adding the peppers and tomatoes, cook for 2 to 3 minutes. Add the beans and cook 3 minutes longer. Purée the mixture with an immersion blender. (Alternatively, let the mixture cool slightly and use a regular blender. Return the purée to the skillet and cook another 5 minutes.) To finish, add 1 tablespoon of chopped cilantro (optional). Taste the beans and adjust seasonings, if needed. Makes a little over 5 cups.

Frijoles Volteados (refried beans): Start with the *Frijoles Colados con* Chile Pimiento recipe. Put 4 to 5 tablespoons of canola oil in a skillet and fry the bean mixture over medium heat, stirring constantly, until it is very thick and pasty, it no longer sticks to the skillet, and it can be shaped into any form. This will take 20 to 30 minutes. Traditionally, Guatemalans shape refried beans like a small American football.

Sopa de Frijoles con Panitos (black bean soup with croutons): Start with the *Frijoles Colados con* Chile Pimiento recipe. Add 2 1/2 to 3 cups of chicken or vegetable stock and season with freshly ground black pepper to taste. Simmer the mixture to heat it through, about 3 to 5 minutes. Serve with a swirl of *crema*, crumbled cheese, tiny croutons, chives, or chopped cilantro.

Frijoles con Chorizo y Tocino (beans with chorizo and bacon): Start with the *Frijoles Parados con Pitos* recipe, but replace the pito buds with 1/4 cup cooked chopped bacon and 1/2 cup sliced cooked chorizo. Taste the mixture and adjust seasonings, if necessary.

Maleta de Frijoles con Arroz (refried beans with rice): Start with the *Frijoles Volteados* recipe. Add 3/4 to 1 cup of cooked rice, mix well, and heat the mixture through. Traditionally, Guatemalans shape refried beans and rice like a small American football.

Caldo de Frijoles (black bean broth) is the liquid resulting from the cooked basic black bean recipe seasoned with salt to taste, or leave out the salt if the broth is used in conjuction with another recipe.

Amalia's Note

To t-score an onion, make a 1/2-inch-deep cross-shaped cut at the narrowest end of the onion. The onion remains whole.

Sopa de Frijoles con Panitos (page 62)

ARROZ NEGRO CON CHILE PIMIENTO

Black Rice with Red Bell Peppers

A This is an attractive and delicious dish. The black rice contrasts beautifully with the red bell peppers, and the mellow flavor pairs well with grilled meats or any of the stews in chapter 5 (page 133). For a spicy twist, add chopped hot peppers to the mixture.

Serves 4 to 6 people

1 cup long-grain white rice

1 tablespoon canola oil

1/2 cup finely diced yellow onion

1/2 teaspoon minced garlic

1/2 cup julienned red bell pepper

1/2 cup finely diced Roma tomatoes

2 cups black bean broth and 1/2 cup black beans

Kosher salt and freshly ground black pepper

Adorno (Garnish)

1/2 cup thinly sliced green onions

1/4 cup red bell pepper strips (2 inches long), sautéed

1. In a medium skillet, sauté the rice in the oil with the onions, garlic, pepper, and tomatoes until the rice is well coated with oil (2 to 3 minutes).

2. Add the black bean broth and beans, then season with salt and pepper to taste. Bring to a quick boil, lower the heat, and simmer covered until rice has absorbed most of the liquid (15 to 20 minutes).

3. Garnish with onions and pepper strips.

Amalia's Note

Refer to *Frijoles Chapines* (basic Guatemalan black beans and variations, page 61) for black bean broth. Alternatively, use canned beans and adjust the liquid with chicken stock. One 15-ounce can of beans will yield exactly 1/2 cup of broth, so add 1 1/2 cups of chicken or vegetable stock to make 2 cups of bean broth for this recipe.

PILOYADA ANTIGÜEÑA

La Antigua Red Bean and Chorizo Salad

Piloyes are red beans native to Guatemala. They are rounder, flatter, and bigger than black beans. *Piloyada* is a dish from La Antigua, Guatemala, a charming colonial city and the former capital of Guatemala. *Piloyada* is a beautiful and tasty dish that serves equally well as a main meal, a side, or a snack. Some of the traditional toppings are the Guatemalan sausages chorizo and *longaniza*. This recipe is inspired by my sister's friend Lorena, who is from Antigua and who makes this delicious dish often to entertain family and friends.

Serves 4 to 6 people

2 cups dried *piloyes* (or red kidney beans), free of debris and rinsed

1/2 pound pork loin, cut into 2-inch cubes

1 whole medium yellow onion, peeled and t-scored

1 whole unpeeled garlic head

5 cups water

Vinagreta (Vinaigrette)

1 ounce (1/8 cup) champagne vinegar or white wine vinegar

1 teaspoon minced garlic

1 whole bay leaf

1/4 teaspoon dried thyme

2 ounces (1/4 cup) olive oil

Kosher salt and freshly ground black pepper

Adorno (Garnish)

1/4 cup Spanish chorizo, thinly sliced on the diagonal

1/4 cup strips (2 inches long) of boiled ham

1/4 cup bite-size pieces of Serrano ham (or diced boiled ham)

1/4 cup finely diced Roma tomatoes

1/2 cup crumbled Guatemalan *queso seco* (or Cotija cheese)

1/4 cup julienned red bell pepper

1 tablespoon julienned red onion

1/4 cup finely chopped flat-leaf parsley

1. Combine the beans, pork, onion, garlic, and water in a medium Crock-Pot set on high. Cover and cook until the beans are tender, about 3 1/2 hours. (Alternatively, soak the beans in the water overnight, then cook them in the same water with the pork, onion, and garlic on the stovetop over medium-low heat until tender, about 1 1/2 hours.) Discard the onion and garlic. Let cool.

2. Combine all the vinaigrette ingredients in a blender and process to a fine consistency.

3. Transfer the beans and pork to a serving bowl with 1 1/2 cups of broth. (Save the rest of the broth for another recipe.) Add the vinaigrette and mix well. Taste and adjust seasonings if needed. The beans are unseasoned, so you may have to work a bit to reach the right *sazón* with salt and pepper. Let the mixture stand at least 30 minutes to allow the flavors to blend.

4. Top the salad with garnishes in the order listed. Distribute the garnishes attractively and evenly over the dish.

Amalia's Note

This dish can be eaten either at room temperature or cold. A cold temperature can weaken the flavors, so when you serve it cold, taste and adjust the seasonings before garnishing. Eat with crusty French bread or corn tortilla chips.

Piloyes beans (page 67)

FRIJOLES BLANCOS CON ESPINAZO
White Beans and Pork Stew with Cumin and Oregano

A When you grow up eating beans, you learn to like and appreciate the many varieties that exist within Guatemala. This is a dish my mom made. We used to sprinkle dried crumbled cheese on top and sometimes even chopped parsley. This dish is as delicious, nutritious, and filling as a bowl of American chili. It goes well with bread or tortillas. Pork *espinazo* (spine) is a stew meat available at Latino markets in the United States. Country-style pork ribs and pork shoulder are good substitutes.

Serves 4 to 6 people

- 2 cups dried white beans (great northern or navy), free of debris and rinsed
- 3/4 to 1 pound pork *espinazo* (or country-style pork ribs or shoulder), cut into 2- to 3-inch chunks
- 1 whole medium yellow onion, peeled and t-scored
- 1 whole unpeeled garlic head
- 5 cups water

- 1 cup quartered Roma tomatoes (about 2 large tomatoes)
- 3/4 yellow onion, quartered
- 2 large garlic cloves
- 1 zambo (or mulato) chile, seeded
- 1/2 cup water

- 1 tablespoon canola oil

Sazón (Seasonings)
- 1/8 teaspoon cumin
- 1/2 teaspoon crumbled dried oregano
- Kosher salt and freshly ground black pepper

- 1 tablespoon tomato paste dissolved in 3 tablespoons water

Adorno (Garnish)
- 1/2 cup crumbled Guatemalan *queso seco* (or Cotija cheese)

1. Combine the beans, pork, whole onion, garlic head, and water in a medium Crock-Pot set on high. Cover and cook until beans are soft, about 3 1/2 hours. (Alternatively, soak the beans in the water overnight, then cook them in the same water with the pork, onion, and garlic on the stovetop over medium-low heat until tender, about 1 1/2 hours.) Discard the onion and garlic. Purée 1 cup of the cooked beans. Set aside.

2. Combine the tomatoes, onion, garlic, chile, and water in a medium saucepan and bring to a quick boil. Reduce the heat to low, cover, and simmer until tender (5 to 7 minutes). Purée the vegetables to fine consistency.

3. In a medium-hot skillet, fry the purée in the oil and add the seasonings. Add the tomato paste liquid, the beans and pork, and the bean purée. Simmer uncovered for 20 minutes, stirring occasionally. Taste and adjust seasonings, if needed.

4. Serve garnished with cheese.

Guatemalan Kitchen

DOBLADAS DE FRIJOLES Y QUESO
Refried Beans and Cheese–Filled Tortillas
with Spicy Tomato Sauce

A The word *dobladas* means "folded." *Dobladas* make an easy, tasty, and healthy snack. My grandmother used to spread leftover beans and cheese on a soft tortilla, fold the tortilla, and griddle it on a dry *comal*. This is my dressed-up version of my grandmother's recipe. Traditional dobladas are fried and have other fillings.

Makes 6 *dobladas*

Chirmol de Tomate y Chile (Tomato and Chile Sauce)

  1 tablespoon canola oil

  2 cups finely diced Roma tomatoes

  1 cup finely diced yellow onion

  1 teaspoon finely diced chiltepe (or hot chile of choice)

  Kosher salt and freshly ground black pepper

  6 corn tortillas

  1 cup crumbled *queso fresco* (fresh Latino cheese)

  1/2 cup refried black beans (page 62)

  Canola oil

Adorno (Garnish)

  1/2 cup crumbled Guatemalan *queso seco* (or Cotija cheese) or *queso fresco* (fresh Latino cheese)

  Flat-leaf parsley

1. Put the tablespoon of oil in a hot skillet. Add the tomatoes, onions, chiles, and salt and pepper. Cook until saucy (3 to 5 minutes). Taste and adjust seasonings, if needed.

2. In a skillet over high heat, warm the corn tortillas for about 30 seconds per side. Keep the tortillas warm and flexible in a tortilla warmer or wrapped in kitchen towels.

3. Combine 1/2 cup of *queso fresco* and the beans in a bowl. Divide into 6 equal portions and spread on each tortilla. Gently fold the tortillas in half.

4. Preheat a skillet or griddle. Brush the stuffed tortillas on both sides with a light coating of canola oil and place them immediately on the hot griddle for about 1 1/2 minutes per side. Place the cooked *dobladas* on a platter and cover them with kitchen towels to keep them warm until you're ready to eat.

5. Serve the *dobladas* garnished with sauce, cheese, and parsley.

FRIJOLES COLORADOS CON CHORIZO ESPAÑOL
Red Bean Stew with Spanish Chorizo and Pumpkin Seeds

A This recipe is inspired by a bean stew my mother used to make with *copetines*. *Copetines* are tiny, tasty sausages from Guatemala. Spanish chorizo is as tasty as *copetines* and makes a great substitute. The pumpkin seeds and the sausage combine to make this dish scrumptiously special.

Serve 4 to 6 people

2 cups dried red beans, free of debris and rinsed

1 whole medium yellow onion, peeled and t-scored

1 whole unpeeled garlic head

5 cups water

1 cup thinly sliced (on the diagonal) Spanish chorizo

Recado (Sauce)
1/2 tablespoon canola oil

1 cup finely chopped yellow onions

1 teaspoon minced garlic

1 cup finely chopped Roma tomatoes (about 2 large tomatoes)

Sazón (Seasonings)
1 1/4 tablespoons ground roasted pumpkin seeds

Kosher salt

Adorno (Garnish)
Crema (Latino table cream)

1. Combine the beans, onion, garlic, and water in a medium Crock-Pot set on high. Cover and cook until the beans are tender, about 3 1/2 hours. (Alternatively, soak the beans in the water overnight, then cook them in the same water with the onion and garlic on the stove-top over medium-low heat until tender, about 1 1/2 hours.) Discard the onion and garlic.

2. In a hot skillet, sauté the chorizo until fat starts to appear (about 3 minutes). Add the oil and the onions, and cook until the onions are medium brown. Add the garlic and cook 1 minute. Add the tomatoes and cook until saucy (3 to 5 minutes). Combine this mixture with the beans. Season with the pumpkin seeds and salt. Simmer for 20 to 30 minutes to blend flavors. Taste and adjust seasonings, if needed.

3. Serve the stew garnished with *crema* (Latino table cream).

PURÉ DE HABAS CON CHICHARRONES

Fava Beans Purée with Cilantro-Tomatillo *Sofrito* Topped with Pan-Roasted Pork

A Fava beans are a nice break from other legumes that you may consume regularly. If you are lucky enough to find them fresh, then use those for this recipe. The crispy pork works really well with the spicy fava bean purée. For a vegetarian version, substitute the pork with fried tofu and the chicken stock with vegetable stock.

Serves 4 to 6 people

1 pound pork shoulder, cut into 2-inch cubes, seasoned with salt and pepper

1 tablespoon olive oil

1 cup quartered Roma tomatoes (about 2 large tomatoes)

1 cup roughly chopped cilantro (stems and leaves)

3/4 to 1 cup quartered onion (about 1 small onion)

1 garlic clove

1 15-ounce can fava beans, drained and rinsed (or 2 1/2 cups fresh fava beans)

2 cups fat-free, low-sodium chicken stock

1 tablespoon olive oil

Sazón (Seasonings)

1 bay leaf

1/8 teaspoon cumin

1/2 teaspoon cobán chile powder (or smoked piquín or árbol chile powder)

Kosher salt and freshly ground black pepper

Adorno (Garnish)

Finely chopped cilantro leaves

1. In a medium hot skillet, sauté the pork in 1 tablespoon of oil to medium brown. Transfer the cooked pork to a plate lined with paper towels to absorb excess oil. Discard the oil. Set aside the skillet.

2. Put the tomatoes, cilantro, onion, and garlic in a blender or food processor. Purée to a fine consistency.

3. Purée the beans with the stock in a blender or food processor. In the same skillet used for the pork, fry the tomato purée in 1 tablespoon of oil. Add the bay leaf, cumin, chile powder, salt, and pepper, and cook for 2 to 3 minutes. Add the bean purée to the tomato mixture and cook uncovered on low heat for 10 to 15 minutes, stirring occasionally. Taste and adjust seasonings, if needed.

4. Transfer the purée to a bowl or platter and top with the pork. Serve garnished with cilantro leaves.

GALLO PINTO

Spicy Rice and Black Beans, with Bell Peppers, Bacon, and Cilantro

*A*ᵉ *Gallo pinto* (speckled rooster) is a traditional Central American dish. Rice and beans with a variety of other ingredients is a popular dish in Guatemala and elsewhere in the Latino Caribbean. I discovered *gallo pinto* while vacationing in Costa Rica. I loved it. I ate it at breakfast, lunch, and dinner. The key to a great *gallo pinto* is Lizano sauce, a Costa Rican sauce available at most Latino markets in the United States or online.

Serves 4 to 6 people

1 cup finely chopped onion
3/4 cup diced multicolored bell peppers
1/2 cup finely chopped cooked bacon
1/2 to 1 cup canned black beans, drained and rinsed
3/4 to 1 cup washed, finely chopped cilantro (stems and leaves)
2 tablespoons canola oil
1 1/2 tablespoons Lizano sauce (or Worcestershire sauce)
1/2 tablespoon Tabasco sauce
Kosher salt and freshly ground black pepper
2 cups long-grain white rice cooked in fat-free, low-sodium chicken stock

Adorno (Garnish)
1/2 cup roughly chopped cilantro leaves

1. Sauté the onions, peppers, bacon, beans, and cilantro in the oil over medium-high heat for about 3 minutes. Season with Lizano sauce (or Worcestershire or both), Tabasco sauce, salt, and pepper. (Keep in mind that the seasoning sauces already contain salt, so salt with a light hand.) Continue sautéing for 2 more minutes.

2. Add the rice gradually, making sure it gets well coated with sauce. Use a firm spatula to break any large clumps of rice. Sauté for 2 minutes. Taste and adjust seasonings, if needed.

3. Serve the *gallo pinto* garnished with cilantro.

GUISO DE POLLO, LENTEJAS Y GARBANZOS

Lentils, Garbanzo, and Chicken Braised in Saffron-Rosemary *Sofrito* Sauce

A Guatemalans eat many Spanish-inspired dishes adapted to local tastes. This dish was inspired by some of my favorite Spanish flavors. Lentils and garbanzo pair well with just about any flavor and taste great with this *sofrito* sauce. You can expand it by adding chopped Serrano ham or Spanish chorizo. Make this dish vegetarian by substituting the chicken with white beans, soybean sprouts, green soybeans, or pigeon peas and substituting the chicken stock for vegetable stock. The dish is naturally gluten-free.

Serves 4 to 6 people

4 to 6 skinless chicken thighs, visible fat removed, rubbed with 1 1/2 teaspoons Spanish *pimentón* (paprika) and seasoned with salt and pepper

1 tablespoon olive oil

Recado (Sauce)

1 tablespoon olive oil

1 tablespoon minced garlic

3/4 cup julienned yellow or red bell peppers

1 bay leaf

1 1/2 teaspoons finely chopped fresh rosemary

1/2 teaspoon Spanish saffron threads soaked in 1/3 cup good quality white wine

2 tablespoons tomato paste dissolved in 1 cup fat-free, low-sodium chicken stock

1 15-ounce can lentils, drained and rinsed

1 15-ounce can garbanzo beans, drained and rinsed

Kosher salt and freshly ground black pepper

Adorno (Garnish)

1/4 cup finely chopped flatleaf parsley (optional).

1. In a wide shallow skillet over medium heat, brown the chicken in 1 tablespoon of oil for about 4 minutes per side. Transfer the cooked chicken to a dish and keep it warm.

2. Add 1 tablespoon of oil to the same skillet and sauté the garlic for about 1 minute. Add the peppers and herbs, and sauté 1 minute more. Deglaze the skillet by adding the wine and saffron and loosening the bits of food stuck to the skillet with a rubber spatula. Cook about 2 minutes. Add the tomato paste and stock and the lentils and garbanzos.

3. Return the chicken to the skillet and nestle it within the legumes. Bring to a quick boil, reduce the heat, and braise partially covered until the chicken is fully cooked and the liquid has reduced by about one-third and formed a nice thin sauce (25 to 30 minutes). Taste and adjust seasonings, if needed.

4. Serve garnished with parsley (if using).

ARROZ CON FRIJOLES Y COCO
Coconut Rice and Beans

Rice and beans are popular in Garifuna country, such as the port city of Livingston in Guatemala's Izabal department, and throughout the Latino Caribbean. Cooking rice with coconut milk can be tricky, but this recipe offers an easy and foolproof way to make delicious coconut rice and beans. For a superb combo, pair the rice with grilled or panfried seafood and plantains.

Serves 4 to 6 people

1 1/2 cups coconut milk

1/2 cup bean broth (from can of beans)

1/2 cup canned red beans (or black beans)

2 tablespoons finely sliced green onions

2 teaspoons minced garlic

1/4 cup julienned red bell pepper

1/2 habanero chile, seeded, deveined, and minced

2 sprigs fresh thyme (or 1/2 teaspoon dry thyme)

1 bay leaf

1/2 teaspoon kosher salt

Freshly ground black pepper

1 cup long-grain white rice

Adorno (Garnish)

1/4 cup finely sliced chives or green onions

1. In a medium hot saucepan or skillet, combine the coconut milk and bean broth with the onions, garlic, peppers, habanero, thyme, bay leaf, salt, and black pepper. Bring to a quick boil.

2. Add the rice, reduce the heat, and simmer covered until the rice is tender (15 to 20 minutes), stirring halfway through.

3. Serve the rice and beans garnished with chives or green onions.

HABICHUELAS DE LIMA EN JOCÓN
Spicy Lima Beans with Chicken, Tomatillo, and Cilantro Stew

A This delicious and versatile recipe combines *jocón*, a Mayan stew, with lima beans—or any other legume or protein. The stew is delicious by itself or pairs well with rice. For a vegetarian version, substitute the chicken stock with vegetable stock and omit the chicken.

Serves 4 to 6 people

1 15-ounce can lima beans, drained and rinsed

1 batch *Jocón* (chicken, tomatillo, and cilantro stew, page 139)

Adorno (Garnish)

Cilantro leaves

1. Combine the lima beans with the *jocón* and heat through.

2. Serve the stew garnished with cilantro.

ENSALADA DE FRIJOLES
Multicolored Spicy 16-Bean Salad with Lime and Herbs

A If you cook the beans the day before, you can make this easy and delicious salad in minutes. Or, you can use multicolored canned beans. This dish is a great vegetarian and gluten-free option for a buffet. For a vegan version, omit the cheese. Combine this salad with cooked rice to add flavor and nutritional value.

Makes about 4 1/2 cups

1 package (2 cups) 16-bean mixture (see note following recipe)

1 small whole onion, peeled and t-scored

1 whole unpeeled head of garlic

5 cups water (or chicken or vegetable stock)

1 batch *Chilito* sauce (page 325)

2 tablespoons chopped cilantro leaves

2 tablespoons chopped flat-leaf parsley leaves

1 tablespoon chopped mint

1 cup crumbled queso fresco (fresh Latino cheese)

1/2 cup finely chopped red bell pepper

Sazón (Seasonings)

Freshly squeezed lime juice

1/8 teaspoon *diente de perro* chile powder (or piquín or árbol chile powder)

Kosher salt and freshly ground black pepper

1. Combine the beans, onion, garlic, and water in a medium Crock-Pot set on high. Cover and cook until beans are tender, about 3 1/2 hours. (Alternatively, soak the beans in the water overnight, then cook them in the same water with the onion and garlic on the stovetop over medium-low heat until tender, about 1 1/2 hours.) Discard the onion and garlic. Strain and rinse the beans. Reserve the broth for another recipe.

2. Combine the beans with the rest of the ingredients and season. Taste and adjust seasonings, if needed.

3. Serve immediately or chill until you're ready to eat.

Amalia's Note

Grocery stores usually offer dried bean mixtures packaged for use in soups. Use the mixture of your choice or combine two or three different types of dried beans to make the equivalent of 2 cups.

This is a very flexible recipe. You may choose to add or leave out ingredients of choice. Tomatoes, bell peppers, and other vegetables could also be a part of this salad. Make sure to taste and adjust seasonings if you increase or decrease the number of ingredients.

DESAYUNO CHAPÍN
GUATEMALAN BREAKFAST

Papayas

NOURISHMENT FOR A FULL DAY

*E*very day, Guatemalans look forward to a good breakfast. Guatemalans consider breakfast and lunch to be the most important meals of the day. These meals are usually larger than the evening meal. Families with school-age children pay special attention to serving nutritious breakfasts. Balance and quality are both important.

Because fresh fruits and vegetables are abundant and varied in Guatemala, it's easy to make a nutritious meal during a busy morning. Guatemalan breakfast dishes are simple but tasty and wholesome.

Mosh (creamy whole oats with cinnamon and milk) is a favorite of the young and the old. Eggs are prepared in many styles, depending on the day of the week. On weekdays they can be soft-boiled, hard-boiled, or scrambled. On the weekend, they can be *huevos estrellados con chirmol frito* (egg sunny-side up with tomato and onion pan sauce) or *huevos revueltos con tomate y cebolla ó* tortilla (scrambled eggs with tomatoes and onions or corn tortilla bits). The typical accompaniments for eggs are black beans in any style and either corn tortillas or Guatemalan-style French bread (an elongated crusty loaf divided into bunlike sections, with a delicious gummy core).

Another breakfast option for the weekend or for brunch is *panqueques con miel de abeja* (pancakes with honey). These are medium-thick crepelike cakes that can be made in minutes. Panfried plantains are a good complement to any meal. For heavier appetites, Guatemalan chorizo and *longaniza* sausages make a great side.

In my grandmother's town in the countryside, *tamalitos de elote* (fresh corn and butter mini-tamales topped with fresh cream) were a very special treat. She made them, especially when we had visitors. *Guineo mojoncho con leche* was another favorite breakfast dish. This is red-skinned bananas grilled over charcoals, peeled, cut into chunks, mashed, and added to hot milk in a bowl. We ate this dish like cereal. At school, whole (not rolled) oats were cooked in milk.

Traditional breakfast drinks include freshly squeezed orange juice and *licuados* (blended drinks made with seasonal fresh fruit and milk). Guatemalan *café con leche* (coffee with hot milk) is also popular.

In my own home, I have had a breakfast routine for years. My son sits at the breakfast bar and watches me prepare his food. Unconsciously he is learning to make good choices about food—especially when he is away from home—just as I learned by watching my grandmother. I've developed simple menus mimicking my childhood breakfasts to show him that cooking and eating good, fresh food isn't hard. Here's our typical breakfast routine (in this order): a multivitamin, a small plate of 3 or 4 different fruits cut into small pieces, *mosh* or whole-grain cereal with skim milk, and eggs in different styles. I vary the routine occasionally to include other choices and to prevent boredom. My biggest reward is that now he can make his own breakfast with good food choices.

DESAYUNO CHAPÍN

Traditional Guatemalan Breakfast Options

Jugo de naranja (freshly squeezed orange juice)

Fruta de la época (seasonal fruit)

Licuados de frutas (blended fruit drinks)

Mosh (creamy whole oats with cinnamon and milk)

Huevos y variantes (various Guatemalan egg recipes)

Frijoles y variantes (various Guatemalan black bean recipes)

Panqueques con miel de abeja (corn pancakes with honey)

Plátanos cocidos ó fritos (cooked or fried plantains)

Chorizos *y longanizas* (Guatemalan chorizo and longaniza sausages)

Tamales *colorados* (red chicken and pork tamales in banana leaves)

Tamales *negros* (corn and rice masa chicken tamales with chocolate sauce)

Paches (spicy potato and pork tamales)

Tamalitos de elote (fresh corn and butter tamales)

Tortillas *de maíz* (fresh corn tortillas)

Pan francés (Guatemalan French bread)

Café Guatemalteco (Guatemalan coffee)

Condimentos (condiments and toppings such as *queso, crema,* and *chilito*)

A WORD ABOUT *ATOL*

*G*uatemala is an *atol*-loving country. *Atol* is a hot traditional drink of Mayan origin that is popular in Guatemala and neighboring countries. *Atol* varies by region. It can be sweet or savory. It may be based on dried legumes, fresh corn, corn masa, roasted *maíz*, rice, other grains, grain starch, fruits, and more. *Atol* can be flavored with cinnamon, chiles, roasted seeds, *panela*, sugar, or salt.

Atols are cozy and nutritious drinks. They are pleasing in the morning and in the afternoon, and they give much comfort to the sick. Moms make them for breakfast, and grandmas make them for their grandkids for afternoon snacks. *Atols* are made at home as well as in the street. They're often sold at church atriums, parks, plazas, festivals, and religious celebrations.

Throughout this book you will find my favorite *atol* recipes. The most popular are *Atol de Elote* (fresh corn *atol* topped with cinnamon and *crema*, page 347), *Atol de Plátano* (sweet plantain *atol*, page 103), and *Atol de Arroz con Leche* (rice, cinnamon, and milk *atol*, page 92).

LICUADOS DE FRUTAS
Blended Fruit Drinks

A *Licuados* are sold in most *mercados* (markets) and in the streets throughout Guatemala. They are the drink of choice for many Guatemalans. *Licuados* can contain water or milk and ice as a base. Sometimes they are packaged in a small *bolsita* (bag) with a straw for convenience. I am pleased to say that soda is an afterthought in a country with abundant fresh fruit drinks. Guatemalans drink soda only occasionally—usually at parties.

Serves 2 people

2 cups of ripe fruit (such as pineapple, cantaloupe, strawberries, blackberries, or mangoes)

1 cup of water

1 tablespoon sugar

Ice

1. In a blender, process the fruit with the water and sugar until smooth. Taste and adjust the sugar, if needed. If you like, strain the drink. Or leave in the fruit pulp for more fiber.

2. Serve the *licuado* over ice.

 **Amalia's Notes**

You can also make a *licuado* using milk instead of water.

Make a lighter drink by adding more liquid, such as orange juice or any other juice, to the fruit mixture. Strain the *licuado* and add fruit bits at the end.

In lieu of fresh fruit, use frozen tropical fruit pulp, such as passion fruit, coconut, papaya, guava, tamarind, or others. Fruit pulp is available at Latino grocery stores.

LICUADO DE BANANO Y FRESA
Banana and Strawberry Smoothie

A This *licuado* is a popular, nutritious, and filling drink that takes minutes to make. Both kids and adults love it. It is a nice afternoon snack.

Serves 2 people

1 banana, peeled, broken in half

1/2 cup washed, stemmed, halved strawberries

2 cups milk

1/2 teaspoon vanilla extract

1/2 teaspoon almond or hazelnut extract

1 tablespoon sugar

Adorno (Garnish)

2 strawberries

1. In a blender, process the first 6 ingredients until smooth. Taste and adjust the sugar, if needed.

2. Serve each *licuado* garnished with a strawberry.

Huevos Tibios (page 95)

Dobladas (page 73)

Mosh (page 91)

MOSH

Creamy Oats with Cinnamon and Skim Milk

*A*malia *Mosh* is very common in Guatemalan households because it's nutritious, delicious, and easy to make. People drink thin *mosh* out of a mug and eat thick *mosh* from a bowl. To make it even more nutritious, top it with sliced bananas and berries. For chewier and nuttier-tasting *mosh*, make it with steel-cut oats (Irish oats). Or make a delicious *Frescavena* (oats and vanilla cooler, page 390). It's so refreshing during hot weather.

Serves 2 people

1/2 cup whole-grain old-fashioned oats
2 cups skim milk
1/3 stick *canela* (Ceylon cinnamon)
1/2 teaspoon kosher salt
1 1/2 tablespoons sugar

Sliced bananas and berries

1. Combine the first 5 ingredients in a small saucepan and bring to a quick boil. Keep a close eye on the mixture, as it can quickly boil over. Adjust the heat to low and continue to cook until creamy, stirring occasionally (about 5 minutes). Taste and adjust seasonings, if needed.

2. Serve the *mosh* in mugs or cups and top it with sliced bananas and berries.

Amalia's Notes

Alternatively, soak the oats in the milk overnight in the refrigerator and follow the same recipe. This accelerates the cooking process and makes even creamier *mosh*. My sister soaks the oats in water at room temperature overnight and then cooks it in the morning and mixes with milk.

If you're making this recipe with steel-cut oats, cook the *mosh* until it's soft and chewy, about 35 minutes.

ATOL DE ARROZ CON LECHE
Hot Rice and Cinnamon Drink

*A*tol de Arroz con Leche is the Guatemalized version of rice pudding that came to Latin America through Spain. It varies by region and by country. You can transform it from a breakfast drink into a dessert by using half the milk. You may eat it hot or cold. Here it is presented as an elegant drink and as dessert.

Serves 2 people

1/3 cup long-grain rice
1 cup water
1/3 stick *canela* (Ceylon cinnamon)
2 cups skim milk
1/4 teaspoon kosher salt
1 1/2 tablespoons sugar

Adorno (garnish)
Ground (or whole) cinnamon, or berries and mint

1. Combine the rice, water, and *canela* in a small saucepan and bring to a quick boil. Adjust the heat to low and cook uncovered for 5 minutes.

2. Add the milk, salt, and sugar, and bring to a quick boil again. Keep a close eye on the mixture, as it can quickly boil over. Adjust the heat to low and continue to cook, stirring occasionally, until the rice is soft (12 to 15 minutes). Taste and adjust seasonings, if needed.

3. Serve the *atol* hot in mugs, warm in tall glasses, or cold in cups.

4. Garnish.

CORAZÓN DE TRIGO
Guatemalan Wheat Farina

A Either as a breakfast porridge or an afternoon snack, kids and adults really like *Corazón de Trigo*. It is nutritious and delicious. Top it with your favorite fruit to make it even heartier. Guatemalan wheat farina is available at some Latino and Guatemalan stores in the United States. It is yellow and a bit finer than American Cream of Wheat.

Serves 2 people

- 1/4 cup Cream of Wheat (or other wheat farina)
- 2 cups skim milk
- 1/3 stick *canela* (Ceylon cinnamon)
- 1/4 teaspoon kosher salt
- 1 1/2 tablespoons sugar
- 1/8 teaspoon vanilla extract
- 1/8 teaspoon almond extract

1. Combine the farina, milk, *canela*, salt, and sugar in a small saucepan and bring to a quick boil. Adjust the heat to low and continue to cook, stirring occasionally, until the mixture thickens (about 5 minutes). Taste and adjust seasonings, if needed.

2. Turn the heat off and add the vanilla and almond extract. Stir well and serve.

INCAPARINA

Fortified Corn and Milk with *Canela*

Incaparina is a delicious alternative to *Mosh* (page 91). It is a powder made of corn and soy. It is high in protein, folic acid, iron, and zinc. Children, pregnant women, and elders often consume Incaparina as a nutritional supplement. It is also a recommended drink at public schools and day-care centers. My mom made it at home with milk and flavored the drink with *canela*. Incaparina is available at Latino stores in the United States and online.

Serves 2 people

1/3 cup Incaparina
2 cups skim milk
1/3 stick *canela* (Ceylon cinnamon)
1/4 teaspoon kosher salt
1 1/2 tablespoons sugar

1. Dissolve the Incaparina well in the milk. Combine all ingredients in a small saucepan and bring to a quick boil. Adjust the heat to low and continue to cook, stirring occasionally, until the mixture thickens (about 5 minutes). Taste and adjust seasonings, if needed.

2. Serve the drink hot.

HUEVOS TIBIOS CON ACEITE DE OLIVA
Soft-Boiled Eggs with Olive Oil

A This egg dish is a favorite in my home. We call it Danish-style eggs because we eat this dish often when we visit Denmark (my husband's homeland). Soft-boiled eggs are delicious, easy to prepare, and pretty. Danes don't add olive oil to their eggs, but some Guatemalans do.

Serves 2 people

2 eggs
3 cups water
Olive oil
Kosher salt and freshly ground black pepper

1. Bring the water to a rolling boil. Immerse the eggs carefully with a slotted spoon. Cook medium to large eggs for 4 1/2 minutes and jumbo eggs for 5 minutes.

2. Remove the tops of the eggs with a table knife. Serve the eggs with oil, salt, and pepper on the side.

Recipe Variation

Huevos Duros con Salsita de Tomate Ciruela (hard-boiled eggs with quick plum tomato sauce): Immerse 2 eggs in cold water and bring to a quick boil. Cook the eggs for 10 minutes from boiling point, until they're hard-boiled. Cut the eggs in wedges and put them on 2 warm corn tortillas. Top with *Salsita de Tomate Ciruela* (quick plum tomato sauce, page 328) and add the cheese of your choice. Eat as an open-faced sandwich.

HUEVOS REVUELTOS CON TOMATE Y CEBOLLA

Scrambled Eggs with Tomatoes and Onions

This delicious and easy recipe is as Guatemalan as corn tortillas. Try it when you're getting tired of the same old scrambled eggs. Guatemalans modify the recipe in many ways. For example, sometimes people add corn tortilla bits instead of tomatoes and onions. Accompany the eggs with *Frijoles Chapines* (Guatemalan black beans, page 61) and Tortillas *de Maíz* (corn tortillas, page 25). Or serve the eggs atop a panfried corn tortilla with beans on the side.

Serves 2 people

2 large or 3 small eggs
1 tablespoon canola oil
2 1/2 tablespoons finely diced Roma tomatoes
1 tablespoon finely diced yellow onion
1/4 teaspoon kosher salt

1. Beat the eggs until fluffy and set aside.

2. Add the oil to a heated medium nonstick skillet. Add the tomatoes and onion and season with salt. Cook at medium heat until saucy and thick (about 3 minutes). Taste and adjust salt, if needed.

3. Add the eggs and combine well with the sauce. Continue to cook until eggs are cooked and smooth (2 to 3 minutes).

HUEVOS ESTRELLADOS CON CHIRMOL FRITO

Eggs Sunny-Side Up with Guatemalan *Sofrito*

A *Huevos Estrellados* literally means "crashed eggs." When topped with *Chirmol Frito* (page 311), a tomato and onion pan sauce, they are also known as *Huevos Rancheros*. The sauce can contain chiles in addition to tomatoes and onions. Sometimes Guatemalans panfry corn tortillas after frying the eggs, put the eggs on top of the tortillas, and smother them with the sauce.

Serves 2 people

1 tablespoon canola oil

2 large eggs

1 batch *Chirmol Frito* (page 311)

Panfried corn tortillas (optional)

1. Heat the oil in a nonstick skillet. Add the eggs, cover, and fry until set and crispy on the edges (about 2 minutes). Transfer the eggs to a plate and keep them warm.

2. Top the eggs with the sauce.

HUEVOS CON TORTILLA
Tortilla Egg Scramble

 In Guatemala scrambled eggs can contain a wide variety of ingredients besides tomatoes, onions, or tortillas. If you like, add diced chayote squash, squash blossoms, or cooked chorizo during step 2.

Serves 2 people

2 large or 3 small eggs

1/4 teaspoon kosher salt

1 tablespoon canola oil

3 tablespoons corn tortillas, finely diced

1. Beat the eggs with the salt until fluffy and set them aside.

2. Put the oil in a heated medium nonstick skillet. Add the diced tortillas and fry them for 1 minute. Add the eggs and mix well with the tortilla pieces. Continue to cook until eggs are cooked and smooth (2 to 3 minutes).

HUEVOS CON CHORIZO CHAPÍN
Scrambled Eggs with Guatemalan Chorizo

A Use Chorizo *Chapín* (Guatemalan red sausage, page 181) or store-bought chorizo in this recipe. For a delicious twist, replace the chorizo with *Longaniza* (Guatemalan spicy white sausage with mint, onion, and sour orange, page 183).

Serves 2 people

2 large or 3 small eggs
1/8 teaspoon kosher salt

3 tablespoons chorizo

1 teaspoon canola oil

1. Beat the eggs with the salt until fluffy and set them aside.

2. Add the chorizo to a heated medium nonstick skillet. Cook the sausage, stirring often, until it's almost crispy (about 5 minutes).

3. Add the oil and stir well. Add the eggs and cook until set and smooth (2 to 3 minutes).

 Amalia's Note

Beware of using too much salt. Chorizo already contains plenty of it.

PANQUEQUES DE MAÍZ CON MIEL DE ABEJA Y FRAMBUESAS

Corn Pancakes with Honey and Raspberries

 Guatemalan pancakes resemble thick crepes. Traditional pancakes are made with wheat flour. Corn pancakes are just as easy to make and are equally delicious.

Makes 7 to 10 *panqueques*

2/3 cup skim milk

2 large eggs

2 tablespoons canola oil

3/4 cup stone-ground corn flour

1/4 cup all-purpose flour

1 tablespoon sugar

1/8 teaspoon kosher salt

Honey for drizzling

1 cup raspberries

1. Combine the first 7 ingredients in a bowl. Mix them with a stainless steel whisk until the batter is thick but still pourable.

2. Heat a medium nonstick skillet. Pour about 3 tablespoons of the batter into the pan and swirl it around to coat the bottom of the skillet. Cook over medium heat just until the pancake appears dry on the surface and can be turned with a soft spatula (about 1 1/2 minutes on 1 side and 1/2 minute on the other side).

3. Serve the pancake drizzled with honey and garnished with raspberries.

Amalia's Note

I recommend using Bob's Red Mill stone-ground corn flour. This brand is available at most grocery stores in the United States.

PLÁTANOS

Basic Guatemalan Plantains and Variations

A Guatemalans eat green and ripe plantains cooked in many ways. Plantains are used for tasty treats such as *Frituras de Plátano Verde* (spicy shrimp green plantain fritters, page 119) or *Tapado* Garifuna (seafood chowder with tomatoes, green plantains, and coconut, page 238). Plantains are starchier than bananas. You must cook them before you eat them. Buy plantains that look already yellow and let them ripen even more, until the peels darken almost to black. This will take several days or up to a week. A very ripe plantain has high sugar content, and this is ideal for panfrying and for all the following recipes. The first recipe is a basic one that you can modify in various ways.

Serves 4 people

2 ripe plantains, unpeeled, washed, cut into
    2-inch slices

1/2 stick *canela* (Ceylon cinnamon)

2 tablespoons sugar

2 cups water

Crema (Latino table cream)

1. Combine the plantains, *canela*, sugar, and water in a medium saucepan and bring to a quick boil. Reduce the heat to low, cover, and simmer until the plantains are cooked (3 to 5 minutes). When cooked, the plantains look shiny and swelled up.

2. Peel the plantains. Serve them topped with a dollop of *crema* or use them as a base for *Atol de Plátano* (hot plantain drink) recipe below.

Recipe Variations

Atol de Plátano (hot plantain drink): Start with the recipe above, but omit the cream. In a blender, process the peeled plantains with the cooking liquid to make a thick purée. Thin the purée by adding 1 1/2 to 2 cups of hot water. Heat through, taste, and adjust sugar if needed.

Plátanos Asados (grilled plantains): Grill plantains following the procedure in Mole de *Plátano* (grilled plantains in chocolate and chile sauce, page 153). Top the plantains with a dollop of *crema*.

Plátanos Fritos (panfried plantains): Peel the plantains and slice them 1/2 inch thick on the diagonal. Panfry the slices in batches in 3 tablespoons of canola oil over medium heat until medium brown (about 1 1/2 minutes per side). Adjust the oil if needed as you fry each batch. Transfer the plantains to a plate lined with paper towels to absorb excess oil.

Plátanos Horneados (baked plantains with butter and cinnamon): Peel the plantains and slice them 1/2 inch thick on the diagonal. Lay the slices on a large piece of foil. Drizzle them with about 1/2 cup of melted butter, 1 1/2 tablespoons brown sugar, and 1 teaspoon ground *canela* (Ceylon cinnamon). Wrap the package and seal it tightly. Bake at 375°F for 12 to 15 minutes.

Plátanos en Gloria (plantains in spiced syrup): Start with the *Plátanos Fritos* recipe. Then wipe the skillet with paper towels to remove most of the oil. Add 2 cups of very hot water, 1 cup of brown sugar, 1/3 stick *canela* (Ceylon cinnamon), 2 cloves, 2 allspice berries, 1 teaspoon of lime zest, and 1 teaspoon of orange zest. Cover the skillet and simmer until aromatic (about 5 minutes). Uncover, increase the heat to high, and reduce until the sauce is very bubbly and has thickened to syrup (about 15 minutes). Strain the syrup and drizzle it over the panfried plantains.

ENTRADAS, BOQUITAS Y CHUCHERÍAS
APPETIZERS, TAPAS, AND STREET FOOD

Pirujos bread (page 127)

STREET GOURMET

Street food is present in every country, culture, and subculture. In my travels, I have noticed that the more economically challenged a country is, the more street vendors it has.

In Guatemala, street food is everywhere. On weekdays street vendors congregate in areas where there's a lot of work-related foot traffic. On weekends street vendors set up shop in church atriums, plazas, and parks and outside movie theaters, discos, and anywhere they find large crowds. A variety of vendors cater to almost every need. They offer breakfast, lunch, dinner, and even late-night snacks. The foods include egg or bean sandwiches, open-faced stuffed tortillas, spicy fresh fruit snacks, ceviches, and much more. The daily routine runs smoothly, even though it's unplanned. As the morning vendors dismantle their stands, the lunch ones get up and running.

Street vendors are not always highly skilled cooks. Pedestrians know that they are eating at their own risk. So why do they buy street food? The main reasons are affordability and easy access. Street food is fast food in countries outside the United States. Also, food seduces. When food is around, it awakens every sense. And street vendors know how to lure customers. They prepare mouth-watering dishes in a flash right in front of their potential customers. Some Guatemalans claim that they are "cured" of getting sick from eating street foods. There might be a bit of truth in this, as one's tolerance to disease grows with constant exposure—up to a point.

Some Guatemalan street food is also bar food. In Guatemalan bars, each drink is traditionally accompanied by a tasty treat—whether the customer requests it or not. Pair street food with traditional and popular Guatemalan drinks found in chapter 15 (page 393). This chapter shows you how to make many scrumptious street foods. You can adapt them as light or heavy appetizers, small plates or tapas, for gatherings with family and friends. Street food is versatile and can be adapted to any style and occasion. It is also a fun and delicious way to entertain guests.

YUCA *CON CHICHARRÓN Y* CHILE
Yuca with Spicy Lime Cabbage Slaw and Crispy Pork Rind

A This recipe was inspired by the street vendors of the east-central region of Guatemala, where buses full of passengers travel from the capital on the Atlantic highway, passing by many food shacks along the way. When the buses stop for fuel, eager street vendors rush toward them with large flat baskets full of cooked treats. Sometimes they even board the buses, filling the air with delicious aromas.

Serves 2 to 4 people

6 cups water

1 teaspoon kosher salt

1 1/2 pounds fresh peeled yuca, cut into 1-inch slices

1 batch *Curtido Crudo* (spicy lime cabbage slaw, page 263) or 1 batch *Curtido con Rábanos* (spicy radish-cabbage slaw, page 263)

1/2 cup crushed crispy pork rind

1. In a medium saucepan, bring the water to a quick boil and add the salt. Add the yuca and cook it until it's soft, but not mushy (about 15 minutes). Alternatively, steam the yuca until cooked (25 to 30 minutes).

2. Drain the yuca in a colander in the sink. Let the yuca cool slightly. Take out the stringy inner core (if visible) and discard it. With a fork, break the yuca pieces into small chunks, but do not mash them.

3. Serve the yuca topped with the slaw and pork rind and add additional lime juice, if desired.

Amalia's Notes

Frozen yuca is available at Latino markets throughout the United States. It is also available fresh at some grocery stores. It takes a bit of time and effort to cut and peel the fresh yuca, but this can save you some money. Peel it as you would peel potatoes.

Crispy pork rind is available at Latino markets by the meat section.

TOSTADAS *GUATEMALTECAS*
Crispy Corn Tortillas Topped with Guacamole, Beans, and Salsa

Tostadas are one of my family's favorite dinners at home, especially when we have very little time to prepare a full meal. Tostadas are not only fun to prepare, but also delicious to eat. They can make dinnertime fun for kids. Set up a tostada bar and have the kids form a line and assemble their own tostadas. To make the tostadas more substantial, add store-bought rotisserie chicken, *carne asada*, roasted pork, or any other protein to the traditional ingredients listed in this recipe. In Guatemala, tostadas are sold on the street at sidewalk shacks, festivals, fairs, church atriums, plazas, and parks. This is my healthy version, which uses baked tostadas instead of the traditional fried ones.

Serves 4 to 6 people

12 to 16 corn tortillas

1 batch *Salsita de Tomate Ciruela* (quick plum tomato sauce, page 328)

1 batch *Guacamol para Tostadas* (Guatemalan guacamole for tostadas, page 289)

1 batch *Frijoles Colados con* Chile Pimiento (bean purée with red bell pepper *sofrito*, page 62)

Adorno (Garnish)

1 cup thinly julienned red or yellow onion

1 cup chopped flat-leaf parsley

Guatemalan *queso seco* (or Cotija cheese), crumbled

1. Bake the tortillas in a toaster oven at 350°F until they're crispy (5 to 7 minutes). Keep a close eye on them, as they can burn easily. Weigh them down with a small wire cooling rack to keep them from curling up. Once the tortillas are crispy, tostadas keep for days.

2. Prepare all the remaining ingredients.

3. Set up all the ingredients in salad bar fashion. Or set up all the ingredients at the table. Invite diners to assemble their own tostadas.

4. Assembly suggestion: Spread salsa, guacamole, or beans on a tostada. Add garnishes in the order listed. Top the tostada with your protein of choice, if you like.

MIXTAS Y SHUCOS
Guatemalan Hot Dogs

A Mixtas are stacked open-faced corn tortilla sandwiches. In Guatemala City, mixtas are a common street food. They contain *salchichas* (hot dogs), guacamole, and herbed pickled cabbage slaw. *Mixtas* may have originated with German settlers in Guatemala. *Shucos* are similar to *mixtas*, except *shucos* are made with *pirujos* (Guatemalan elongated bread) or hot dog buns instead of tortillas. *Shucos* may contain chorizo *colorado* (red sausage), *longaniza* (white sausage), *salchicha* (hot dogs), and other ingredients. They are topped with condiments such as mayonnaise, ketchup, mustard, or hot sauce.

Serves 4 to 6 people

8 to 12 corn tortillas or 4 to 6 hot dog buns, halved and grilled on the inside

1 batch *Guacamol Chapín* (Guatemalan guacamole, page 289)

1 to 2 packages low-fat beef hot dogs or sausage of choice, halved lengthwise, griddled until medium brown

1 batch *Curtido* (herbed pickled cabbage slaw, page 263) or 1 batch *Curtido Crudo* (spicy lime cabbage slaw, page 263)

Condimentos (Condiments)

Mustard

Mayonnaise

Hot pepper sauce

Ketchup

1. To make *mixtas*, warm tortillas in a preheated toaster oven for about 1 1/2 minutes or heat them in a nonstick skillet for 1 minute per side. Top each corn tortilla with 1 or 2 teaspoons of guacamole, a half or whole hot dog, slaw, mustard, mayonnaise, hot sauce, and plenty of ketchup.

2. To make *shucos*, spread 2 teaspoons of guacamole on one side of the bun and mayonnaise, mustard, and ketchup on the other side. Add a whole hot dog and top with slaw and hot sauce.

Amalia's Note

To save time, make the slaw ahead. The herbed pickled slaw keeps well in the refrigerator for up to a month.

GUATEMALAN ENCHILADAS

Lettuce Cups with Spiced Beef, Marinated Vegetables, Tortilla Crunchies, Egg, and Cheese

A traditional Guatemalan enchilada is a delicious, messy, fancy tostada with layers of ingredients piled on top of one other. It is a popular street food at fairs, festivals, and *mercados*. It can also be prepared as an elegant fork-and-knife salad or in casual lettuce cups, a more casual food. Most ingredients can be prepped the day before, making this dish perfect for a build-your-own enchilada party.

Serves 4 to 6 people

Carne (Meat)

1 pound flank steak

Kosher salt and freshly ground black pepper

1 tablespoon canola oil

1 1/2 cups fat-free, low-sodium beef stock

1/2 yellow onion, quartered

2 bay leaves

1/3 cup finely diced yellow onion

1/4 teaspoon thyme

1 bay leaf

1 1/2 teaspoons garlic, minced

1 tablespoon canola oil

1/3 cup canned crushed tomatoes

Kosher salt and freshly ground black pepper

Salsa (Sauce)

1 cup roughly chopped Roma tomatoes

1/2 cup roughly chopped yellow onion

1/2 cup water

1 teaspoon minced garlic

3/4 to 1 teaspoon thyme

Kosher salt

Adorno (Garnish)

4 to 6 leaves of butter lettuce, washed and spun dry

1 batch *Curtido para* Enchiladas (pickled slaw for Guatemalan enchilada lettuce cups, page 277)

1 cup finely shredded Cotija cheese

1/2 cup julienned yellow onions

1 cup finely chopped flat-leaf parsley leaves

2 hard-boiled eggs, chopped or cut into wedges

Tortilla crunchies (page 26)

1. Season the steak with salt and pepper. In a hot, medium-size, deep skillet, sear the meat on both sides in the oil until medium brown, about 4 minutes per side. Add the stock, onion, and bay leaves, and bring to a quick boil. Lower the heat, cover, and braise until the meat fibers separate easily when pulled (about 1 1/2 hours). Check the meat during cooking and make sure the liquid stays at about 1 1/2 cups at all times. Add 1/2 cup of stock or water at a time as needed. When the meat is done, transfer it to a cutting board and let it cool. Discard the onion and bay leaves. Pour the broth into a cup and set it aside.

2. Cut the meat into uniform 2-inch chunks and chop them coarsely in a food processor, in batches, using the pulsing function for better control. In the same skillet in which you cooked the steak, panfry the onion, thyme, bay leaf, and garlic in the oil until aromatic (about 2 minutes). Add the tomatoes and the reserved broth, taste, and adjust the seasonings if needed. Add the meat to this mixture and cook over low heat, stirring occasionally, until most of the liquid has evaporated (8 to 10 minutes).

3. Combine all the sauce ingredients in a medium saucepan and bring to a quick boil. Reduce the heat and simmer covered until all the vegetables are tender (5 to 8 minutes). Purée the cooked vegetables with an immersion blender or regular blender. Return the purée to the pan, reheat it, taste it, and adjust the seasonings if needed.

4. Assemble the salad in individual portions (or on a platter) by layering ingredients attractively beginning with the lettuce, followed by a thin layer of *curtido* (drained), the meat, another thin layer of *curtido*, sauce, cheese, onion, parsley, eggs, and tortilla crunchies.

Amalia's Note

Use leftover meat as a topping for Tostadas *Guatemaltecas* (page 111) or as stuffing for Tacos *Dorados con Guacamol Chapín* (page 117) or Tortillas *con Carne, Longaniza, Pollo, Ó Huevo Duro* (page 121).

TACOS *DORADOS CON GUACAMOL CHAPÍN*
Guatemalan Rolled Crispy Tacos with Guacamole

A Guatemalan tacos are rolled crispy treats stuffed with a variety of ingredients. Street vendors stack tacos in baskets and garnish them with fresh onion rings, chopped parsley, and crumbled dried cheese. When sold to passersby, they are quickly topped with tomato sauce, guacamole, and more.

Makes 16 to 18 tacos

16 to 18 corn tortillas
1 batch *Relleno de Pollo* (chicken and vegetable stuffing, page 205) or 1 batch *Relleno de Cerdo y Res* (pork and beef stuffing, page 206) or 1 batch *Relleno de Verduras* (vegetarian stuffing, page 206)
16 to 18 toothpicks

3/4 cup canola oil

Adorno (Garnish)

3 leaves of butter lettuce
1 batch *Guacamol para Tostadas* (Guatemalan guacamole for tostadas, page 289)
1 batch *Salsita de Tomate Ciruela* (quick plum tomato sauce, page 328)
1 batch *Curtido Crudo* (spicy lime cabbage slaw, page 263)
Guatemalan *queso seco* (or Cotija cheese), crumbled
1/2 cup chopped flat-leaf parsley leaves
1/2 cup julienned yellow onion

1. Warm the tortillas in a preheated toaster oven for about 1 1/2 minutes or heat them in a non-stick skillet for 1 minute per side. Keep the tortillas warm.

2. Place 2 tablespoons of stuffing in the center of each tortilla and distribute the stuffing carefully with your fingers to form a cylinder. Roll the tortilla tightly around the stuffing and secure with a toothpick.

3. Heat a skillet over medium heat. Add the oil. Fry the tacos in small batches of 4 or 5 at a time (1 1/2 to 2 minutes per side). Remove the toothpicks as you turn the tacos to fry their other sides. Transfer the fried tacos to a plate lined with paper towels to absorb excess oil. Keep the tacos warm.

4. Serve the tacos on a bed of lettuce, topped with garnishes in the order listed.

Amalia's Notes

Buy tortillas *para* tacos (tortillas for tacos) at Latino stores. They are smaller than regular corn tortillas. If tortillas *para* tacos are unavailable, use regular-size tortillas.

Save and freeze leftover stuffing for later use.

FRITURAS DE PLÁTANO VERDE

Spicy Shrimp Green Plantain Fritters

These spicy fritters are delicious by themselves or with a light sprinkling of lime juice. *Frituras de plátano verde* with varying ingredients are popular in Garifuna cooking. Serve them as a side or appetizer. You can make them with or without seafood. For a twist on this recipe, use fresh herbs and chile powder instead of fresh peppers.

Makes 16 fritters

1 1/4 cups peeled and shredded green plantains (about 2 plantains)

2 teaspoons minced garlic

2 teaspoons minced Serrano pepper (or other hot chile pepper)

2 ounces frozen tiny salad shrimp, thawed and drained (or other seafood)

1 teaspoon kosher salt

Freshly ground black pepper

About 3/4 cup canola oil

Adorno (Garnish)

Minced red bell pepper

Chopped flat-leaf parsley leaves

1. Mix the plantains, garlic, chile pepper, shrimp, salt, and pepper in a bowl. Form 16 equal-size balls with the mixture. Pick up each ball and mold it like a meatball, then press gently with your hands to flatten the balls into patties.

2. In a deep medium skillet, heat the oil until it sizzles and small bubbles begin to form. Cook the fritters in the oil until their edges look medium brown (about 2 minutes per side). Fry the fritters in batches and don't overcrowd the skillet. With a wide spatula, transfer the crispy fritters to a platter lined with paper towels to absorb excess oil.

3. Serve the fritters garnished with bell pepper and parsley.

GARNACHAS

Tasty Tortilla Morsels Topped with Chicken and Spicy Cabbage Slaw

A *Garnachas* are tasty treats of varying sizes and textures sold at fairs and religious celebrations. Recipes vary from cook to cook. This is my version using a variety of fillings and toppings. In Guatemala the tortilla cups are fried and then filled. A healthier method is to bake the tortillas until the dough is fully cooked, but not crunchy.

Makes 16 *garnachas*

2 cups instant corn masa flour
2 cups chicken stock or water

Canola oil

1/2 batch *Relleno de Pollo* (chicken and
vegetable stuffing, page 205) or 1 batch
Relleno de Cerdo y Res (pork and beef
stuffing, page 206) or 1/2 batch *Relleno de
Verduras* (vegetarian stuffing, page 206)

Adorno (Garnish)
1 batch *Curtido Crudo* (spicy lime cabbage
slaw, page 263) or *Curtido con Rábanos*
(spicy radish-cabbage slaw, page 263) or 1
cup chopped flat-leaf parsley
1 batch *Salsita de Tomate Ciruela* (quick plum
tomato sauce, page 328)
Guatemalan *queso seco* (or Cotija cheese),
crumbled

1. Combine the flour with the stock or water to
make a very moist dough. It should not stick to
your hands. If the dough feels dry, add a little
more liquid. If it's too wet, add more flour.
When you form it into a ball, the dough should
hold its shape and not crack when pressed.
Keep the dough covered with a damp cloth, as
it tends to dry quickly.

2. Divide the dough into 16 equal parts and form
them into balls. Line a tortilla maker with plastic
wrap on both sides. Flatten the balls in the tortilla maker to about 1/4 inch thick (about 3
inches in diameter).

3. On a preheated griddle or nonstick skillet over
medium heat, cook the tortillas until the edges
loosen, about 1 minute. Turn with a wide spatula and cook for another minute. Transfer to a
tortilla warmer or cloth. The tortillas will not be
fully cooked. When the tortillas are cool
enough to handle, pinch the edges with your
fingers to make cups. Form a wall around the
perimeter of each tortilla, pulling as much
dough from the center to the sides as possible.
Flatten the center with your thumb. Panfry the
tortilla cups in batches in canola oil until light
brown or bake them at 400°F until the dough is
cooked (about 4 minutes). Keep a close eye on
the tortilla cups as they cook.

4. Fill the tortilla cups with the stuffing of your
choice and top with slaw, parsley, sauce,
and cheese.

TORTILLAS *CON CARNE, LONGANIZA, POLLO, Ó HUEVO DURO*

Open-Faced Soft Corn Tortilla Sandwiches with *Carne Asada*, *Longaniza*, Chicken, or Hard-Boiled Eggs

A Tortillas *con carne* are popular at carnivals, festivals, and *mercados abiertos* (open markets) where people shop for fresh seasonal vegetables or other items. Eager vendors take advantage of the crowds and open small shops with improvised grills, where they make tortillas piled with ingredients of the customer's choice. Street vendors live a nomadic life. They often take their stores down as easily as they assemble them, sometimes leaving behind only a trace of their presence. Then they quickly pop up at other celebrations.

Serves 4 to 6 people

12 to 18 white, yellow, or blue corn tortillas

Rellenos (Fillings)

Choose 1 or 2 of the following:

1 batch sliced *Carne Asada con Chirmol* (orange and onion–marinated flank steak with charred tomato and mint salsa, page 173)

1 batch *Longaniza* (Guatemalan spicy white sausage with mint, onion, and bitter orange, page 183)

1 batch *Relleno de Pollo* (chicken and vegetable stuffing, page 205) or 1 batch *Relleno de Cerdo y Res* (pork and beef stuffing, page 206) or 1 batch *Relleno de Verduras* (vegetarian stuffing, page 206) or 1 batch store bought rotisserie chicken

4 to 6 hard-boiled eggs, quartered lengthwise

Adorno (Garnish)

1 batch *Salsita de Tomate Ciruela* (quick plum tomato sauce, page 328)

1 batch *Chilito* (bird's eye chile, onion, lime, and olive oil sauce, page 325)

1 cup cherry tomatoes, quartered

½ cup English cucumber, thinly sliced and quartered

½ cup thinly sliced cabbage

½ cup yellow bell peppers, thinly sliced

1 avocado, peeled, pitted, thinly sliced

3/4 cup chopped flat-leaf parsley or cilantro leaves

1 cup thinly sliced yellow or green onions

Crema (Latino table cream) (optional)

1. Warm the tortillas in a preheated toaster oven for about 1 1/2 minutes or heat them in a non-stick skillet for 1 minute per side. Keep the tortillas warm.

2. Assembly for tortillas with *Carne Asada con Chirmol*: Fill tortillas with sliced grilled meat and garnish with the *chirmol* sauce.

3. Assembly for tortillas with *longaniza*, chicken, stuffing, and eggs: Fill tortillas with your proteins of choice and garnish as desired.

Amalia's Note

For a hearty, balanced meal, accompany this dish with *Arroz Guatemalteco* (Guatemalan vegetable rice, page 287), *Guacamol Chapín* (Guatemalan guacamole, page 289), and *Frijoles Colados con* Chile Pimiento (bean purée with red bell pepper *sofrito*, page 62).

ELOTES ASADOS CON LIMÓN Y SAL DE MAR
Grilled Fresh Corn with Lime and Sea Salt in Corn Husks

For street food, it doesn't get any simpler than this. *Elotes Asados* (grilled corn on the cob) is a common barbecue item and street food in Guatemala City. Street vendors grill the corn in rustic grills, rub them generously with lime and salt, and serve them on fresh corn husks. The corn is also boiled in the husks, peeled, and rubbed with lime and salt or varnished with mayonnaise, hot sauce, and other condiments. (See Crazy Corn variation following this recipe.) Grilled corn is more nutritious than boiled corn.

Serves 4 to 6 people

4 to 6 ears of fresh corn, husked
husks of 4 to 6 ears of corn
2 limes, halved
Sea salt

1. Grill the corn over very hot charcoal until the corn is charred all over. Keep a close eye on the corn, as it cooks fast. Turn corn when charring and popping begins. Keep the cooked corn warm.

2. Serve the corn on the husks, rubbed with lime and sprinkled with sea salt.

Recipe Variation

Elotes Locos (Crazy Corn): Cook the ears of corn in the husks in salted boiling water for 5 to 8 minutes. Then carefully remove the husks—beware of the steam—cool slightly, and varnish the corn with a light coating of low-fat mayonnaise. Sprinkle the corn with dried Cotija cheese, bottled hot chile sauce, and cobán chile powder (page 6).

Amalia's Note

Alternatively, remove the kernels from the cob with a sharp knife, sprinkle them with lime juice and salt, and serve them as a side dish.

PANES
Guatemalan Sandwiches

A *Panes* literally means "breads." *Panes* can be simple or elaborate sandwiches. They are a popular street food and a common item in school lunch boxes. Often *panes* are stuffed with the previous day's leftovers, such as beans and cheese, holiday turkey, or delicious chiles *rellenos*. Make them at home with *carne asada* or the proteins of your choice.

Makes 4 to 6 sandwiches

4 to 6 *pirujos* (elongated bread), halved lengthwise

Rellenos (Fillings)
Choose 1 of the following:

1 batch Chiles *Rellenos* (fire-roasted peppers stuffed with chicken and vegetables, page 129)

3 cups shredded *Pavo Navideño* (Guatemalan holiday roasted turkey, page 211)

1 batch *Frijoles Colados con* Chile Pimiento (bean purée with red bell pepper *sofrito*, page 62)

1 batch *Relleno de Pollo* (chicken and vegetable stuffing, page 205)

1 batch *Relleno de Cerdo y Res* (pork and beef stuffing, page 206)

1 batch *Relleno de Verduras* (vegetarian stuffing, page 206)

Adorno (Garnish)
1 head Bibb or leaf lettuce, washed and spun dry

1 cup thinly sliced onion

1 cup sliced tomatoes

1/2 cup chopped flat-leaf parsley

1 cup crumbled *queso fresco* (fresh Latino cheese)

1 batch *Salsita de Tomate Ciruela* (quick plum tomato sauce, page 328)

Condimentos (Condiments)
Light mayonnaise

Bottled hot sauce or *Chilito* (page 325)

1. Assembly 1: Spread mayonnaise on both sides of the bun, add lettuce, and top with a chile *relleno*, a little onion, parsley, *salsita de tomate ciruela*, and hot sauce.

2. Assembly 2: Spread mayonnaise on both sides of the bun, add lettuce, and top with shredded turkey, a little onion, tomato, *salsita de tomate ciruela*, and hot sauce.

3. Assembly 3: Spread beans on both sides of the bun, add 2 tablespoons crumbled fresh cheese, and top with some *salsita de tomate ciruela* and hot sauce.

4. Assembly 4: Spread beans on both sides of the bun, add lettuce, add 3 tablespoons of the *relleno* of choice, and top with a little onion, tomato, and hot sauce.

Amalia's Note
Many Latino grocery stores in the United States have bakeries. Substitute *pirujos* with *bolillos* or any other bread of similar texture.

CHILES *RELLENOS*
Fire-Roasted Peppers Stuffed with Chicken and Vegetables

Chiles *rellenos* are a favorite street food and home treat stuffed with a variety of fillings. As a street food, chiles *rellenos* are made into sandwiches with lettuce, tomato, onions, and parsley. At home they are often served accompanied by rice, salad, and corn tortillas. Traditionally, chiles *rellenos* are coated in egg batter and deep-fried. This is my healthier and easier version. It omits the egg batter and deep-frying, replacing those with fire-roasting and broiling. In Guatemala, chiles rellenos are made with fresh pimiento chiles, but Anaheim and poblanos are good substitutes.

Serves 4 to 6 people

4 to 6 fresh Anaheim or poblano peppers

1/4 cup white wine vinegar

1 batch *Relleno de Pollo* (chicken and vegetable stuffing, page 205) or 1 batch *Relleno de Cerdo y Res* (pork and beef stuffing, page 206) or 1 batch *Relleno de Verduras* (vegetarian stuffing, page 206)

Adorno (Garnish)

1 batch *Salsita de Tomate Ciruela* (quick plum tomato sauce, page 328)

1/2 cup flat-leaf parsley leaves

1/2 cup julienned yellow onion

1. Roast the peppers directly over a flame on the stovetop or on a very hot grill to char all sides evenly. Wrap the peppers in plastic or seal them in a plastic bag and let them sit for about 10 minutes to loosen the skins. (Alternatively, dip the peppers in very hot oil for 1 to 2 minutes to blister the skins.) Remove the skins using damp paper towels. Make a slit on 1 side of each pepper, and carefully remove the seeds, ribs, and inner core with the help of scissors. Brush the peppers with vinegar inside and out and let them sit for 10 minutes.

2. Stuff the peppers, broil them for 3 to 5 minutes, and serve them garnished with *salsita de tomate ciruela*, parsley, and onion.

Amalia's Note
Save and freeze leftover stuffing for later use.

Recipe Variation

For the traditional version of chiles *rellenos*, replace step 2 with the following steps.

Huevo Batido (Egg Batter)
> 2 large eggs, separated
> 1/8 teaspoon kosher salt
> 1 tablespoon all-purpose flour

> Flour
> Canola oil

1. Beat the egg whites until stiff peaks form. Add the yolks, salt, and flour. Beat 1 minute to make a soft batter.

2. Heat a medium skillet and add about 2 tablespoons of oil.

3. Work with one pepper at a time. Pat dry and stuff each pepper with the stuffing of your choice. Dust the pepper with a little flour and dip it quickly in the batter to coat it very lightly.

4. Panfry the battered peppers in small batches. Place them facedown first to seal the open side. Use a wide spatula to turn the peppers and cook all sides to medium brown (about 1 minute per side). Keep a close eye on the peppers, as the egg batter cooks fast. Adjust the oil as you cook each batch, and adjust the heat if the batter is browning too fast. Transfer the fried peppers to a platter lined with paper towels to absorb excess oil.

FRUTA CON PEPITA, LIMÓN Y CHILE COBANERO

Fresh Fruit with Lime, Sea Salt, and Cobán Chile

This is a very popular snack sold by street cart vendors throughout Guatemala. Vendors peel the fruit, cut it into medium-size pieces, pack the pieces tightly in *bolsitas* (small bags), and hang them from the side of the cart. Large mangoes are shaped like a flower and sold on a stick. As fruit is sold, it is garnished with toppings of the customer's choice. This snack is easy, healthy, and addicting. It can serve as a light dessert, too. For a flavorful twist on this recipe, grill the fruit before seasoning it.

Serves 4 to 6 people

4 to 6 2-inch cubes of each of the following fruits: green mango, seeded cucumber, papaya, pineapple, orange, and cherry tomatoes

4 to 6 skewers

Juice of 2 limes

Kosher salt

1/2 cup ground roasted pumpkin seeds

1/2 teaspoon cobán chile powder (or smoked piquín or árbol chile powder)

1. Assemble the fruit attractively on the skewers.

2. Brush the fruit all over with lime juice, then sprinkle it with salt, ground pumpkin seeds, and chile powder.

Amalia's Note

Fruit and vegetable skewers make an attractive and healthy snack, appetizer, or side dish. Use firm (not mushy) ingredients that hold well on skewers.

Culantro (cilantro)

GUISOS MAYAS Y CALDOS
MAYAN STEWS AND SOUPS

From top to bottom:

Red bell pepper,
Poblano,
Serrano (top),
Anaheim (under),
Jalapeño,
Fresno,
Habanero (left), and
Bird's Eye (Thai) chiles

THE BACKBONE OF GUATEMALAN CUISINE

Mayan cuisine is the ancient foundation upon which modern Guatemalan cuisine is built. Mayan cuisine is also a key element of Guatemalan culture. Mayan stews give Guatemalan cuisine its strength and character. The stews carry Mayan names and vary from region to region. Prior to the arrival of Europeans, Mayan stews, tamales and other dishes, contained only native chiles and ingredients. Today they blend Old World and New World ingredients and techniques. Although Mayan stews are eaten in their areas of origin regularly, in Guatemala City, some are eaten only on special occasions and at *restaurantes típicos* (traditional Guatemalan food restaurants).

Mayan stews all combine fresh native ingredients, lively colors, velvety textures, and spicy flavors to create a symphony for the palate. Most of the stews share some ingredients, such as tomatoes, tomatillos, and dried or fresh chile peppers. But each stew has a distinctive flavor, texture, color, and aroma achieved by the use of other typical ingredients. Common spices and herbs in Mayan cooking are bay leaves, thyme, oregano, cumin, cinnamon, mint, cilantro, and epazote (a very pungent herb). Common thickeners are masa (fresh corn dough) or instant corn masa flour, blackened corn tortillas, roasted or grilled plantain peel, toasted rice, rice soaked in water, sweet or savory bread, all-purpose flour, yuca, and potatoes. The combination of native ingredients is what makes Mayan stews Guatemalan—and what differentiates them from the stews of other ancient civilizations.

Pepián can be black, yellow, or red. It's characterized by the use of pan-roasted sesame and pumpkin seeds. Mole must contain chiles, tomatoes, and sometimes chocolate in addition to seeds. *Kaqik* must contain the herb *zamat*, cobán chile, mint, and achiote. *Jocón* must contain fresh ingredients that yield a bright green sauce, such as fresh chiles, green onions, cilantro, tomatillos, and more.

Dried chile peppers play a special role in Guatemalan cuisine, especially in Mayan stews. These peppers are native to Guatemala and have very distinctive aromas and flavors as well as varying degrees of heat. Pan roasting is a technique Guatemalans often use to develop and intensify the flavor of chile peppers. Soaking is needed to reconstitute and soften the dried peppers for easier blending. Achieving the right balance of flavor and spiciness is important when using Guatemalan chile peppers. One too little or one too many can have a significant impact on the finished dish. The main kinds of dried peppers used in Mayan stews and soups are guaque (also used fresh), pasa, zambo, and cobán.

The most common fresh chile peppers used in Guatemalan cooking, stews, and sauces are morrón (sweet chile resembling a bell pepper), pimiento (red or green lightly hot chile used for chiles rellenos), verde or chocolate (a skinny tapered chile, used mostly in *paches* and available fresh and dried), chiltepe (a fiery tiny pepper with varying colors depending on ripeness), and chamborote (used to garnish *fiambre*—a spicy pepper that resembles the habanero in looks, but is larger and less spicy). Chiltepe is the Guatemalan national pepper and is the spicy pepper of choice in nearly every Guatemalan dish, from ceviches to soups to sauces. Other types of chile peppers, including *diente de perro* (dog's tooth) and *siete caldos* (seven broths), are used in some Guatemalan recipes. Jalapeño and Serrano peppers are not Guatemalan, but Guatemalans often cook with them. Anaheim, poblano, habanero, and

Fresno are not Guatemalan either, but I like to use them because of their texture, great flavor, and looks, in chiles rellenos, chowders, rice, ceviche, and even for garnish. They are good substitutes when fresh Guatemalan peppers are not available.

While vacationing in Thailand once, I took a cooking class and discovered that bird's eye chile (Thai chile) is as tasty and fiery as a Guatemalan chiltepe. If you can't find fresh chiltepe, use bird's eye chile as a substitute. It is widely available at grocery stores and Asian markets. Guatemalans say that chiltepe doesn't irritate the stomach as other hot peppers do, and neither does bird's eye chile.

The list of Mayan stews is longer and more varied than the one offered in this chapter. The recipes in this chapter represent the prominent Mayan regions of Guatemala, the western and central highlands. In 2007 the Guatemalan government declared the Mayan stews *Jocón* (page 139), *Pepián* (page 143), *Kaqik* (page 141), and Mole (page 315) collectively a cultural patrimony (heritage) of Guatemala. *Lasaña Maya* is not a stew at all, but rather a fusion recipe combining a Mayan stew with other Guatemalan flavors. Without sacrificing flavor or quality, I've simplified all the recipes in this chapter and have adapted them to the modern kitchen. I have also made them healthier and tastier by substituting lard with healthier fats and replacing water with low-fat, low-sodium stocks.

Kitchen

JOCÓN

Chicken, Tomatillo, and Cilantro Stew

A *Jocón* (pronounced ho-CON) is a dish from Huehuetenango, a department located in western Guatemala, and the surrounding region. The recipe varies slightly from family to family. This is my simplified version. It is not only easy to make, but also hearty and delicious. The sauce has a vibrant green color. You can also use it to top grilled meats, such as beef, pork, or chorizo.

Serves 4 to 6 people

4 to 6 skinless chicken thighs, visible fat removed

1 cup fat-free, low-sodium chicken stock

1 small whole onion, peeled and t-scored

1/2 cup cilantro (unchopped, stems and leaves included)

1 cup trimmed green onions cut into 1-inch pieces

2 large garlic cloves, peeled

1 1/2 cups tomatillos (about 10 tomatillos), husked and quartered

1/2 cup seeded, chopped green bell pepper

1 poblano pepper, seeded and chopped (3/4 to 1 cup)

1 cup roughly chopped cilantro (stems and leaves)

1 whole Serrano pepper, seeds and veins included (optional)

2 corn tortillas, torn into small pieces

1 cup fat-free, low-sodium chicken stock

1 teaspoon kosher salt

Freshly ground black pepper

Adorno (Garnish)

Fresh cilantro sprigs

1. Cook the chicken in the stock with the onion and cilantro in a medium saucepan until the chicken is tender (20 to 30 minutes).

2. While the chicken is cooking, cook the rest of the ingredients (except the seasonings and garnish) in a separate saucepan. Bring to a quick boil. Reduce the heat and simmer covered until the vegetables are soft (5 to 8 minutes).

3. When the chicken is done, transfer it to a dish and set it aside. Reserve the onion, cilantro, and stock.

4. Combine the vegetable mixture with the onion, cilantro, and stock. In a blender or food processor, purée the mixture until it's smooth. Pour the purée back into the pot and add the chicken. Stir and cook for 10 to 15 minutes longer. The sauce should look smooth, velvety, and bright green.

5. Season the stew with salt and pepper. Taste and adjust seasonings if needed.

6. Serve the stew garnished with cilantro sprigs.

Recipe Variation

Jocón Crudo (*jocón* with raw sauce): Cook the chicken in stock only. Then purée all the vegetables raw in a blender or food processor. (Soak the tortillas beforehand in some hot stock.) Finally, panfry the vegetable mixture in 1 tablespoon of canola oil. Combine the mixture with the chicken and stock and heat through.

Amalia's Notes

To t-score an onion, make a 1/2-inch-deep cross-shaped cut at the narrowest end of the onion. The onion remains whole.

For an outstanding meal, serve *jocón* with corn tortillas, *Arroz Guatemalteco* (Guatemalan vegetable rice, page 287), *Tamalitos de Queso* (fresh cheese mini-tamales in banana leaves, page 32), and *Frijoles Chapines* (Guatemalan black beans, page 61).

Peel tomatillos under running water if you find the husks hard to remove.

KAQIK
Red Chile Turkey Soup

A *Kaqik* is a hearty soup from Cobán, Alta Verapaz, in north-central Guatemala, a rain forest–like region with a large population of Mayas who have deeply rooted traditions. *Zamat* (a wild plant with flavor similar to cilantro) and cobán chile (a tasty, fiery chile pepper) are native to this region and give *Kaqik* its character. Achiote enhances the eye appeal of the soup.

Serves 4 people

2 skinless turkey thighs, visible fat removed (or 4 to 6 chicken thighs)

6 large whole garlic cloves, peeled

1/2 cup unchopped cilantro (stems and leaves included)

4 cups fat-free, low-sodium chicken stock

1 cup quartered Roma tomatoes (about 2 large tomatoes)

1/2 cup husked, quartered tomatillos (3 to 4 large tomatillos)

2 large whole garlic cloves, peeled

1 guaque chile (guajillo), seeded

1/2 chile pasa (ancho), seeded

3/4 cup trimmed green onions cut into 2-inch pieces

2 tablespoons roughly chopped fresh mint leaves

1/2 cup roughly chopped fresh cilantro (stems and leaves included)

1/2 cup roughly chopped *zamat* (or cilantro) leaves

1 to 1 1/2 teaspoons ground achiote dissolved in a little water

Sazón (Seasonings)

1/2 teaspoon cobán chile powder (or smoked piquín or árbol chile powder)

1 teaspoon kosher salt

Freshly ground black pepper

Adorno (Garnish)

Thinly sliced green onions or chives

Finely chopped mint leaves

Finely chopped cilantro leaves

1. In a medium pot, cook the turkey with the garlic and cilantro in the stock until the turkey is tender (30 to 45 minutes). Remove and reserve the garlic and cilantro. Set aside the pot of turkey and stock.

2. Heat a skillet for 2 minutes at medium heat. Add the tomatoes, tomatillos, and garlic. Adjust the heat to medium-low and pan roast until the vegetables are charred all over and mushy (about 8 minutes).

3. Separately, pan roast the chiles at medium-low heat for about 3 minutes. Keep a close eye on the chiles, as they burn easily. Then soak the roasted chiles in 1 cup of very hot water for 10 minutes.

4. Combine the roasted vegetables, the reserved garlic and cilantro, 1 cup of hot stock, the soaked chiles, half the soaking water, and the green onions and the fresh herbs in a blender. Purée the mixture to a fine consistency. The purée should look smooth and velvety. Add this purée to the pot of turkey and stock, stir well, and simmer the soup until it's aromatic (5 to 10 minutes).

5. Mix in the achiote liquid, chile powder, salt, and pepper. Taste and adjust seasonings if needed. Cook for 5 minutes longer.

6. Serve the soup garnished with green onions or chives, mint, and cilantro.

Amalia's Note

Peel tomatillos under running water if you find the husks hard to remove.

PEPIÁN NEGRO

Spicy Chicken and Pork Vegetable Stew

A *Pepián negro* (black *pepián*) is from Guatemala department (which contains Guatemala City) in the south-central part of the country. It takes its name from the blackened tortillas used in the sauce. There are also red and yellow *pepián* with varying ingredients, made with turkey, chicken, beef, or pork, in Quetzaltenango, Suchitepéquez, and other regions. All varieties have some ingredients in common, such as pan-roasted seeds, peppers, and tomatoes, but they may have different finishing touches. *Pepián* can be made with any kind of protein. Serve it with *Arroz Guatemalteco* (Guatemalan vegetable rice, page 287) and *Tamalitos de Queso* (fresh cheese mini-tamales in banana leaves, page 32), which provide a nice break between spicy bites.

Serves 4 to 6 people

- 3 skinless, boneless chicken thighs, cut into 2-inch pieces
- 1/2 pound pork loin, cut into 2-inch pieces
- 2 cups fat-free, low-sodium chicken stock
- 1 small whole onion, peeled and t-scored
- 1/2 cup unchopped cilantro (stems and leaves included)

- 1 cup quartered Roma tomatoes (about 2 large tomatoes)
- 1/2 cup husked, quartered tomatillos (3 to 4 large tomatillos)
- 1 small yellow onion, cut into thick slices
- 2 large garlic cloves, peeled

- 1 guaque (guajillo) chile, seeded
- 1 zambo (mulato) chile, seeded

Para Espesar (Thickeners)

Choose 1 of the following:

- 2 corn tortillas blackened in toaster oven to medium brown, soaked in hot stock for 10 minutes or
- 2 tablespoons instant corn masa flour, browned in a dry pan over medium-low heat until medium brown
- 2 tablespoons white rice, browned in a dry pan over medium-low heat until medium brown, then soaked in cold water 10 minutes

- 1 tablespoon canola oil

Sazón (Seasonings)

- 1 tablespoon ground pan-roasted pumpkin seeds
- 1 tablespoon ground pan-roasted sesame seeds
- 1/8 teaspoon ground *canela* (Ceylon cinnamon) (optional)

Arroz Guatemalteco (page 287)

1/8 teaspoon ground cloves

1 teaspoon kosher salt

Freshly ground black pepper

1 cup loosely packed, finely chopped fresh
cilantro leaves

1/2 cup small cubes of potatoes, cooked al
dente

1/2 cup fresh green beans cut into 1-inch
pieces, cooked al dente

1/2 cup carrots sliced on the diagonal, cooked
al dente

1/2 cup *güisquil* (chayote squash) cut into
1-inch cubes, cooked al dente

Adorno (Garnish)

Cilantro leaves, whole or finely chopped

1. In a medium pot, cook the chicken and pork in
the stock with the onion and cilantro over low
heat until the chicken and pork are tender (20
to 30 minutes). Remove and reserve the onion
and the cilantro. Set aside the pot of chicken,
pork, and stock.

2. Heat the skillet for 2 minutes over medium heat
and add the tomatoes, tomatillos, onion, and
garlic. Adjust the heat to medium-low and pan
roast the vegetables until they're charred all
over and mushy (about 8 minutes).

3. Separately, pan roast the chiles over medium-low heat for about 3 minutes. Keep a close
eye on the chiles, as they burn easily. Then soak
the roasted chiles in 1 cup of very hot water for
10 minutes.

4. Combine the roasted vegetables, the reserved
onion and cilantro, the soaked chiles, half the
soaking water, and 3/4 cup of the hot stock in a
blender. Add the thickener and purée to a fine
consistency. The purée should look smooth
and velvety.

5. Heat the oil in a medium skillet. Add the purée
and seasonings. Add the 1 cup of finely
chopped cilantro. Cook for about 3 minutes.
Add the sauce to the pot of chicken, pork, and
stock. Add the al dente vegetables and stir.
Simmer covered to blend the flavors (about 15
minutes). The sauce should be medium thin—
about the consistency of steak sauce. If the
sauce is too thin, cook the stew a bit longer to
thicken it. If the sauce is too thick, add more
stock or water. Taste and adjust seasonings,
if needed.

6. Serve the stew garnished with cilantro.

Amalia's Note

To t-score an onion, make a 1/2-inch-deep cross-shaped cut at the narrowest end of the
onion. The onion remains whole.

Arroz Guatemalteco (page 287)

SUBANIK

Pork and Chicken Stew

A*Subanik* is a traditional hearty stew from Chimaltenango, located about 35 miles west of Guatemala City. It is scrumptious and easy to make. It is a perfect one-dish meal for a gathering. This delicious velvety red stew goes well with *Arroz Guatemalteco* (Guatemalan vegetable rice, page 287) and *Tamalitos de Queso* (fresh cheese mini-tamales in banana leaves, page 32), which provide a break between spicy bites.

Serves 4 people

3 skinless, boneless chicken thighs, cut into 2-inch pieces

1/2 pound pork loin cut into 2-inch pieces

Kosher salt and freshly ground black pepper

1 tablespoon canola oil

2 cups fat-free, low-sodium chicken stock

1 cup quartered Roma tomatoes (about 2 large tomatoes)

1/2 cup husked, quartered tomatillos (3 to 4 large tomatillos)

1 small yellow onion, quartered

2 large garlic cloves, peeled

1 1/2 cups seeded, chopped red bell peppers

1 guaque (guajillo) chile, seeded

1/2 pasa (ancho) chile, seeded

1/2 zambo (mulato) chile, seeded

2 corn tortillas, torn into pieces

1 teaspoon ground achiote dissolved in a little water

Sazón (Seasonings)

1/4 to 1/2 teaspoon dry thyme

1 bay leaf

1/2 teaspoon cobán chile powder (or smoked piquín or árbol chile powder)

1 teaspoon kosher salt

Freshly ground black pepper

Adorno (Garnish)

Chives or sautéed julienned red bell pepper

1. Season the chicken and pork with salt and pepper. Brown the chicken and pork together in the oil, in a large deep skillet over medium heat. Transfer the chicken and pork to a dish and keep them warm. Save the oil and fat left in the skillet for panfrying the sauce.

2. In a medium pot, combine the chicken stock, tomatoes, tomatillos, onions, garlic, peppers, chiles, and tortilla pieces. Bring to a quick boil, reduce heat, and simmer covered until all the ingredients are soft (15 to 20 minutes). Using an immersion blender (or a regular blender after cooling slightly), purée the mixture to a fine consistency.

3. Use all or some of the oil and fat left in the skillet to panfry the puréed sauce over medium heat. Add the achiote liquid, thyme, bay leaf, chile powder, salt, and pepper. Put the chicken and pork back into the skillet and simmer, covered, for about 15 minutes. Taste and adjust seasonings, if needed. The sauce should have the consistency of ketchup. If it's too thin, cook it a bit longer to thicken it. If the sauce is too thick, add a little stock or water.

4. Garnish with chives or sautéed julienned red bell pepper

Amalia's Note

Peel tomatillos under running water if you find the husks hard to remove.

PULIQUE
Chicken and Epazote Stew

A Throughout the central Mayan highlands, in Quiché (northwest of Guatemala City) and Sololá (southwestern Guatemala), people make *pulique* using chicken, beef, turkey, or pork. Every family has its own recipe with varying amounts of spices and herbs and vegetables, but most recipes share tomatoes, tomatillos, and achiote. *Pulique* differs from other Mayan stews because the sauce starts out raw and is then combined with the cooked meats.

Serves 4 to 6 people

4 to 6 skinless chicken thighs, visible fat removed

1 small whole onion, peeled and t-scored

1/2 cup parsley (unchopped, stems and leaves included)

2 cups fat-free, low-sodium chicken stock

1 cup quartered Roma tomatoes (about 2 large tomatoes)

1/2 cup husked, quartered tomatillos (3 to 4 large tomatillos)

1/2 to 3/4 cup diced red bell pepper

1 small yellow onion, cut into thick slices

2 large garlic cloves, peeled

2 to 3 tablespoons chopped epazote (or 1/2 cup chopped cilantro)

Para Espesar (Thickener)

1 1/2 ounces (3 tablespoons) rice soaked in 1/2 cup hot water for 20 minutes, or 2 corn tortillas, torn into small pieces and soaked in 1/2 cup hot water for 10 minutes

1 to 1 1/2 teaspoons ground achiote dissolved in a little water

Sazón (Seasonings)

1 bay leaf

1/4 to 1/2 teaspoon thyme

Pinch of ground cloves

Kosher salt and freshly ground black pepper

1/2 cup *güisquil* (chayote squash) cut into 1-inch cubes, cooked al dente

1/2 cup carrots sliced on the diagonal, cooked al dente

1/2 cup peeled, sliced potatoes, cooked al dente

Adorno (Garnish)

Epazote (or cilantro) sprigs

1. In a medium pot, cook the chicken, the onion, and the parsley in the stock until the chicken is tender (20 to 30 minutes). Remove and reserve the onion and parsley. Set aside the chicken and stock.

2. In a blender or food processor, purée the tomatoes, tomatillos, red bell pepper, onions, garlic, epazote, soaked rice and liquid, and the reserved onion and parsley.

3. Add the purée, achiote liquid, bay leaf, thyme, cloves, salt and pepper, and al dente vegetables to the pot of chicken and stock. Simmer covered for 8 to 10 minutes. Taste and adjust seasonings, if needed.

4. Serve the stew garnished with epazote.

Amalia's Notes

To t-score an onion, make a 1/2-inch-deep cross-shaped cut at the narrowest end of the onion. The onion remains whole.

Epazote is available fresh at most Latin stores. It is an earthy herb with a strong, unique flavor. If you're unfamiliar with it, use just a little at a time. Taste and add more, if you like.

Peel tomatillos under running water if you find the husks hard to remove.

SAQUIC
Chile and Chicken Stew

A *Saquic* is a stew from Alta Verapaz department (north-central Guatemala) and the surrounding region. *Saquic* is traditionally made with turkey. Pork, chicken, other meats, or a combination would be delicious, too. This stew is simpler and easier to make than the other stews in this chapter, but it's equally delicious.

Serves 4 to 6 people

4 to 6 skinless chicken thighs, visible fat removed

1 small whole onion, peeled and t-scored

3 garlic cloves, peeled

2 cups fat-free, low-sodium chicken stock

1 1/2 cup quartered Roma tomatoes (about 3 large tomatoes)

1/2 cup husked, quartered tomatillos (3 to 4 large tomatillos)

1/2 cup roughly chopped cilantro (stems and leaves included)

1 teaspoon ground achiote dissolved in a little water

Sazón (Seasonings)

1 teaspoon cobán chile powder (or smoked piquín or árbol chile powder)

1/8 teaspoon ground *canela* (Ceylon cinnamon)

1/8 teaspoon ground cloves

1 teaspoon kosher salt

Freshly ground black pepper

2 tablespoons instant corn masa flour dissolved in a little water

Adorno (Garnish)

Cilantro sprigs

1. In a medium pot, cook the chicken thighs with the onion and garlic in the stock until the chicken is tender (20 to 30 minutes). Transfer the chicken to a dish and set it aside. Reserve the onion, garlic, and stock.

2. Heat the skillet for 2 minutes over medium heat and add the tomatoes and tomatillos. Adjust the heat to medium-low and pan roast them until they're charred all over and mushy (about 8 minutes).

3. In a blender or food processor, purée the tomatoes, tomatillos, cilantro, reserved onion and garlic, and reserved stock until smooth. Pour the purée back into the pot and combine with the chicken.

4. Add the achiote liquid and season the stew with chile powder, cinnamon, cloves, salt, and pepper, and stir well. Lastly, add the flour liquid and stir well. Cook for about 15 minutes longer. Taste and adjust seasonings, if needed.

5. Garnish with cilantro sprigs.

Amalia's Note

To t-score an onion, make a 1/2-inch-deep cross-shaped cut at the narrowest end of the onion. The onion remains whole.

MOLE *DE PLÁTANO*

Grilled Plantains in Chocolate and Chile Sauce

A Mole is a versatile Mayan sauce from Guatemala City that varies from maker to maker. Traditionally it is served with fried plantains. For a healthier and tastier version, grill the plantains instead. Moles are dark brown or lighter brown. They can be sweet or savory. They can be used to top grilled pork or chicken or as a base for a stew. Two key ingredients in this mole are Guatemalan chocolate and *canela* (Ceylon cinnamon), both of which are very flavorful and fragrant. Mole pairs well with red wine, berries, and mint.

Serves 4 to 6 people

3 very ripe plantains, peeled
Canola oil

1 recipe Mole (chocolate and chile sauce, page 315)

Adorno (Garnish)
1 tablespoon pan-roasted sesame seeds
1 cup berries
3 to 4 mint sprigs

1. Brush the plantains with a heavy coating of canola oil. Grill over natural charcoal at medium heat until the plantains are brown on all sides (10 to 15 minutes).

2. Leave the plantains whole or slice them on the diagonal and arrange the slices attractively on a platter. Top them with the mole.

3. Serve the plantains garnished with sesame seeds, berries, and mint.

Recipe Variation

Traditional Mole *de Plátano* (panfried plantains with chocolate and chile sauce): Peel and slice plantains on the diagonal 1/2 inch thick. Panfry them in batches in 3 tablespoons of canola oil over medium heat until the slices are medium brown (about 1 1/2 minutes per side). Adjust the oil as you panfry each batch. Transfer the plantains to a plate lined with paper towels to absorb excess oil. Add the plantains to the sauce and simmer for 3 to 5 minutes.

REVOLCADO DE POLLO

Chicken in Dried Chile Peppers and Tortilla Sauce

*A*revolcado* is a stew from the area around Guatemala City. It is traditionally made with a pig's head and organ meats. After it's cooked, the entire head is cut into small pieces and then mixed with the delicious brown sauce. The recipe varies slightly depending on who prepares it. This is my version of the exotic dish using chicken instead.

Serves 4 to 6 people

4 to 6 skinless chicken leg quarters
1 small whole unpeeled onion, t-scored
1 cup fat-free, low-sodium chicken stock

1/2 cup chopped Roma tomatoes (about 1 large tomato)
1/2 cup chopped tomatillos (3 to 4 large tomatillos)
1/2 cup seeded, chopped red bell pepper
1 cup sliced green onions
2 teaspoons minced garlic
1 guaque (guajillo) chile, seeded
1 zambo (mulato) chile, seeded
1 corn tortilla, torn into small pieces (or 1 tablespoon bread crumbs)
1 cup fat-free, low-sodium chicken stock

1 tablespoon achiote oil

1 teaspoon kosher salt
Freshly ground black pepper

Adorno (Garnish)
Sautéed julienned red bell pepper or thinly sliced green onions

1. Cook the chicken and onion in the stock for 20 to 30 minutes. Remove and reserve the onion. Set aside the chicken and stock.

2. In a medium pot, combine the tomatoes, tomatillos, pepper, green onions, garlic, chiles, tortilla pieces, and stock, and bring to a quick boil. Lower the heat and simmer covered until the vegetables are soft (5 to 8 minutes). Combine this mixture with the reserved onion and purée to a fine consistency.

3. Heat the achiote oil in a deep skillet over medium heat. Add the purée and panfry the sauce until bubbly and medium thick.

4. Add the sauce to the reserved chicken and stock. Simmer, partially covered, to concentrate flavors and to thicken the sauce further (25 to 30 minutes). Season and taste.

5. Serve the stew garnished with red bell peppers or green onions.

Amalia's Notes

To make achiote oil, heat 1/2 cup of canola oil in a small skillet until small bubbles start to form. Turn the heat off and add 1 tablespoon of achiote seeds. Allow the seeds to color the oil for 5 to 10 minutes or longer, strain the oil, and discard the seeds. The oil should be deep orange, not brown. Keep leftover achiote oil in the refrigerator for up to a month.

Peel tomatillos under running water if you find the husks hard to remove.

To t-score an onion, make a 1/2-inch-deep cross-shaped cut at the narrowest end of the onion. The onion remains whole.

HILACHAS

Spicy Shredded Beef and Potato Stew

A *Hilachas* (shreds), from Suchitepéquez department in southwestern Guatemala, is the Guatemalan cousin of Cuban *Ropa Vieja* (old clothes stew) and Venezuelan *Carne Mechada* (shredded beef stew). This type of stew came to Latin America through Spain. It is a scrumptious, crowd-pleasing heavy stew that tastes even better on day two. People make this dish in a variety of ways throughout the Guatemala City area and in Salamá, Baja Verapaz. This is my easy version. Serve the stew with *Arroz Guatemalteco* (Guatemalan vegetable rice, page 287) and *Frijoles Chapines* (Guatmalan black beans, page 61), which provide a break between spicy bites.

Serves 4 people

1 pound flank steak

Kosher salt and freshly ground black pepper

1 tablespoon canola oil

2 cups fat-free, low-sodium beef stock

1 small yellow onion, quartered

2 bay leaves

1 cup quartered Roma tomatoes (about 2 large tomatoes)

1/2 cup husked, quartered tomatillos (3 to 4 large tomatillos)

1 cup seeded, chopped red bell pepper

1 small yellow onion, cut into thick slices

2 large garlic cloves, peeled

1 guaque (guajillo) chile, seeded

1 pasa (ancho) chile, seeded

1 corn tortilla, torn into small pieces (or 1/4 cup bread crumbs)

1 1/2 cups fat-free, low-sodium beef stock

1 tablespoon achiote oil

Sazón (Seasonings)

1 bay leaf

1/2 teaspoon thyme

1 teaspoon kosher salt

Freshly ground black pepper

2 cups sliced small russet potatoes, cooked al dente

Adorno (Garnish):

Fresh thyme and bay leaves or red bell pepper strips, sautéed

1. Season the steak with salt and pepper. In a hot, deep medium skillet, sear the meat on both sides in a little oil until medium brown (about 4 minutes per side). Add the stock, onion, and bay leaves, and bring to a quick boil. Lower the heat, cover, and braise until the meat fibers separate easily when pulled (about 1 1/2 hours). Check the meat while it cooks and make sure the liquid stays at about 1 1/2 cups at all times (adding 1/2 cup of stock or water at a time as needed). When the meat is done, transfer it to a cutting board and let it cool. Cut it in half against the grain and shred it. Reserve the stock and onion. Set aside.

2. In a medium pot, combine the tomatoes, tomatillos, pepper, onion, garlic, chiles, tortilla, and stock and bring to a boil. Lower the heat and simmer covered until soft (15 to 20 minutes).

3. Using an immersion or regular blender, purée the cooked vegetables and the reserved onion and stock to a fine consistency.

4. Heat the achiote oil in the pot used to cook the beef. Add the purée, bay leaf, thyme, salt, and pepper. Add the shredded beef and potatoes. Simmer to let the flavors blend (20 to 25 minutes). Taste and adjust seasonings, if needed. The sauce should be about the consistency of beef stew. If it's too thin, cook it a bit longer. If it's too thick, add some stock or water.

Amalia's Notes

To make achiote oil, heat 1/2 cup of canola oil in a small skillet until small bubbles start to form. Turn the heat off and add 1 tablespoon of achiote seeds. Allow the seeds to color the oil for 5 to 10 minutes or longer, strain the oil, and discard the seeds. The oil should be deep orange, not brown. Keep leftover achiote oil in the refrigerator for up to a month.

Peel tomatillos under running water if you find the husks hard to remove.

POLLO EN CHICHA
Braised Sweet and Sour Chicken

A *Pollo en chicha* is a dish I treasure from my childhood with my grandmother. Various versions of the dish exist in Guatemala City and in Oriente (eastern Guatemala). *Chicha* is an alcoholic mixture of fermented fresh fruit, corn, *panela*, purified water, *canela*, ginger, and other ingredients. As a delicious drink on the rocks, it is also known as *fresco de súchiles*, popular especially during *Cuaresma* (Lent). In Guatemala, *fresco de súchiles* is also available bottled. *Chicha* makes an exquisite sauce base in this sweet and sour stew traditionally made with rooster. When *chicha* is not available, you can imitate some of the flavors by making a substitute. Accompany with *Arroz Guatemalteco* (Guatemalan vegetable rice, page 287) and *Ensalada Rusa* (marinated green beans, carrots, potatoes, and baby peas in light aioli, page 265).

Serves 4 to 6 people

4 to 6 chicken leg quarters, seasoned with salt and pepper

1 tablespoon canola oil

1/2 cup finely chopped Roma tomatoes

1/2 cup finely chopped red bell pepper

3/4 cup finely chopped yellow onion

1 teaspoon minced garlic

1/2 pasa (ancho) chile, seeded, soaked 10 minutes in very hot water

1/2 tablespoon grated fresh ginger

1/2 cup water

Sazón (Seasonings)

1 bay leaf

1/2 teaspoon thyme

1/8 teaspoon ground *canela* (Ceylon cinnamon)

Pinch of ground cloves

Kosher salt and freshly ground black pepper

1 1/2 cups *chicha* (or 2 tablespoons apple cider vinegar, 2 tablespoons *panela* or brown sugar, and 1 1/2 cups fat-free, low-sodium chicken stock)

Adorno (Garnish):

Fresh thyme sprigs and bay leaves

1. In a hot medium-sized skillet, brown the chicken in the oil over medium heat, about 4 minutes per side. Transfer the chicken to a dish and keep it warm.

2. In a blender, combine the tomatoes, pepper, onion, garlic, chile, ginger, and water. Purée the mixture to a fine consistency.

3. In the same skillet used to brown the chicken, fry the purée and add the seasonings. Add the *chicha*. Return the chicken to the skillet and simmer partially covered for 20 to 30 minutes. Taste and adjust seasonings, if needed.

POLLO EN CREMA Y LOROCOS
Chicken with Loroco Flower Buds and Cream Sauce

A *Pollo en crema y lorocos* is a delectable dish from Oriente in eastern Guatemala. Loroco is the flower bud of a plant native to Central America. It is delicate, aromatic, has a strong flowery-earthy flavor, and holds up well during cooking. Loroco is best when eaten fresh. Alternatively, use frozen buds. Loroco is great in stews, and when mixed with cheese, it makes an excellent filling for *Empanadas de Loroco y Requesón* (loroco flower buds and ricotta cheese-stuffed corn masa cakes, page 27).

Serves 4 to 6 people

4 to 6 skinless chicken thighs, visible fat removed

1 1/2 cups fat-free, low-sodium chicken stock

2 corn tortillas, torn into small pieces

1/2 cup julienned yellow onion

2 minced garlic cloves

3/4 cup julienned red bell pepper

1/2 cup small-diced roma tomatoes

1 tablespoon butter

1/3 cup frozen loroco flower buds, thawed and separated

1/2 cup fresh Guatemalan *crema* (or Latino table cream)

1 teaspoon kosher salt

Freshly ground white pepper

Adorno (Garnish)

1/2 cup minced red bell pepper, sautéed

1. In a medium pot, cook the chicken in the stock with the tortilla pieces for 20 to 30 minutes. Transfer the chicken to a dish and keep it warm. Mash the tortillas and stock until they are well incorporated. Set aside.

2. In a medium skillet, sauté the onion, garlic, pepper, and tomatoes in the butter for 3 to 4 minutes. Add the loroco and sauté 1 minute. Add the cream and the thickened stock. Season the mixture with salt and pepper. Return the chicken to the skillet and spoon the sauce over the chicken. Simmer covered for 5 to 10 minutes. Taste and adjust seasonings, if needed.

3. Serve the dish garnished with minced red peppers.

LASAÑA MAYA
Mayan Lasagna

 This fusion recipe is a layered baked dish that layers the Mayan stew *Jocón* (page 139) with corn tortillas and other traditional Guatemalan ingredients. You can make this dish with any other stew in this chapter, too.

Serves 4 to 6 people

1 recipe *Jocón* (chicken, tomatillo, and cilantro stew, page 139)

Canola oil spray

12 to 20 corn tortillas

1 cup *requesón* (Latino ricotta cheese)

Aluminum foil

Adorno (Garnish)

1 cup *crema* (Latino table cream)
1 cup crumbled *queso fresco* (fresh Latino cheese) (optional)
1/2 cup julienned yellow onions
1/2 cup chopped cilantro

1. Preheat the oven to 350°F.

2. Put the chicken and sauce in separate bowls. Shred the chicken using 2 forks.

3. Spray the bottom and sides of a Pyrex pie pan, or any other baking dish of choice, heavily with oil. Cover with 3 tortillas and spray lightly with canola oil.

4. Add half of the chicken and some sauce and distribute evenly on top of the layered tortillas.

5. Cover the first layer with 3 tortillas and spray lightly with oil. Add the ricotta cheese and spread evenly.

6. Cover the second layer with 3 tortillas and spray lightly with oil. Add the rest of the chicken and some sauce and distribute evenly. Save about 1 cup of the sauce.

7. Cover the third layer with 3 tortillas and spray lightly with oil. Seal with foil and bake for 30 to 40 minutes. Let the dish set, covered, for 20 minutes.

8. Garnish the dish. Begin with the rest of the sauce, then use a thin layer of *crema*, followed by *queso fresco* (if using), onions, and cilantro.

TIRAS

Honeycomb Beef Tripe in Spicy Tomato-Guajillo Sauce

A *Tiras* (strips) is a tasty dish from Baja Verapaz (central Guatemala) that is also popular in the *mercados* of Guatemala City. For the adventurous cook or foodie, this can be a new and exciting dish to try. Others may find it a bit too adventurous. *Tiras* is made with tripe, or stomach tissue. It's loved by Guatemalans and eaten cold as a salad. Alternatively, you can make the dish with pork or chicken instead of tripe. Serve it with *Arroz Guatemalteco* (Guatemalan vegetable rice, page 287), *Güicoyitos con Mantequilla y Cebolla* (steamed baby squash with onion butter, page 291), and Tortillas *de Maíz* (corn tortillas, page 25).

Serves 4 to 6 people

1 1/2 pounds beef honeycomb tripe
6 cups water
5 cups water
1 tablespoon salt
1 lemon, thinly sliced
6 cups cold water

1 1/2 cups roughly chopped Roma tomatoes
3/4 cups husked, roughly chopped tomatillos
1 cup green onions cut into 2-inch pieces
2 whole cloves garlic, peeled
1/2 to 1 guaque (guajillo) chile, seeded
1 cup roughly chopped cilantro (stems and leaves included)
1/2 cup water

1 tablespoon canola oil

Sazón (Seasonings)

1 bay leaf
Kosher salt and freshly ground black pepper

Adorno (Garnish)

1/2 cup chopped cilantro leaves

1. In a medium pot on the stovetop, cook the tripe submerged in 6 cups of water over medium-low heat until tender, about 2 hours. Transfer the tripe to the sink and drain the water. Add 5 cups of water again and return to the stovetop. Add 1 tablespoon of salt and cook over medium-low heat for 1 hour. Drain the salted water, add the sliced lemon, add 6 cups cold water, and let sit for 30 minutes or longer. Drain the water. Slice tripe into 3-inch-long strips about 1/2 inch wide.

2. In a medium saucepan, combine the tomatoes, tomatillos, green onions, garlic, chile, and cilantro with the 1/2 cup of water, and bring to a quick boil. Lower the heat and simmer covered until all vegetables are tender (5 to 8 minutes). Purée with an immersion or regular blender to a medium consistency.

3. Heat the oil in a deep medium skillet and sauté the tripe for 2 to 3 minutes. Add the purée and seasonings and cook for 20 to 30 minutes to blend flavors and thicken the sauce to the consistency of puréed salsa. Taste and adjust seasonings, if needed.

Amalia's Notes

Honeycomb tripe comes from the first three chambers of a cow's stomach. It is available fresh at Latino markets and is packaged and frozen at some grocery stores. It is labeled as "honeycomb beef tripe."

Peel tomatillos under running water if you find the husks hard to remove.

CHURRASCO GUATEMALTECO
GUATEMALAN BARBECUE

TAKE IT OUTSIDE

*I*n Guatemala, the word *churrasco*, like the English word *barbecue*, can refer to either grilled meats or a gathering at which grilled meats will be served. During a *churrasco* gathering, family and friends congregate around the *parrilla* (grill) to share a good time and to celebrate. *Churrascos* are the perfect mix of socializing and eating fun, casual, and delicious food.

When I lived in Guatemala City, I recall getting together with coworkers annually for the company barbecue. Everyone would participate in the preparation and cooking, and this helped people bond outside the office. Thinking back, I see that we were actually team-building during these events.

Preparing for a Guatemalan barbecue is easy. Simply plan a menu around one or a few proteins and complement these with a few sauces and vegetables that are conducive to grilling. *Churrasco* options are many. This chapter presents some of my favorites—the ones that are not only scrumptious, but take only minutes to prepare. You are in for a tasty treat with a *plato chapín* (traditional Guatemalan barbecue plate) containing *Carne Asada con Chirmol* (orange and onion–marinated steak with charred tomato and mint salsa, page 173) complemented with *Guacamol Chapín* (Guatemalan guacamole, page 289), *Elotes Asados con Limón y Sal de Mar* (grilled fresh corn with lime and sea salt in corn husks, page 125), *Frijoles Volteados con Queso Fresco* (refried black beans with fresh farmer cheese), and *Plátanos Asados* (grilled plantains, page 103). Tortillas (corn torti-

ABOUT NATURAL CHARCOAL

In my commercial kitchen, I grill on a gas grill or griddle for ease and convenience. But at home, I prefer to grill with natural charcoal because it contains no additives that can be transferred to the food through the smoke. Use natural fire starters, such as pine sticks or even paper, instead of lighter fluid. The flavor of grilling with natural charcoal is superior to using charcoal briquets, and it's better for your health and the environment, too. Natural charcoal and fire starters are available at supermarkets and home improvement stores in the United States and online.

Don't fret if you don't own a charcoal grill. Gas grills are very popular in the United States. If you use a gas grill, your grilled foods will still be delicious.

llas, page 25), *Chilito* (bird's eye chile, onion, lime, and olive oil sauce, page 325), and a cold beer are the perfect pairings.

Guatemala is home to many good Argentinean and Uruguayan steak houses, so *Chimichurri* (garlic, parsley, and organo sauce, page 336), *papa horneada* (baked potato), and *ensalada mixta* (lettuce, red onion, avocado, and tomato with olive oil and red wine vinegar) are also popular barbecue foods. Sometimes you will encounter a hybrid barbecue party where these foods and Guatemalan foods come together. The combination is divine. If you ever visit Guatemala, stop at one of the steak houses where you can cook your own steak right at your table. It is a fun experience for everyone.

EASY GRILLING TIPS

Grilling is very personal. Everyone has a unique style and preferences. These are mine.

After you've lit the coals and they've become ashy, group or spread the coals according to the degree of heat you want. Follow this guide:

High heat: Use high heat for beef, pork, and chicken; for searing and grilling marks; for grilling corn on the cob without the husks; for grilling tomatoes, conch, and fish wrapped in foil; and for grilling any foods very quickly. Pile the coals in the middle of the grill for concentrated high heat in the center zone.

Medium-high heat: Use medium-high heat for vegetables, chicken, pork, meat patties, shrimp, and plantains. Spread the coals evenly on the center base of the grill for even heat in this zone.

Medium-low heat: Medium-low heat is good for slower grilling or for finishing after searing or marking foods; for finishing marinated pork tenderloin or boneless country-style pork ribs; and for slow-grilling meat patties and plantains. Push the coals toward the perimeter of the grill for indirect heat in the center of the grill.

Always season your grill. Right before you put foods on a hot grill, rub the cleaned hot grate with a rag saturated in canola oil. This will prevent foods from sticking to the grate. Don't turn meats prematurely. If they stick to the grill, that means they are not ready to be turned, and they will shred.

For gas grilling, set the temperature according to the grilling guide on your gas grill. Then follow the tips above.

CARNE ASADA CON CHIRMOL
Orange and Onion–Marinated Flank Steak with Charred Tomato and Mint Salsa

A *Carne Asada con Chirmol* is the Guatemalan barbecue basic. It is one of my favorite dishes because it's not only delicious and healthy, but also easy to prepare. The sauce elevates the steak to a five-star status. For another dimension of flavor, serve the steak on top of two soft corn tortillas with refried black beans in between, and finish with the *chirmol*. On rainy or snowy days, grill the tomatoes on the stovetop and grill the steak in a pan or on a griddle.

Serves 4 to 6 people

Salmuera (Marinade)

  2 unpeeled oranges, sliced thinly

  1/2 cup julienned yellow onion

  1 teaspoon crumbled dried oregano

  2 tablespoons canola oil

  1/2 teaspoon kosher salt

  Freshly ground black pepper

  1 1/2 to 2 pounds flank steak (or 4 to 6 top sirloin steaks), seasoned generously with kosher salt and freshly ground black pepper

  1 batch *Chirmol* (charred tomato and mint salsa, page 309)

1. To make the marinade, combine the orange slices, onion, oregano, oil, salt, and pepper in a large ziplock bag. Seal the bag and squeeze the ingredients with your hands to mix them and to force the juice out of the orange slices. Add the steak, seal the bag, and work the marinade into the steak with your hands, making sure it gets well coated. Marinate the steak for 1 to 3 hours or overnight.

2. Preheat the grill.

3. Take the steak out of the bag. Discard the orange and onion. Grill the steak over medium-high heat for about 4 minutes on one side and 2 to 3 minutes on the other side for medium-rare. Or cook more or less according to taste, using the guide following this recipe. Prior to slicing, rest the steak for 5 to 10 minutes tented with foil.

4. Slice the steak on the diagonal and top it with *chirmol*.

Amalia's Notes

Steaks will continue to cook after you take them off the grill. Resting lets the steak reach the proper temperature without overcooking and helps the steak retain its juices. The following guide shows the temperature that steak would reach after resting.

To grill steaks on the stovetop on a pan or griddle, start with a medium-hot dry pan, use the following guide, and rest the steak before slicing.

- Rare (very red center, tender and very juicy): 125°F. Cook 4 to 5 minutes on one side and 1 to 2 minutes on the other side.

- *Medium-rare* (red center, tender and juicy): 130° to 135°F. Cook 4 to 5 minutes on one side and 2 to 3 minutes on the other side.

- Medium (brown and pink center, less tender and a bit dry): 140° to 145°F. Cook for 4 to 5 minutes on one side and 3 to 4 minutes on the other side.

- Medium-well (brown, less tender and dry): 150° to 155°F. Cook 4 to 5 minutes on one side and 4 to 5 minutes on the other side.

- Well-done (brown, tough and dry): 160°F. Cook 4 to 5 minutes on one side and 5 to 6 minutes on the other side.

CEBOLLITAS A LA LLAMA
Flamed Green Onions with Lime

Cebollitas are popular at some restaurants in Guatemala City and at barbecue parties. *Llama* means "flame," and it refers to the flames the oil generates during grilling. I like to complement a *plato chapín* (traditional Guatemalan barbecue plate) with two grilled onions because they take minutes to make, are delicious, and add a nice look.

Makes 18 to 20 onions

2 bunches green onions, trimmed, washed, and patted dry

Canola oil

Kosher salt and freshly ground black pepper

Freshly squeezed lime juice

1. Preheat the grill.

2. Brush the onions generously with the canola oil. Grill for 1 minute per side and use tongs to turn them over.

3. Drizzle the onions with lime juice and season them with salt and pepper.

176 | Amalia's Guatemalan Kitchen

POLLO AL CARBÓN

Grilled Chicken Marinated in Sour Tangerine and Cumin Sauce

A Marinating the chicken in this sauce produces a deliciously moist chicken. The sauce takes minutes to prepare, and it can be used with pork, ribs, beef, or fish with equally delicious results. *Carbón* means "charcoal." It refers to the cooking method, but it can also mean natural charcoal.

Serves 4 to 6 people

Salmuera (Marinade)

1 cup freshly squeezed tangerine juice

1/3 cup freshly squeezed lemon juice

1 teaspoon finely chopped lemon zest

1 tablespoon canola oil

1/2 cup thinly sliced onion

1 tablespoon minced garlic

1 teaspoon ground cumin

1 teaspoon crumbled dried oregano

1 tablespoon chopped fresh mint

1 tablespoon chopped fresh cilantro

1 teaspoon kosher salt

Freshly ground black pepper

4 to 6 skinless chicken thighs, fat removed, rinsed, patted dry

1. Combine all the marinade ingredients in a zip-lock bag and mix them well.

2. Place the chicken in the bag of marinade, seal it, and work the marinade into the chicken until all the pieces are well coated. Marinate in the refrigerator for 3 to 5 hours or overnight.

3. Preheat the grill.

4. Grill the marinated chicken on medium-high heat until cooked, 3 to 4 minutes per side. (Alternatively, roast in the oven at 375°F until cooked, 20 to 25 minutes.)

LOMITO ADOBADO

Grilled Guajillo, Achiote, and Tomatillo Sauce– Marinated Pork Tenderloin

*A*dobo is a wet marinade that enhances the flavor of proteins. In Guatemala *carne adobada* usually means pork marinated in the sauce presented in this recipe and then grilled. However, adobo can be used with chicken or any other protein. Adobo is easy to make and gives meat not only great flavor and color, but also an inviting aroma. *Lomito Adobado* goes well with warm Tortillas *de Maíz* (corn tortillas, page 25) and *Guacamol Chapín* (Guatemalan guacamole, page 289).

Serves 4 to 6 people

1 batch Adobo (guajillo, achiote, and tomatillo salsa, page 313)

2 pork tenderloins (1 pound each) or 2 1/2 pounds boneless country-style pork ribs

1. Prepare the adobo. Marinate the pork in the sauce in a ziplock bag overnight or up to 3 days. (Alternatively, freeze the pork after for later use marinating it overnight.)

2. Preheat the grill.

3. Grill the pork over natural charcoal to an internal temperature of 135°F (15 to 20 minutes). During grilling time, turn the pork every 2 to 3 minutes until it's evenly brown. Alternatively, sear it on the stovetop until it's medium brown all over and then transfer it to a preheated 375°F oven and roast it to an internal temperature of 135°F (for 10 to 15 minutes). Let the pork rest for 5 to 10 minutes tented with a piece of foil to help it reach an internal temperature of 145°F.

4. Slice the tenderloins on the diagonal and serve.

Amalia's Notes

Resting helps the pork reach the proper temperature while retaining its juices.

Boneless country-style pork ribs require slower cooking for a longer time to be tender. To inject charcoal flavor, cook them on a grill over medium-high heat for 4 to 5 minutes on one side and 2 to 3 minutes on the other side. Transfer the ribs to a preheated 325°F oven and braise them with the marinade, in a small pan covered with foil, until the ribs are tender (45 minutes to 1 hour).

CHORIZO *CHAPÍN*

Grilled Guatemalan Red Sausage

A Chorizo is popular throughout Guatemala, and everyone has a special recipe. Chorizos can be spicy or mild. They can be red, white, or black, depending on the region and purpose. Chorizo patties make an excellent burger, or cook the chorizo on the stove top and add it to scrambled eggs. Chorizo is usually stuffed into pig's intestines in an elongated shape. Pig's intestines go through a process that rids them of bacteria and makes them safe for cooking. They come dried and must be soaked in warm water to make them flexible and stuffable. Commercial chorizos are stuffed by machine, but in the rural areas of Guatemala, they are still made by hand with the help of a handheld tool. Chorizos usually have added back fat or bacon. This easy recipe is a healthier version using only the fat contained in the ground pork.

Makes 4 to 6 patties

1 1/2 teaspoons minced garlic

2 quartered Roma tomatoes

2 tomatillos, husked and halved

2 tablespoons guaque (guajillo) chile, seeded and torn into small pieces

2 teaspoons pasa (ancho) chile, seeded and torn into small pieces

1 teaspoon zambo (mulato) chile, seeded and torn into small pieces

1/2 teaspoon ground cumin

1/2 teaspoon crumbled dried oregano

2 teaspoons *pimentón* (Spanish paprika)

1/4 teaspoon ground achiote

1 1/2 tablespoons white wine vinegar

1 teaspoon kosher salt

Freshly ground black pepper

1 pound ground pork

1. Put all the ingredients except the pork in a blender and purée them to a fine consistency. Pulse the blender on and off. With a soft spatula, carefully push the ingredients down into the blade. Do not add any liquid; the tomato, tomatillo, and vinegar provide the moisture needed to blend all the ingredients. (Alternatively, you may soak the dried peppers to soften them first.)

2. In a medium bowl, combine the blended ingredients with the pork. Wearing disposable gloves, mix everything with your hands to combine thoroughly. To check the seasonings, panfry a small amount of the mixture and taste it.

3. Marinate the mixture in the refrigerator for 1 to 3 hours or overnight. Fresh sausage will keep in the refrigerator for 3 days.

4. Preheat the grill.

5. Form 4 to 6 equal-size sausage patties and either grill them over medium-high heat until cooked, or freeze them for later use.

LONGANIZA

Grilled Guatemalan Spicy White Sausage
with Mint, Onion, and Sour Orange

A *Longaniza* is a delicious sausage that's often part of an open-faced tortilla sandwich topped with *Chirmol de Miltomate* (spicy tomatillo salsa, page 312). You can cook *longaniza* and chorizo ahead of time and then combine them with scrambled eggs for a tasty breakfast treat. The flavor of *longaniza* is quite different from Chorizo *Chapín* (Guatemalan red sausage, page 181), yet the sausages share some of the same ingredients. *Longaniza* usually contains added back fat or bacon. This is a healthier version using only the fat contained in the ground pork.

Makes 4 to 6 patties

1 teaspoon garlic, mashed to a paste

1/2 cup thinly sliced green onion (green parts only)

2 tablespoons finely chopped fresh mint

1 to 2 minced bird's eye chiles (Thai chiles)

1/4 teaspoon guaque (guajillo) chile, powder or flakes

1/2 teaspoon crumbled oregano

1/2 teaspoon freshly ground nutmeg

1 tablespoon white wine vinegar

1 tablespoon freshly squeezed orange juice

1 tablespoon freshly squeezed lime juice

1 teaspoon kosher salt

Freshly ground black pepper

1 pound ground pork

1. Put all the ingredients in a medium bowl. Wearing disposable gloves, mix them well until they're thoroughly combined. To check the seasonings, panfry a test batch and taste it.

2. Marinate the mixture in the refrigerator for 1 to 3 hours or overnight. Fresh sausage will keep in the refrigerator for 3 days.

3. Preheat the grill.

4. Form 4 to 6 equal-size patties and grill them over medium-high heat until they're cooked, or freeze them for later use.

CAMARONES A LA PARRILLA CON CHOJÍN

Avocado Halves Stuffed with
Grilled Spicy Shrimp and Radish and Mint Slaw

A Traditionally this dish is topped with pork rind or *buche* (cooked, diced cow's esophagus). The spicy grilled shrimp, the tangy slaw, and the creamy avocados produce an explosion of flavors and textures. Alternatively, top the dish with roasted pork bits or *carne asada* strips.

Serves 4 to 6 people

1 teaspoon roughly chopped garlic
1 bird's eye chile (Thai chile)
1 tablespoon finely chopped cilantro leaves
2 tablespoons olive oil
Kosher salt and freshly ground black pepper
8 to 12 medium shrimp, deveined, tails on

Chojín (Radish and Mint Slaw)

1 cup finely chopped radish
2 tablespoons finely diced vine-ripened
   tomatoes
1 tablespoon finely diced onion
1 tablespoon finely diced mint leaves
1 tablespoon freshly squeezed lime juice
1 teaspoon freshly squeezed orange juice
1/2 teaspoon kosher salt

4 to 6 avocados
Lime juice
Kosher salt and freshly ground black pepper

Adorno (Garnish)

Radish slices
Mint and cilantro sprigs
Tortilla crunchies (page 26)

1. Preheat the grill.

2. Purée the garlic, chile, cilantro, oil, salt, and pepper in a blender or food processor. Pour the purée over the shrimp and marinate for 10 to 15 minutes. Grill or griddle the shrimp over medium-high heat until they're opaque and tender (about 2 minutes per side). Set them aside in the refrigerator.

3. Mix all the slaw ingredients. Taste and adjust seasonings, if needed. Set the slaw aside in the refrigerator.

4. Cut the avocados in half widthwise. Remove the pits and slice off a bit of the curved shell so the avocados will lie still when you set them faceup on top of each other. Brush each avocado half with lime juice and season it with salt and pepper. Top 4-6 avocado halves with 2 teaspoons of slaw and garnish it with the shrimp, lime slices, mint and cilantro sprigs, and tortilla crunchies. Use the other 4-6 halves facedown as a pedestal for the filled avocado halves.

FILETE DE LOMITO CON CHIRMOL DE MILTOMATE

Filet Mignon with Spicy Tomatillo Salsa

A This recipe is an upscale alternative to *Carne Asada con Chirmol* (page 173). Tomatillos give the salsa a different flavor dimension. This salsa's tangy flavor, chunky texture, and green color look and taste great on a steak. Vary the recipe by chosing different sauces from chapter 12 (page 305).

Serves 4 to 6 people

4 to 6 cuts filet mignon (1 1/2 inches thick), coated with canola oil and seasoned generously with kosher salt and freshly ground black pepper

1 batch *Chirmol de Miltomate* (spicy tomatillo salsa, page 312)

1. Preheat the grill.

2. Grill the steaks over medium-high heat for 4 to 5 minutes on one side and 2 to 3 minutes on the other side for medium-rare steak. Or cook more or less according to taste, using the guide following this recipe. Prior to cutting, rest the steak for 5 to 10 minutes tented with foil.

3. Top with *Chirmol de Miltomate*.

Amalia's Notes

Steaks will continue to cook after you take them off the grill. Resting lets the steak reach the proper temperature without overcooking and helps the steak retain its juices. The following guide shows the temperature that steak would reach after resting.

To grill steaks on the stovetop on a pan or griddle, start with a medium-hot dry pan, use the following guide, and rest the steak before slicing.

- Rare (very red center, tender and very juicy): 125°F. Cook 4 to 5 minutes on one side and 1 to 2 minutes on the other side.

- *Medium-rare* (red center, tender and juicy): 130° to 135°F. Cook 4 to 5 minutes on one side and 2 to 3 minutes on the other side.

- Medium (brown and pink center, less tender and a bit dry): 140° to 145°F. Cook 4 to 5 minutes on one side and 3 to 4 minutes on the other side.

- Medium-well (brown, less tender and dry): 150° to 155°F. Cook 4 to 5 minutes on one side and 4 to 5 minutes on the other side.

- Well-done (brown, tough and dry): 160°F. Cook 4 to 5 minutes on one side and 5 to 6 minutes on the other side.

PINCHOS DE VERDURAS

Grilled Herbed Tomato, Green Onion, and Chile Skewers

 This is a simple, easy, and delicious side to accompany grilled meat or fish. Or place on top of *Gallo Pinto* (rice and black beans with bell peppers, bacon, and cilantro, page 77) to create a striking dish.

Serves 4 to 6 people

4 to 6 metal or bamboo skewers soaked in water for 10 minutes

4 to 6 whole, washed Roma tomatoes

1 yellow bell pepper, seeded, deveined, cut into 1 1/2-inch chunks

4 to 6 whole washed, trimmed green onions

Canola oil

Freshly squeezed lime juice

Chile powder of choice (optional)

1/2 cup finely chopped flat-leaf parsley

Kosher salt and freshly ground black pepper

1. Preheat the grill.

2. Skewer the tomatoes, peppers, and green onions folded in half, in that order.

3. Brush the skewered items generously with the oil.

4. Grill the skewers over medium-high heat until charred all over, but not mushy (3 to 5 minutes). Don't overcook or the tomatoes will fall off the skewers.

5. Drizzle the skewers with lime juice and sprinkle with chile powder, flat-leaf parsley, salt, and pepper.

CARACOL DE MAR CON MANTEQUILLA DE AJO, LIMÓN Y CILANTRO

Grilled Conch with Garlic, Lime, Cilantro, and Achiote Butter

A Grilling doesn't get any easier than this! This recipe is inspired by *Caracol a la Plancha* (griddled conch), a specialty in Guatemala's Izabal region on the Caribbean. When conch is fresh, it smells briny and is sweet and tender and a bit crunchy. Conch is available in Florida. Or you can purchase it frozen or order it through your local fishmonger and online. Sushi-grade conch makes great ceviche. See Ceviche *de Caracol de Mar* (conch and green mango in habanero sauce, page 234).

Serves 4 to 6 people

4 to 6 conch fillets, 4 to 5 ounces each
Canola oil
Kosher salt and freshly ground black pepper

1 batch *Mantequilla de Ajo, Limón y* Cilantro
(garlic, lime, cilantro, and achiote butter,
page 327)

Adorno (Garnish)
Cilantro leaves
Lime slices

1. Preheat the grill.

2. Brush the conch fillets with a light coating of oil and season them with salt and pepper.

3. Grill the fillets over high heat for 1 to 2 minutes per side. Conch cooks very fast and can become tough and rubbery when overcooked. Ideally, it should be lightly cooked on the outside and rare on the inside.

4. Top the fillets with the *Mantequilla de Ajo, Limón y* Cilantro and garnish them with cilantro and lime.

Amalia's Note

To save time and effort, ask your fishmonger to filet the conch for you.

SALMÓN CON CHIRMOL DE AZAFRÁN Y VINO EN HOJA DE BANANO

Grilled Salmon with Saffron-Wine *Sofrito* and Capers in Banana Leaves

A Steaming food in banana leaves is an ancient Mayan technique that already existed when the French created a similar technique called *en papillote*. This recipe fuses Guatemalan techniques and Spanish flavors with a nontraditional fish. The tangy tomato sauce goes beautifully with the highly nutritious salmon, and the dish is beautiful.

Serves 4 people

Chirmol de Azafrán (Saffron-Wine Sofrito)

 1 tablespoon olive oil
 1 cup finely diced vine-ripened tomatoes
 1/2 cup finely diced onion
 1/2 teaspoon minced garlic
 1 teaspoon fresh thyme (or 1/2 teaspoon dry thyme)
 1 bay leaf
 1/2 teaspoon fresh rosemary
 1/2 teaspoon Spanish saffron threads soaked in 1/3 cup good-quality dry white wine
 1/2 teaspoon kosher salt
 Freshly ground black pepper

 4 5-ounce Altantic salmon filets (preferably wild, not farmed)
 Olive oil
 Kosher salt and freshly ground black pepper

 4 12x6-inch banana leaves, wiped on both sides with a damp cloth
 4 12x17-inch pieces aluminum foil

 Spanish capers

Adorno (Garnish)
 Frisée or chopped parsley

1. Preheat the grill or oven.

2. Combine all the *sofrito* ingredients in a hot skillet and cook the mixture until it's saucy (about 5 minutes). Let it cool.

3. Brush the salmon filets with a light coating of oil and season them with salt and pepper.

4. Place a banana leaf (matte side up) on top of each aluminum foil sheet. Put a salmon fillet on top of each banana leaf. Distribute the saffron *sofrito* equally over all four fillets. Top each fillet with 2 teaspoons of capers. Wrap and seal each fillet tightly inside the foil.

5. Place the foil packets on a very hot grill. Cover the grill and cook the salmon until it's medium rare (10 to 15 minutes). Or cook the salmon in the oven at 375°F for 10 to 12 minutes.

Amalia's Note

Undercooking the salmon is important because the salmon will continue to cook in the foil packets when you remove them from the grill or oven. Medium-rare salmon appears pink and flaky on the surface and is moist and juicy inside. For medium salmon, cook it a bit more (1 to 2 minutes longer).

HAMBURGUESAS DE BISONTE CON PAPITAS

Grilled Bison Burgers with Guacamole, Black Beans, Spicy Chile Ketchup, Tomato, Red Onion, and Butter Lettuce with Roasted Herbed Fries

A I discovered bison while living in Minnesota. Grass-fed bison is delicious and not at all gamy. It's leaner, lower in calories, and more nutritious than beef. It reminds me of the taste of *carne asada* (grilled beef) from my grandmother's town—probably because cows there also ate grass, and that makes a big difference in the flavor of the meat. Try the amazing taste and quality of bison steaks and burgers—you will be hooked for life! Bison also works in place of all other beef recipes in this book. Burgers adapted to local tastes are popular in Guatemalan restaurants. This is my version based on my experience eating burgers at Guatemalan Chinese restaurants (which made some of the best burgers in town), Guatemalan burger chains, and mom-and-pop joints. For a fun burger party, mix bison burgers with other patties, such as *Chorizo Chapín* (Guatemalan red sausage, page 181), *Longaniza* (Guatemalan spicy white sausage with mint, onion, and sour orange, page 183), and *Tortitas de Carne con Salsa de Dos Tomates* (Dad's favorite beef patties with tomato and tomatillo sauce, page 209). The gourmet fries in this recipe are healthier than conventional fries, too, as they are oven-roasted instead of deep-fried. Oven roasting is easy. It mimics the flavor of crispy, crunchy fried foods, and it speeds cleaning as well.

Serves 2 to 4 people

Tortitas (Patties)

- 1 pound ground round bison
- 1 cup finely diced yellow onion
- 1 cup finely diced Roma tomatoes
- 1/2 cup finely chopped celery
- 1 egg, beaten
- 1 to 2 tablespoons cornflake crumbs or herbed bread crumbs
- Kosher salt and freshly ground black pepper

Adorno (Toppings)

- 2 to 4 butter lettuce leaves, washed and spun dry
- 2 to 4 slices salad tomatoes
- 2 to 3 thinly sliced red onion
- 1 16-ounce can organic, fat-free refried black beans or *Frijoles Volteados* (refried black beans, page 62)
- 4 to 6 cilantro sprigs
- 1 batch *Guacamol Chapín* (Guatemalan guacamole, page 289)
- 1/2 cup crumbled *queso* (Cotija cheese or *queso fresco*)

Spicy Chile Ketchup

3/4 to 1 cup Heinz ketchup

2 to 3 minced bird's eye (Thai) chiles

2 teaspoons lime juice

Freshly ground black pepper

2 to 4 Latino buns, sliced and grilled (or whole-wheat buns)

1. In a bowl, combine the bison with the rest of the patty ingredients. Form four equal-size patties (or size them according to taste). Set the patties aside.

2. Prepare all the toppings and arrange them attractively on a platter. Set them aside.

3. Mix all the ketchup ingredients in a small bowl. Taste and adjust seasonings, if needed.

4. Heat the grill (or griddle) and cook the patties over medium-high heat to desired doneness. Slice and grill the buns.

5. Assemble the burgers. Spread some guacamole and sprinkle some cheese on one side of the bun, and then spread black beans on the other side. Add 1 slice of lettuce, then a patty, followed by the spicy chile ketchup, tomatoes and onions, and cilantro sprigs. Serve.

PAPITAS (Oven-Roasted Herbed Fries)

Serves 2 to 4 people

2 to 4 unpeeled russet potatoes, soaked, scrubbed, cut into eighths lengthwise

Olive oil

1 tablespoon *pimentón* (Spanish paprika)

1 tablespoon dried cilantro, thyme, oregano, and parsley (combined)

Kosher salt and freshly ground black pepper

1. Preheat the oven to 450°F.

2. Prepare the potatoes. After cutting the potatoes, pat them dry with paper towels or the seasonings will not stick. Place them in a medium bowl and drizzle them with enough olive oil to coat them thinly and thoroughly. Sprinkle the paprika and herbs, and season generously with salt and pepper. Use your hands to toss the potatoes and coat them well with oil and spices.

3. Lay the potatoes faceup on a baking sheet lined with parchment paper or foil. Roast them in 10-minute intervals, turning the baking sheet around after each interval to roast the potatoes evenly. Roast until the potatoes are medium brown and puffy. Total roasting time should be 20 to 25 minutes.

Amalia's Notes

You can purchase or order bison through the meat department of your local grocery store. It is also available online.

Latino buns are available at some grocery stores and Latino bakeries.

COMIDA CASERA
GUATEMALAN HOME COOKING

THE WAY TO ANYONE'S HEART

The old saying declares, "The way to a man's heart is through his stomach." I think the way to *anyone's* heart is through the stomach. My heart is in my grandmother's and mother's home cooking. This is the everyday food I looked forward to eating while growing up in Guatemala. It is simple yet nutritious food that anyone can cook.

Guatemalan home cooking in Guatemala City is mild but not bland, with spicy sauces on the side. It is the food that most Guatemalans eat daily. It is closer to Spanish cuisine than to Mayan cooking, although it does have a Mayan touch. For example, most Guatemalans consume tamales at least once a week. One dish in this chapter is neither Spanish nor Mayan, but rather a Chinese transplant. *Chao Mein* (page 221) was one of my dad's favorite dishes—and mine, too. It's a nostalgic dish for me. In Guatemala, Mayan stews and other elaborate traditional meals are eaten only on special occasions and at *restaurantes típicos* (traditional Guatemalan food restaurants).

Many dishes that came to Latin America from Spain went through a transformation in name and ingredients as home cooks in the New World blended them with native ingredients and adapted them to local tastes. This is why there are many versions of the same dish from country to country and from family to family throughout Latin America. For example, the dish called *Hilachas* (page 157) in Guatemala is called *Ropa Vieja* in Cuba and *Carne Mechada* in Venezuela. The basic dish, shredded beef in tomato sauce, is the same, but the recipe varies a bit from country to country. The original recipe likely came from Spain. Another good example is paella. Many versions, including *Fideua* (a paellalike dish made with vermicelli noodles instead of rice), exist within Spain as well as in Latin America.

Guatemalans today still shop at the *mercados abiertos* (open markets) routinely for their daily cooking. My sister shops once a week on market day to buy the freshest produce. It is customary to bargain over the price of fruits and vegetables. Locals seldom pay what vendors ask. Shopping at a Guatemalan market is a game of give-and-take. My mom is a bargaining expert. She wheels and deals with vendors until they agree on a price. If she is losing the battle after a few minutes of bargaining, she may threaten to go to the next stall—and that is when vendors give in. Bargaining over small-ticket items may seem senseless, but it is common practice in Guatemala. It's a trait of a thrifty culture. Guatemalans do it because it feels good to save money—even if it's just a penny.

SUPERMERCADO
LA MEXICANA
1522 E. LAKE ST. MPLS., MN 65407

CANELA
$12.99/lb $4.29
0.33 lb

SUPERMERCADO
LA MEXICANA
1522 E. LAKE ST. MPLS., MN 65407

$.98
0.4 lb $12.9/b

$5.20
2.99/lb   Aug 15, 12

Canela (page 8)

Guatemalan *mercados* are great places to find the foods in this book. (But be aware that you eat market foods at your own risk, as sanitation is not always the best.) *Mercados* are also great places to observe culinary customs. For example, at a Guatemalan market, you'll see many cuts of meats you won't see in the United States. Guatemalans eat just about every part of the animal, from the head to the tail. They make scrumptious dishes from pigs' heads, cows' stomachs, pigs' feet, organ meats, and even skin. The fresh fish and seafood at a Guatemalan market comes from the neighboring Pacific and Atlantic oceans and from the country's many lakes and rivers. Typical offerings include *lenguado* (sole), *conchas* (black clams), *jutes* (river snails), and *jaibas* (river crabs). The bounty is interesting not only to see, but also to eat.

PREVALENT SEASONINGS IN GUATEMALAN HOME COOKING

Guatemalan home cooking often uses combinations of seasonings in a single recipe. The "duo" (bay leaves and thyme) and the "trio" (bay leaf, thyme, and oregano) are the most common combinations. In addition, Guatemalan home cooking often uses sweet peppers alone or in combination with tomatoes and other vegetables.

Mayan dishes prominently feature fresh and dried chiles and powders, both hot and mild. Home cooking uses chiles more sparingly. The following list outlines the seasonings most common in home cooking.

Culantro (cilantro)

Perejil (parsley)

Yerbabuena (mint)

Zamat (wild cilantro)

Laurel (bay leaves)

Tomillo (thyme)

Orégano (oregano)

Azafrán (saffron)

Pimentón (Spanish paprika)

Pimienta gorda (allspice)

Clavos de olor (cloves)

Comino (cumin)

Canela (Ceylon cinnamon)

Pimienta de castilla (black pepper)

Nuez Moscada (nutmeg)

Semilla de mostaza (mustard seed)

Achiote (annatto) is used for coloring and not for seasoning

LENGUA FINGIDA

Guatemalan Meat Loaf Stuffed with Hard-Boiled Eggs

A *Lengua* means "tongue," and *fingida* means "faux." The name of this dish has nothing to do with its contents. Another more appropriate name is *Carne Fría* (cold beef roll). This dish probably came to Guatemala and Latin America from Spain. Traditionally, the elongated meat loaf is wrapped in corn husks, cheese-cloth, or a kitchen towel, and then poached in a flavored liquid that can become part of the sauce. *Lengua Fingida* is eaten cold or warm and topped with tomato sauce. My mom liked to coat each slice with egg batter and then fry it. She used the poaching liquid to make a sauce with browned flour. This recipe is a quicker but equally delicious version.

Serves 6 to 8 people

1 1/2 pounds extra-lean ground beef
3/4 cup finely diced yellow onion
1 1/2 teaspoons minced garlic
1 cup minced red bell pepper
4 eggs, beaten until very fluffy
2 teaspoons freshly ground nutmeg
2 teaspoons cumin
2 teaspoons kosher salt
Freshly ground black pepper

4 hard-boiled eggs, peeled
Good quality plastic wrap
14 cups water

1 recipe *Salsita de Tomate Ciruela* (quick plum tomato sauce, page 328)

1. In a medium bowl, combine all ingredients except the hard-boiled eggs and water. Wearing disposable gloves, mix the ingredients with your hands to ensure seasonings are well integrated into the meat. Panfry a test batch. Taste and adjust seasonings, if needed.

2. Shape the meat into a roll and make a crevice with the side of your hand. Deepen and widen the crevice gradually to make room for the eggs. Lay the eggs in the crevice along the length of the roll. Carefully enclose the eggs inside the meat. Wrap the roll firmly with plastic. Wrap at least 4 times widthwise and 4 times lengthwise, making sure all the meat is well covered.

3. Place the roll and the water in a wide, heavy-bottomed pot. Bring to a quick boil, reduce the heat to medium, cover the pot, and simmer until the roll is fully cooked, about 1 1/2 hours.

4. Remove the roll from the hot water and let it cool for about 30 minutes. Remove and discard the plastic. Slice the meat loaf and serve it with the *salsita de tomate ciruela*.

Amalia's Note

Alternatively, let the roll cool completely and refrigerate it overnight. Slice and serve it cold.

CHULETAS MIGADAS
Breaded Marinated Pork Cutlets

A This dish is a quick and delicious Guatemalan twist on the Italian Milanese or the Austrian *Wiener Schnitzel* (breaded veal cutlets). *Chuletas migadas* is popular not only in Guatemala, but also throughout Latin America. This quick, healthy recipe marinates pork and then uses cornflakes instead of bread crumbs for the breading. Eat *chuletas migadas* accompanied with *Ensalada de Remolacha con Sal de Mar* (fresh beets with onion, lime, and sea salt, page 281) and *Puré de Papas con Perejil* (potato purée with olive oil and parsley, page 300), or make a sandwich with the cutlets, lettuce, tomatoes, pickled jalapeños, and your favorite condiments.

Serves 4 people

Juice of 1 orange

1 tablespoon fresh lemon juice

1/2 teaspoon garlic powder

1/2 teaspoon cumin

1 pound (about 5) boneless thin pork loin cutlets (or thinly sliced pork chops)

Kosher salt and freshly ground black pepper

3/4 cup cornflake crumbs mixed with 1 teaspoon oregano and 1/2 teaspoon red chile flakes

Canola oil

1. In platter, mix the orange juice, lemon juice, garlic powder, and cumin. Place the pork in the platter and marinate it for 20 to 30 minutes. Turn over the pork halfway through the marinating time to ensure even marinating. Shake off the excess juice and season the cutlets on both sides.

2. Spread the cornflake mixture on a plate. Press each pork chop firmly against the crumbs and repeat to cover the other side.

3. Add 2 teaspoons or more of oil to a hot medium skillet and cook the cutlets until medium brown (2 to 3 minutes per side). Add more oil to the pan as needed.

4. Transfer the pork to a platter lined with paper towels to absorb excess oil, and keep the cutlets warm.

RELLENO DE POLLO
Chicken and Vegetable Stuffing

A *Relleno* (also called *picadillo*) means "filling," "stuffing," or "hash" in Latin America. This delicious dish can be used for stuffing chicken or turkey or as a stuffing for empanadas, rolled crispy tacos, chiles *rellenos*, or sandwiches. Or eat it as a side dish with corn tortillas, rice, and beans. *Relleno* can be made with beef or pork and with varying vegetables. Substitute the meat with cooked garbanzo beans or lentils for a tasty vegetarian dish.

Makes about 6 cups

1 cup finely diced yellow onions

2 teaspoons finely chopped fresh thyme leaves (or 1 teaspoon dry thyme)

2 fresh bay leaves

2 tablespoons canola oil

3/4 cup julienned green beans

3/4 cup julienned carrots

3/4 cup finely diced potatoes

2 teaspoons minced fresh garlic

1 cup canned crushed tomatoes

1 tablespoon plus 2 teaspoons champagne vinegar or white wine vinegar

1 teaspoon kosher salt

Freshly ground black pepper

4 cups chopped skinless store-bought rotisserie chicken

1. In a large skillet over medium heat, sauté the onions, thyme, and bay leaves in the oil for about 2 minutes. Add the green beans, carrots, and potatoes and sauté until aromatic, about 5 minutes. Add the garlic, tomatoes, and vinegar, and sauté 3 minutes. Season with salt and pepper.

2. Add the chicken, stir well to combine all ingredients, and sauté 3 minutes. Adjust the heat to low and continue to cook the chicken and vegetable mixture uncovered, stirring from time to time, until the vegetables are tender and all liquid has evaporated (10 to 15 minutes). Taste and adjust seasonings, if needed.

3. Serve immediately with warm corn tortillas. If you're using the mixture for stuffing, let it cool completely.

Recipe Variations

Relleno de Cerdo y Res (pork and beef stuffing): Follow the recipe but substitute the chicken with 2 cups cooked chopped pork and 2 cups cooked chopped round of beef.

Relleno de Verduras (vegetarian stuffing): Follow the recipe but substitute the chicken with 4 cups cups cooked garbanzo beans, lentils, a combination of beans, or any other vegetable protein you like.

Amalia's Note

Save unused portions of stuffing and freeze them for another recipe.

TORTITAS DE CARNE
CON SALSA DE DOS TOMATES
Dad's Favorite Beef Patties with Tomato and Tomatillo Sauce

A In the United States, beef patties are used mostly for burgers. In Guatemala, *tortitas* (patties) are mixed with vegetables and seasonings and topped with tomato sauce. As the protein on the plate, they go well with *Ensalada de Aguacate, Lechuga, Tomate y Cebolla Roja* (avocado, Bibb lettuce, tomato, and red onion salad with red wine vinaigrette, page 271), and *Arroz con Espárragos* (rice with asparagus and cheese, page 209). *Tortitas* also make an exceptional Guatemalan burger with lettuce, tomato, avocado, pickled jalapeños, and refried beans.

Makes 8 2-ounce patties

1 pound extra-lean ground beef

1 egg, slightly beaten

3/4 cup finely chopped Roma tomatoes

3/4 cup finely chopped yellow onion

1 teaspoon minced garlic

1 to 2 tablespoons corn flake crumbs or
    herbed bread crumbs

Kosher salt and freshly ground black pepper

1 tablespoon canola oil

Salsa *de Dos Tomates* (Tomato and Tomatillo Sauce)

1 tablespoon canola oil

1 cup finely diced Roma tomatoes

1/2 cup finely diced tomatillos

3/4 cup chopped yellow onion

1/2 cup water

Kosher salt and freshly ground black pepper

1. In a medium bowl, combine the beef with the egg, tomatoes, onion, garlic, crumbs, salt, and pepper. Do a test batch by cooking 1 tablespoon of the meat mixture in a hot skillet. Taste and adjust the seasonings, if needed.

2. Form 8 2-ounce patties with the beef mixture, or make larger patties if you like.

3. Add the oil to a medium hot skillet and panfry the patties in batches until medium brown on both sides (about 2 1/2 minutes per side). Transfer the patties to a plate and keep them warm.

4. Combine all the sauce ingredients in a medium hot skillet and cook them until saucy (3 to 5 minutes). Taste and adjust seasonings, if needed. Serve the patties on top of the sauce or smother them in it.

PAVO NAVIDEÑO
Guatemalan Holiday Roasted Turkey

A Guatemalans eat pavo (turkey) at Christmas and in tamales and in *Kaqik* (page 141). In Guatemala at Christmastime, grocery stores sell turkeys already roasted and festively decorated. The cold turkey is studded with toothpicks that hold radishes, baby corn, baby pickles, black olives, maraschino cherries, and other attractive garnishes. Serve *pavo Navideño* with *Relleno de Pollo* (chicken and vegetable stuffing, page 205), *Relleno de Cerdo y Res* (pork and beef stuffing, page 206), or *Relleno de Verduras* (vegetarian stuffing, page 206) and *Ensalada Rusa* (marinated green beans, carrots, potatoes, and baby peas in light aioli, page 265).

Serves 8 to 10 people

1 10 to 12-pound turkey, rinsed and patted dry

1 tablespoon canola oil

2 tablespoons ground achiote

3 teaspoons thyme

2 teaspoons nutmeg

1 tablespoons guaque (guajillo) chile powder

Kosher salt and freshly ground black pepper

1. Preheat the oven to 325°F. Rub the turkey with the oil, achiote, thyme, nutmeg, chile powder, salt, and pepper.

2. Transfer the turkey to the oven and roast it until done (3 to 3 1/2 hours), or when a meat thermometer reads 165°F. Because of carryover heat, the turkey will continue to cook outside the oven. Its internal temperature will rise about 10°F, bringing the turkey to the proper and safe temperature of 175°F. If you wait until the thermometer reads 175°F to take the turkey out of the oven, it will be overcooked and dry.

3. Serve the turkey with stuffing on the side and drizzle both with the cooking juices.

Amalia's Note

I prefer not to stuff turkeys before cooking them because this increases the cooking time and tends to dry out the meat.

RABO EN SALSA DE TAMARINDO
Oxtails Braised in Tamarind and Wine Sauce

A *Rabo* (tail) and *tamarindo* (tamarind) are a match made in heaven when combined with the right *sazón* (seasonings). Oxtails require long, slow cooking, but they are well worth the wait. This delicious, saucy dish goes well with *Arroz Guatemalteco* (Guatemalan vegetable rice, page 287) and *Verduras Encurtidas* (vegetables marinated in aromatic herb sauce, page 279).

Serves 4 to 6 people

8 to 10 meaty oxtails, seasoned with salt and pepper

5 cups fat-free, low-sodium beef stock

1/2 cup roughly chopped yellow onion

1 teaspoon minced garlic

1 teaspoon chopped raisins

2 teaspoons chopped prunes

1/2 to 3/4 cup tamarind concentrate

1/4 cup good quality dry white wine

Sazón (Seasonings)

1 bay leaf

1/2 to 1 teaspoon thyme

1/8 teaspoon ground cloves

Kosher salt and freshly ground black pepper

1. Preheat the oven to 325°F.

2. Sear the oxtails in a dry hot skillet until medium brown all over. Add the stock and bring to a quick boil. Lower the heat and transfer to the preheated oven. Braise covered with foil until tender, about 2 hours. Transfer the oxtails to a cutting board and remove the excess fat with a paring knife. Degrease the juices by running a spoon slightly under the visible fat and removing a little at a time, or by cooling the juices in the refrigerator until the fat firms up and then removing it.

3. In a blender, combine the onion, garlic, raisins, prunes, and 1 cup of the degreased juices. Purée the mixture to a fine consistency. Add this mixture to the skillet with the rest of the juices. Add the tamarind concentrate, wine, and seasonings.

4. Return the oxtails to the skillet and cover. Braise in the oven for 30 minutes. Turn the oxtails twice during the cooking time. Taste and adjust seasonings, if needed. To thicken the sauce further (if desired), cook at medium heat on the stovetop for 10 to 15 minutes, stirring occasionally.

Amalia's Notes

Tamarind concentrate is available at Latino stores.

In place of step 1 and 2, season the oxtails and sear them in a dry, hot pressure cooker, add the stock, and cook for 40 to 50 minutes. Then follow steps 3 and 4, except return the oxtails to the pressure cooker and braise uncovered for 30 minutes to thicken the sauce. Turn the oxtails twice during the cooking time.

You can make this dish a day ahead. When cooled in the refrigerator overnight, the fat rises to the surface and separates from the stock. You can remove the fat easily with a spoon before you reheat the dish. This results in an even healthier version of the dish.

POLLO CON PEPSI
Chicken Braised in Pepsi Cola Sauce

A This dish makes a delicious, easy weekday meal. It can be ready in 30 minutes or less. Accompany it with white rice, mashed potatoes, or any of the sides in this book. My mom created this dish. Dark meat is great for stewing and braising because it holds well during cooking and stays moist.

Serves 4 to 6 people

4 to 6 skinless chicken thighs, visible fat removed, seasoned with salt and pepper

1 tablespoon canola oil

1 cup finely diced yellow onions

1 cup julienned red bell pepper

Sazón (Seasonings)

1/4 teaspoon thyme

1/4 teaspoon crumbled oregano

1 bay leaf

Kosher salt and freshly ground black pepper

2 teaspoons minced garlic

1 cup finely diced Roma tomatoes

1 3/4 cup Pepsi Cola

1. In wide, shallow skillet, brown the seasoned chicken pieces in 1 tablespoon of the oil over medium heat (about 4 minutes per side). Transfer the chicken to another dish and keep it warm.

2. In the same skillet, sauté the onions for about 1 minute. Add the bell pepper and the seasonings (except salt) and sauté 1 minute more. Add the garlic and sauté another minute. Add the tomatoes and sauté 1 to 2 minutes.

3. Return the chicken to the skillet and nestle it within the vegetables. Add the Pepsi Cola, bring to a quick boil, reduce the heat, and braise partially covered until the chicken is fully cooked and the liquid has reduced by about one-third and formed a thin sauce (25 to 30 minutes). Taste and adjust seasonings, if needed.

LENGUA EN SALSA DE TOMATE, CON ACEITUNAS Y ALCAPARRAS

Beef Tongue Stew with Olives and Capers Tomato Sauce

A My sister, Gilda, makes this delicious dish for her family often. The dish resembles the sauce in cod Biscayne, a Spanish dish. The tongue slices are fork-tender, the olive oil gives it a light richness, and the olives and capers add a tangy dimension.

Serves 4 to 6 people

1 2 1/2-pound beef tongue
1 medium yellow onion, quartered
3 whole peeled garlic cloves
1 bay leaf
5 cups water

1 cup roughly chopped Roma tomatoes
1 cup roughly chopped red bell pepper
1 cup broth from cooking the tongue

1 1/2 tablespoons olive oil
3/4 cup finely diced yellow onion
2 teaspoons minced garlic
1 bay leaf

Kosher salt and freshly ground black pepper

1/2 cup Spanish Manzanilla olives stuffed with pimentos, rinsed and sliced
3/4 cup Spanish nonpareil capers

Adorno (Garnish)
Flat-leaf parsley sprigs

1. Rinse the tongue under cold running water. Cook it with with the onion, garlic, and bay leaf in the water. Method 1: Cook in a pressure cooker for about 45 minutes. Method 2: Cook in a Crock-Pot on the high setting until tender (3 1/2 to 4 hours). Transfer the tongue to a cutting board and let it cool. Peel it. Slice it thinly on the diagonal and set aside. Reserve the vegetables and broth and discard the bay leaf.

2. To make the sauce, combine the tomatoes, bell peppers, reserved vegetables, and 1 cup of reserved broth in a medium pot and bring to a quick boil. Reduce the heat and simmer until vegetables are cooked (5 to 8 minutes). Purée to a medium consistency (like spaghetti sauce) using an immersion blender. Or wait for the mixture to cool and then use a regular blender.

3. In a deep medium-hot skillet, add the olive oil, onion, garlic, and the remaining bay leaf. Sauté for 2 minutes. Add the purée and the remaining broth and cook over medium heat uncovered to thicken the sauce (10 to 15 minutes). Season with salt and pepper. Add the olives, capers, and tongue slices, and simmer covered for 20 to 30 minutes. Taste and adjust seasonings, if needed.

4. Serve garnished with parsley.

BISTEC
Pan-Seared Minute Steaks with Onion and Tomato

A *Bistec* is the Guatemalan term for "beefsteak." (The two words are pronounced about the same.) This is a terrific dish to make when you don't have much time to prepare a meal. For a quick weekday menu, accompany the steaks with *Guacamol Chapín* (Guatemalan guacamole, page 289), or *Güicoyitos con Mantequilla y Cebolla* (steamed baby squash with onion butter, page 291), or *Papitas a la Maggi* (roasted spicy Yukon gold potatoes with Maggi sauce, page 301).

Serves 4 to 6 people

4 to 6 3- to 4-ounce minute steaks
Kosher salt and freshly ground black pepper
2 to 3 teaspoons canola oil

1 teaspoon canola oil
1/2 cup julienned yellow onions
3/4 cup thinly sliced vine-ripened tomatoes

1. Heat a medium skillet over medium-high heat.

2. Season the steaks with salt and pepper.

3. Add the oil to the hot skillet. Sear the steaks for 1 1/2 minutes per side and transfer them to a platter. Keep the steaks warm.

4. Adjust the heat to medium. Add the rest of the oil to the same skillet. Sauté the onion until it's translucent and medium brown (about 3 minutes). Add the tomatoes and sauté 2 minutes. Taste and adjust seasonings, if needed.

5. Top the steaks with the tomatoes and onions.

Amalia's Note

Alternatively, use top sirloin steaks or flattened chicken breasts instead of minute steaks. Follow the same steps, but cook the sirloin steaks for about 3 to 4 minutes per side and the chicken for 4 to 5 minutes per side (or until fully cooked). To flatten chicken breasts, cover them with plastic wrap and pound them with a meat mallet to about 1/2 inch thick or desired thinness.

COCIDO DE RES

Aromatic Beef and Vegetable Soup

*C*ocido means "cooked," and *de res* means "of beef." This recipe was inspired by a Spanish dish with the same name. In Guatemala it's usually eaten for Saturday lunch. It can include 10 or more varieties of vegetables, and the recipe varies from family to family. *Cocido de res* is a 3-course meal. The beef from the soup sometimes becomes a dish called *Salpicón*, a delicious salad of chopped beef, onion, mint, and lime (page 275). The vegetables are taken out of the soup and served on the side. And the broth is served separately. Traditional side dishes are *Arroz Guatemalteco* (Guatemalan vegetable rice, page 287), avocado slices, lime wedges, corn tortillas, and *Chilito* (bird's eye chile, onion, lime, and olive oil sauce, page 325). Traditional *Cocido* is made by cooking all the ingredients together in a pot. This simplified version has great flavor and less fat, has leaner and tenderer beef, and the vegetables are cooked al dente.

Serves 4 to 6 people

1/3 cup roughly chopped shallots or onion

1/3 cup roughly chopped leek

1/3 cup roughly chopped celery

1 teaspoon roughly chopped garlic

1/3 cup roughly chopped green bell pepper

2 bird's eye (Thai) chiles, stems removed

1/3 cup roughly chopped Roma tomato

1 1/2 tablespoons roughly chopped cilantro stems

1 1/2 tablespoons roughly chopped parsley stems

1 tablespoon canola oil

1 fresh bay leaf

2 teaspoons Maggi sauce

1/4 teaspoon kosher salt

Freshly ground black pepper

3 cups fat-free, low-sodium beef stock

1 carrot, peeled, sliced on the diagonal into pieces 1/2 inch thick

1/2 ripe plantain, scrubbed, unpeeled, sliced into pieces 1/2 inch thick

1 ear of corn, sliced into pieces 1/2 inch thick

1/2 acorn squash, scrubbed, peeled, cut into 2-inch cubes

1 small russet potato, peeled, sliced into pieces 1/2 inch thick

1 very small yuca, peeled, sliced into 4 to 5 pieces 1 inch thick

1/4 cabbage cut into 2-inch chunks

1 pound sirloin steak, fat removed, sliced thinly and cut into 2-inch pieces

2 teaspoons freshly squeezed lime juice

Chopped cilantro

Avocado slices

1. Purée the first 9 ingredients in a blender or food processor.

2. Add the oil to a hot, medium-size, heavy pot. Add the purée and bay leaf and fry until aromatic (about 2 minutes). Add the Maggi sauce and cook 1 minute. Season with salt and pepper.

3. Add the stock to the purée, stir well, and cook until very hot. Gradually add the vegetables in the order listed. Cook each vegetable for 2 to 3 minutes or until al dente before adding the next one.

4. Add the beef and cook for 3 to 5 minutes. Transfer the soup to a serving bowl, season with the lime juice, and garnish it with chopped cilantro and avocado slices.

Amalia's Notes

Many Latino stores carry sliced, bagged, mixed vegetables for making beef soup. Maggi sauce is available at most Latino stores and in the ethnic section of many grocery stores in the United States.

Traditionally the beef for this soup comes from tougher, fattier cuts of meat that take longer to cook. Sirloin steak is a tenderer and leaner option. It cooks much faster and is healthier, too.

CHAO MEIN

Guatemalan-Style Chicken Lo Mein Stir-Fry

A This is a nostalgic dish for me. It's not Guatemalan, of course, but it reminds me of home. *Chao mein* is popular in Guatemala City, and it was one of my dad's and my favorite dishes. *Chao mein* packages containing noodles, Chinese soy sauce, and flavorings are readily available at most *mercados abiertos* (open markets) and supermarkets in Guatemala. After combining the package contents with a few vegetables and chicken or other protein, you can have a simple, delicious, and satisfying meal.

Serves 6 to 8 people

Canola oil

1 cup julienned carrots

1 cup julienned celery

1 cup julienned chayote squash, peeled

1 cup julienned multicolored bell peppers

2 cups julienned yellow onions

Salsa (Sauce)

3 teaspoons minced garlic

2 teaspoons freshly grated ginger

1/2 tablespoon canola oil

2 tablespoons cornstarch

1 1/2 cups fat-free, low-sodium chicken stock

3 to 4 tablespoons low-sodium Chinese soy sauce

2 teaspoons Maggi sauce

Freshly ground black pepper

4 cups lo mein noodles, cooked al dente in salted boiling water

3 cups shredded store-bought rotisserie chicken, cooked shrimp, or any other protein

Adorno (Garnish)

1/2 cup thinly sliced green onions

1. Add about 1/2 teaspoon of oil to a hot wok or a medium skillet and sauté the fresh vegetables one at a time in the order listed. Transfer each batch of vegetables to a bowl after you cook it. Adjust the oil as you cook each batch, adding about 1/2 teaspoon each time. Cook all the vegetables al dente (about 2 minutes per batch).

2. Make the sauce in the same wok or skillet used for the vegetables. Sauté the garlic and ginger in the oil for 1 minute. Dissolve the cornstarch in the chicken stock. Add the stock and starch mixture and cook, stirring constantly, until the sauce thickens (about 2 minutes). Season with soy and Maggi sauce and freshly ground black pepper. Do not add any salt, as soy and Maggi sauce are high in salt.

3. Return the vegetables to the wok or skillet and combine with the sauce. Add the noodles and the chicken and mix well. Taste and add more soy sauce and freshly ground black pepper, if you like.

4. Serve the *chao mein* garnished with green onions.

 *Amalia's Note*

Guatemalan packaged *chao mein* typically contains noodles, about 1 tablespoon of Chinese soy sauce, and 2 small packets of *saborín* (MSG). I choose not to use MSG because I have an adverse reaction to it. This recipe is very tasty without it. Use MSG at your own discretion.

Chao Mein packages are available at some Latino stores or online.

PAELLA *FÁCIL Y RÁPIDA*

Rice, Chorizo, Seafood, and Chicken with Saffron, Rosemary, and Wine

A I have vivid memories of eating *Tía* (Aunt) Lidia's paella in Guatemala. She was the best cook in my dad's large family. Special gatherings often took place at her home. Everyone looked forward to her cooking, and this is one of the dishes that I truly relish from my childhood. Traditionally, Spanish paella is made with a special pearly rice called *bomba* or *calasparra* in a *paellera,* or paella skillet. This is where name of the dish comes from. Bomba (or calasparra) rice resembles arborio rice in looks but not in texture, and it requires much more liquid than white rice. In Guatemala, paella is made with long- or medium-grain rice. It is not an authentic paella, but the end result is just as delicious. *Fideua* is another version of paella with vermicelli noodles instead of rice.

Serves 6 to 8 people

1/2 cup thinly sliced Spanish chorizo

4 chicken thighs, seasoned generously with *pimentón* (Spanish paprika), salt, and pepper

3 tablespoons olive oil

3/4 cup finely diced yellow onion

2 teaspoons minced garlic

1/2 cup julienned red bell peppers

2-ounce jar diced pimentos, drained

2 tablespoons olives stuffed with pimentos, sliced

2 tablespoons Spanish capers

1 1/2 tablespoons finely chopped fresh rosemary

1/2 to 1 teaspoon kosher salt

Freshly ground black pepper

1/2 teaspoon saffron soaked in 1/2 cup good quality dry white wine

1/2 cup fresh green beans cut into 2-inch pieces

1 1/3 cup canned crushed tomatoes

2 cups long-grain white rice

1 8-ounce bottle hot clam juice

3 cups hot fat-free, low-sodium chicken stock

4 to 6 clams, scrubbed

4 to 6 mussels, scrubbed and debearded

1/2 cup frozen squid rings, thawed

1/2 cup frozen baby peas, thawed

8 to 12 peeled and deveined medium shrimp seasoned with *pimentón*, salt, and pepper and sautéed in a skillet with a little olive oil (about 1 1/2 to 2 minutes per side)

Adorno (Garnish)

Parsley leaves and lemon wedges

1. In a hot large, deep skillet cook the chorizo to render about 2 tablespoons of fat (about 2 minutes). Transfer the chorizo to a dish and set it aside. In the fat, cook the chicken until medium brown (about 4 minutes per side). Transfer the chicken pieces to the chorizo dish and set it aside.

2. Add the 3 tablespoons of olive oil to the skillet and sauté the onion, garlic, bell peppers, pimentos, olives, capers, and rosemary, and season with salt and pepper. Cook for 2 minutes. Deglaze the pan with the white wine and saffron by loosening the bits stuck to the skillet with a spatula. Cook 3 to 5 minutes to evaporate about three-fourths of the wine.

3. Put in the green beans and crushed tomatoes and cook until saucy (about 3 minutes). Add the clam juice and chicken stock, stir well, and add the rice. Return the chorizo and chicken to the pan and nestle them within the rice and vegetables. Bring to a quick boil, reduce the heat, and simmer covered until the rice has absorbed three-fourths of the liquid (about 20 minutes).

4. Uncover the skillet and add the clams, mussels, squid, and peas, and cover and continue to cook for about 5 minutes or until the shells open and the squid has turned white and is tender. Do not overcook, as overcooked seafood can be tough and rubbery. Lastly, top with the sautéed shrimp and garnish with parsley and lemon wedges.

Amalia's Note

To make paella with *bomba* rice, use 3 cups of stock for each cup of rice.

CEVICHES Y MARISCOS
CEVICHES AND SEAFOOD

THE *CEVICHERÍA*:
A GUATEMALAN INSTITUTION

*C*evicherías (ceviche restaurants) are a Guatemalan institution. There are many of them in Guatemala City and in the coastal areas. All are usually packed on weekends. Guatemalans claim that ceviche is the perfect cure for a hangover.

Ceviche is popular in Guatemala and in other Central and South American countries, as well as in Mexico, the Caribbean, and even the United States. Ingredients and presentation vary from country to country. In Guatemala eating ceviche is a cultural experience. At restaurants waiters bring all the prepped fresh ingredients to the tables of eager customers, who fix their own ceviches to taste. Common ingredients and condiments are tomatoes, onion, mint, cilantro, Worcestershire sauce, lots of limes, and fresh spicy sauces. Traditional accompaniments are *tamalitos* (mini-tamales) or soda crackers and Guatemalan beer, the national drink.

Ceviche is very easy to make. Its key ingredients are usually raw seafood. Because the seafood is eaten raw, freshness is very important. Sushi-grade seafood is ideal for ceviches. Lime juice and salt are typical seasonings, and together they help

LIMONCITO

Guatemalans love limes. They sprinkle lime juice on just about everything—from grilled corn on the cob to beer, from ceviche to tamales, from soups to salads, from seafood to snacks, from fruit desserts to drinks, and the list goes on.

Lime is limón in Guatemala. Limoncito (little lime) is what many Guatemalans call it. When Guatemalans add -ito or -ita at the end of any word or proper name, such as limoncito or cafecito, especially in group settings, they are using a cozy way of naming people and things—including food.

While lemon, or limón amarillo in Guatemala, has been gaining popularity in gourmet settings, it hasn't been the norm in traditional Guatemalan cooking. It tastes different from lime and is not as widely available. Because of this, lime is king.

Lime juice is an affordable, easy, and healthy way to add quick and great flavor to any food. I can't think of a better habit to have in the kitchen and at the table.

kill bacteria. The ascorbic acid in lime juice changes the color and texture of the seafood, making it look cooked. The lime juice also has a pickling effect. It heightens the flavor of the ceviche, which would otherwise be bland.

Depending on where you are in Guatemala, you may encounter variations of the same ceviche that reflect the taste of a family or a restaurant owner. Often friends gather at *cevicherías* not only to eat ceviche, but also to listen to live music. Musicians roam among the tables offering to play requested music at a price. Sometimes these gatherings turn into parties, and people dance, drink, and eat for hours.

Ceviche is also a street food sold from the backs of pickup trucks, shacks, stands, carts, and small mom-and-pop neighborhood stores. Passersby stop to eat a quick ceviche, or vendors pack the ceviche to go in small *bolsitas* (bags) or disposable cups.

> ## CONCHAS, A GUATEMALAN DELICACY
>
> Conchas (black clams) are a specialty of the Latin Pacific region and are considered a delicacy. They resemble cherrystone clams in looks and texture. However, black clams have a unique flavor and color. Conchas can be eaten on the half shell or in ceviches or in other seafood cocktails.

CEVICHE *DE CONCHAS*
Black Clams in Mint and Cilantro Citrus Sauce

A Ceviche *de conchas* is a delicacy and a favorite in Guatemala. The exotic clam is white, black, and orange inside with black juice and a unique flavor. *Conchas* come from mangroves, or tidal swamps on the Pacific coast from about Baja California to the tip of Chile. They must be scrubbed because they are covered with marine silt. Because they are eaten raw, freshness is vital. Fresh *conchas* should smell briny and be alive when prepared. The shells must be tightly closed and should resist the shucking knife. Any slightly opened *conchas* that do not close at the touch should be discarded, as a spoiled *concha* can make people very sick. Ceviche must be consumed the day it is made for optimum texture, flavor, and quality. A few hours after preparation, the lime juice starts breaking down the ingredients. Serve ceviche with soda crackers and pair it with beer—preferably Guatemalan beer. Alternatively, substitute *conchas* with cherrystone clams.

Serves 1 to 2 people

1 dozen *conchas* (or cherrystone clams), scrubbed, shucked, juice included, roughly chopped
1/2 cup finely diced Roma tomatoes
1 tablespoon finely diced red onion
1/2 to 1 bird's eye (Thai) chile, finely chopped
1/2 to 1 tablespoon finely chopped mint leaves
3 to 4 tablespoons freshly squeezed lime juice

Condimentos (Condiments)
1 to 2 teaspoons Worcestershire sauce
Kosher salt

1. Combine the clams with the tomatoes, onion, chile, mint, and lime juice in a medium bowl.

2. Add the sauce and salt gradually. Taste and adjust seasoning, if needed.

3. Serve the ceviche with soda crackers.

Amalia's Note

My sister buys fresh *conchas*, scrubs them with a brush to remove all the silt, and places them in the freezer for a few hours to let the shells open on their own. This reduces time and effort, as she needs the shucking knife only to scrape the meat out of the shells.

CEVICHE *DE CAMARÓN Y CONCHAS DE VIEIRA*

Spicy Shrimp and Scallops in Lime-Orange Sauce

When you make shrimp ceviche, it is important to undercook the shrimp because when it is marinated in the lime juice, it will become firmer. Seafood in ceviche should be tender, not rubbery, so it's best to cook your own instead of buying precooked seafood. Accompany this dish with avocado slices, soda crackers, lime wedges, and hot sauce.

Serves 1 person

6 medium shrimp, deveined, tails removed
Salted water
1/3 cup fresh baby or large (halved) scallops

1 tablespoon roughly chopped onion
5 roughly chopped cilantro stems
1 bird's eye (Thai) chile, stem removed
2 tablespoons freshly squeezed lime juice
1 tablespoon freshly squeezed orange juice
1 teaspoon ketchup (optional)
3/4 teaspoon kosher salt
Freshly ground black pepper

3 finely diced vine-ripened tomatoes
1 tablespoon chopped cilantro leaves

Adorno (Garnish)
1 tablespoon thinly sliced red onion
1 lime slice (optional)
Cilantro leaves

1. Blanch the shrimp in salted hot water until opaque (about 2 minutes). Remove the shrimp from the water and chill immediately in the refrigerator to keep it from cooking further. Repeat the procedure with the scallops, but blanch them for 1 minute.

2. With a mortar and pestle, gradually pound the onion, cilantro, and chile to a fine paste. Add the lime juice and orange juice, ketchup, and seasonings and stir with the pestle to form a saucy mixture. (Or purée the ingredients in a blender or food processor.)

3. In a medium nonreactive bowl, combine the seafood, sauce, tomatoes, and cilantro leaves. Using a soft spatula, mix gently with folding strokes. Taste and adjust seasonings, if needed.

4. Serve the ceviche garnished with onion, lime (if using), and cilantro leaves.

CEVICHE *DE PESCADO*
Fish with Cucumber in Garlic-Lime Sauce

A Ceviche *de pescado* is easy to make. Use a firm fish that doesn't flake easily when cooked, so that it can hold well during marinating. Mahi mahi, sea bass, and tuna are all good choices. The lime juice tends to break down the fish further, so choosing the right texture of fish is a must for the best flavor, texture, and appearance. Serve with soda crackers and pair with beer—preferably Guatemalan beer.

Serves 1 person

1/3 cup bite-size pieces of mahi mahi (or any other firm white fish)
Salted water

1 tablespoon roughly chopped onion
1 teaspoon roughly chopped garlic
5 roughly chopped cilantro stems
1 bird's eye (Thai) chiles, stem removed
2 tablespoons freshly squeezed lime juice
1 tablespoon olive oil
1/4 teaspoon kosher salt
Freshly ground black pepper

1/3 cup thinly julienned unpeeled, seeded cucumber
1 tablespoon thinly julienned red or green bell pepper
1 tablespoon finely chopped cilantro leaves

Adorno (Garnish)
Cilantro sprigs

1. Blanch the fish in salted hot water until opaque (about 2 minutes). Remove from the water and chill immediately in the refrigerator to keep it from cooking further.

2. With a mortar and pestle, gradually pound the onion, garlic, cilantro stems, and chile to a fine paste. Add the lime juice, oil, and seasonings, and stir with the pestle to form a saucy mixture. (Or purée the mixture in a blender or food processor.)

3. In a medium nonreactive bowl, combine the fish, sauce, cucumber, bell peppers, and cilantro leaves. Using a soft spatula, mix gently with folding strokes, taking care not to break the fish. Taste and adjust seasonings, if needed.

4. Serve the ceviche garnished with cilantro sprigs.

CEVICHE *DE CARACOL DE MAR*
Conch and Green Mango in Habanero Sauce

Caracol (conch) is popular in the Caribbean region of Guatemala, where it is either grilled or used raw in ceviche. It is a delicacy. It's delicious and tender, with a sweet and briny taste. It holds well during marinating and cooking. Sushi-grade conch makes great sushi, too. If you are lucky enough to find fresh conch, you are in for a very special treat. Serve this conch ceviche with fresh sliced avocado and soda crackers.

Serves 1 person

1 tablespoon roughly chopped red onion

1/2 teaspoon roughly chopped seeded, deveined habanero

5 roughly chopped cilantro stems

3 tablespoons freshly squeezed lime juice

1/2 teaspoon kosher salt

Freshly ground black pepper

1/3 pound sushi-grade conch, thinly sliced into bite-size pieces

1/3 cup julienned green mango

1 tablespoon thinly sliced red onion

1 tablespoon finely choppped cilantro leaves

Adorno (Garnish)

1 tablespoon minced multicolored bell peppers

Cilantro leaves

1. With a mortar and pestle, gradually pound the onion, habanero, and cilantro stems to a fine paste. Add the lime juice and seasonings, and stir with the pestle to form a saucy mixture. (Or, purée in a blender or food processor.)

2. In a medium nonreactive bowl, combine the sauce, conch, mango, onion, and cilantro leaves. Using a soft spatula, mix gently with folding strokes. Taste and adjust seasonings, if needed.

3. Serve the ceviche garnished with bell peppers and cilantro leaves.

ESCABECHE DE LENGUADO
Pan-Seared Sole with Peppers, Olives, and Capers Herb Vinaigrette

A This dish is perfect for a busy weeknight. It is not only easy to make, but also nutritious and delicious. Accompany it with *Papas al Vapor con Mantequilla de Ajo, Limón y* Cilantro (steamed fingerling potatoes with garlic, lime, cilantro, and achiote butter, page 327) or *Arroz con Espárragos* (rice with asparagus and cheese, page 299).

Serves 4 to 6 people

4 to 6 fillets of fresh sole, corvina, cod, or tilapia (4 to 6 ounces each), rinsed and patted dry
Kosher salt and freshly ground black pepper
Flour
Olive oil

Escabeche (Chunky Sauce)

1 tablespoon olive oil
1/2 cup julienned onions
2 teaspoons minced garlic
2 fresh bay leaves
1 teaspoon fresh thyme (or 1/2 teaspoon dried thyme)
1/4 teaspoon crumbled oregano
1/3 cup julienned poblano pepper
1/3 cup julienned red bell pepper
1/2 cup sliced Spanish olives stuffed with pimentos
2 tablespoons Spanish capers
1/4 teaspoon kosher salt
Freshly ground black pepper

Toque Final (Finishing Touch)

2 teaspoons champagne vinegar or white wine vinegar
1 tablespoon fresh flat-leaf parsley leaves

1. Season the fish generously with salt and pepper on both sides. Dust lightly with flour. Heat a medium nonstick skillet over medium heat. Add the oil and fry the fish 3 to 4 minutes on one side to develop a medium-brown crust. Turn the fillets and panfry the other side until fish appears opaque, flakes easily, and is tender and juicy (2 to 3 minutes). Transfer the fish to a dish, keep it warm, and set it aside.

2. In the same skillet, make the *escabeche*. Heat the olive oil over medium heat. Sauté the onions, garlic, and herbs for about 2 minutes. Add the peppers, olives, capers, salt, and pepper, and sauté 1 1/2 minutes. To finish, turn off the heat, add the vinegar and parsley, and mix well. Taste and adjust seasonings, if needed.

3. Serve the fish topped with the *escabeche*.

COCTEL DE CANGREJO Y AGUACATE
Spicy Crab and Avocado Cocktail

A My mom used to make shrimp and avocado cocktail when we had parties at home. It is delicious and very easy to make, and you can substitute the shrimp with any other seafood you like. I choose to substitute the shrimp with crab and to make the cocktail sauce from scratch. Serve this dish with soda crackers and a cold beer—preferably a Guatemalan beer. This avocado cocktail is meant for sharing, as each portion is large.

Serves 8 people

1 8-ounce jar lump crabmeat, drained, picked over to remove any shell bits or cartilage

1/2 cup thinly sliced red onion

1/2 cup finely diced vine-ripened tomatoes

1 tablespoon finely chopped cilantro

2 teaspoons olive oil

2 teaspoons freshly squeezed lime juice

1/2 teaspoon kosher salt

Freshly ground black pepper

4 avocados, pitted, peeled, halved

Lime juice

Kosher salt and freshly ground black pepper

1 cup Salsa *para Coctel* (spicy cocktail sauce with lime and cilantro, page 326)

Adorno (Garnish)

Cilantro sprigs

Lime slices (optional)

1. Combine the first 8 ingredients in a bowl and mix them gently to keep the crabmeat as chunky as possible. Taste and adjust seasonings, if needed.

2. To prepare the avocados, halve them the long way. Remove the peels and pits. Brush each avocado half with lime juice and sprinkle it with salt and pepper. Cut a small slice off the rounded bottom of each half to flatten it. Invert 1 avocado half on a plate (pitted side down) and place the other half on top of it (pitted side up) and secure in place.

3. Fill each top avocado half with 1 heaping table-spoon of the crab filling. Surround each set of halves with the cocktail sauce.

4. Serve the dish garnished with cilantro sprigs and lime slices (if using).

TAPADO GARIFUNA
Seafood Chowder with Tomatoes, Green Plantains, and Coconut

A *Tapado* is a dish from the city of Livingston on Guatemala's Caribbean coast. *Tapado* means "covered," and it refers to topping or covering the finished dish with a panfried fish fillet. *Tapado* is a signature dish of the Guatemalan Garifuna culture. This chunky, creamy chowder makes a delicious, hearty meal and pairs well with beer—preferably Guatemalan beer.

Serves 1 to 2 people

2 garlic cloves, peeled

1 teaspoon roughly chopped habanero chile

1 1/2 tablespoons roughly chopped cilantro stems

2 tablespoons roughly chopped onion

2 tablespoons roughly choppped red bell pepper

1/3 cup finely diced Roma tomatoes

1 tablespoon canola oil

1/4 to 1/2 teaspoon ground achiote dissolved in a little water

3/4 teaspoon fresh thyme (or 1/4 teaspoon dried thyme)

1 fresh bay leaf

1/4 teaspoon kosher salt

Freshly ground black pepper

1 1/2 cups fish or seafood stock

2 teaspoons fish sauce (or 2 anchovies mashed to a paste)

1/3 cup finely diced green plantain

1/3 cup finely diced green banana

1/3 cup finely diced yuca

3 tablespoons coconut milk

4 2-inch cubes sea bass

2 peeled, deveined shrimp, tails on

3 to 4 squid rings

1 1/2 teaspoons freshly squeezed lime juice

Adorno (Garnish)
Cilantro sprigs

Lime slices

1. With a mortar and pestle, pound the first 6 ingredients to a rough paste. Pound the ingredients one at a time, adding ingredients to the mixture in the order listed. (Alternatively, finely purée all 6 ingredients in a food processor.)

2. Put the oil in a hot, medium-size heavy pot and add the paste or purée, achiote liquid, and herbs, and fry until aromatic (about 2 minutes). Season with salt and pepper.

3. Add the stock, fish sauce, plantains, bananas, and yuca, and cook until tender (about 10 minutes).

4. Add the coconut milk and seafood, stir well, and cook until tender (2 to 3 minutes). Turn the seafood halfway through the cooking time to ensure even cooking.

5. Transfer the chowder to a bowl and season it with the lime juice. Taste and adjust seasonings, if needed.

6. Serve the *tapado* garnished with cilantro sprigs and lime slices.

Amalia's Notes

Fish sauce is available in the ethnic or Asian section of most grocery stores in the United States.

If you like, you can substitute 1 2-ounce fish filet, floured and panfried, for the sea bass. If you choose this option, use the fillet to top the chowder at the end, and then add the garnishes.

BACALAO A LA VIZCAÍNA
Guatemalan Cod Biscayne

A This is another dish inspired by my *Tía* (Aunt) Lidia. I recall inviting aromas coming from her kitchen every time we visited her home. She made delicious food for every event, and family and friends looked forward to her gatherings. *Bacalao* (cod) *a la Vizcaína* (Biscayne) is a Guatemalized version of the original Spanish dish. It's traditionally made with salt cod, but the process is faster and easier with fresh cod. You may substitute the cod with sole or other fish with a similar texture.

Serves 4 to 6 people

2 tablespoons olive oil

1 tablespoon minced garlic

2 tablespoons finely diced yellow onion

1/3 cup puréed roma tomatoes

1/3 cup puréed red bell pepper

2 bay leaves

3 tablespoons canned crushed tomatoes

1 tablespoon tomato paste dissolved in 1 1/2 cup hot seafood stock (or water)

1/3 cup jarred roasted red bell peppers, cut in strips

8 to 10 sliced Spanish olives stuffed with pimentos

2 tablespoons Spanish capers

3/4 teaspoon kosher salt

Freshly ground black pepper

2 cups sliced Yukon gold potatoes, cooked al dente in salted water

1 1/2 to 2 pounds cod, cut into 6 uniform pieces

Adorno (Garnish)

Flat-leaf parsley

1. Put the olive oil in a deep, wide skillet. Over medium-high heat, sauté the garlic and onion until aromatic (about 2 minutes). Add the tomatoes and bell pepper purée, and sauté 2 minutes. Add the bay leaves, canned tomatoes, tomato paste liquid, bell pepper strips, olives, and capers, and season. Cook for 5 minutes.

2. Lower the heat, add the potatoes, and immerse the cod in the sauce. Cook until the cod is opaque and flaky (about 5 minutes). Taste and adjust seasonings, if needed.

3. Serve the dish garnished with flat-leaf parsley.

Amalia's Note

If you use salt cod, soak the cod in cold water in the refrigerator for 3 straight days prior to cooking it in the sauce. Change the water once a day. The fish's excessive saltiness will fade with each water change. On the third day, the fish should be only mildly salty.

MOJARRAS AL AMATITLÁN
Pan-Roasted Perch with Lemon-Lime Parsley Sauce

*M*ojarra is a lake fish similar to perch. This recipe is inspired by *mojarra frita* (fried head-on perch), a dish common in *comedores* (eateries) along the lakeshore of Amatitlán, a small city on a beautiful lake very close to Guatemala City. The fish is often accompanied by rice, a mixed salad, and lime wedges. The aromas of street foods and confections permeate Amatitlán's main street, which is crowded with locals and tourists on weekends.

Serves 4 to 6 people

4 to 6 head-on *mojarras* (perch or any other freshwater fish), scaled, cleaned, rinsed, patted dry

Kosher salt and freshly ground black pepper

1 cup all-purpose flour

Canola oil

1 lime, halved

Adorno (Garnish)

Lime slices

Flat-leaf parsley leaves

1. Sprinkle plenty of salt and pepper on both sides of the fish. Dredge the fish in flour and press the flour gently to make it stick. Set aside the floured fish.

2. Heat about 3 tablespoons of oil in a medium skillet. Panfry the fish over medium-low heat for about 4 minutes on one side to develop a nice brown crust and another 2 to 3 minutes on the other side to fully cook the fish. Test for doneness: If the fish flakes easily when poked with a fork, then it is cooked.

3. Squeeze lime juice over the fish.

4. Serve the fish garnished with lime slices and parsley.

Amalia's Note

Fresh fish smells sweet and briny, not fishy. The gills should be bright pink and feathery, and the eyes should be bulging, not sunken.

PESCADO ENVUELTO EN HUEVO CON SALSA DE TOMATE

Egg-Battered Fish with Potatoes in Tomato Sauce

A *Pescado seco* (dried fish) is sold in *mercados abiertos* (open markets) in Guatemala, especially during *Cuaresma* (Lent). Before cooking, the fish must be soaked in water to reconstitute it and to release the large amount of salt used to dry and cure the fish. Curing in salt is an old food preservation technique that came to Guatemala and Latin America from Spain. This dish is popular during *Semana Santa* (Holy Week), the week leading up to Easter. To save you time and effort, I have suggested fresh tilapia because it takes less time to prepare than dried fish does, and it's equally delicious. You may also use fresh cod or any other fish you like.

Serves 2 people

Salsa *de Tomate* (Tomato Sauce)

- 1/2 cup roughly chopped yellow onion
- 1 teaspoon roughly chopped garlic
- 1 cup roughly chopped Roma tomatoes
- 1/3 cup water

- 2 tablespoons olive oil
- 1/4 teaspoon ground achiote dissolved in a little water
- 1 teaspoon fresh thyme (or 1/2 teaspoon dried thyme)
- 1/4 teaspoon crumbled oregano
- 1 bay leaf
- 3/4 teaspoon kosher salt
- Freshly ground black pepper

Huevo Batido (Egg Batter)

- 1 large egg, separated
- 1/8 teaspoon kosher salt
- 1 tablespoon all-purpose flour

- 2 tilapia filets, rinsed, patted dry
- Kosher salt and freshly ground black pepper

- 2 tablespoons canola oil

- 1 1/2 cups thinly sliced peeled potatoes, cooked al dente

Adorno (Garnish)

- 1/4 cup chopped flat-leaf parsley
- 3 to 4 thinly sliced onion rings

1. Combine the onion, garlic, tomatoes, and water in a blender, and purée them to a fine consistency. Heat the oil in a medium skillet and add the purée, the achiote liquid, the herbs, and the salt and pepper. Cook until the mixture is medium-thick and saucy. Taste and adjust seasonings, if needed.

2. Beat the egg whites until stiff peaks form. Add the yolk, salt, and flour. Beat 1 minute to make a soft batter.

3. Sprinkle both sides of the fish fillets generously with salt and pepper. Press the fish gently on both sides to make the seasonings stick. Heat a medium skillet and add 1 tablespoon of the oil. Dip the first fish fillet in the batter to coat it well on both sides. Panfry the fish over medium heat to medium brown (2 to 3 minutes per side). Transfer the fish to a plate lined with paper towels to absorb excess oil. Add the rest of the oil to the pan and repeat the frying procedure with the second fish fillet.

4. Place the fish in the sauce to cook through for 2 to 3 minutes. Do not stir or turn the fish. Surround it with the potatoes.

5. Serve the dish garnished with parsley and onions.

Amalia's Note

If you use salt cod, soak the cod in cold water in the refrigerator for 3 straight days prior to cooking it in the sauce. Change the water once a day. The fish's excessive saltiness will fade with each water change. On the third day, the fish should be only mildly salty.

EMPANADAS *DE SARDINA*
Spicy Sardine-Stuffed Baked Pastries

 Empanadas (stuffed baked pastries) are popular in Guatemala and throughout Latin America. They vary from country to country and can be sweet or savory. *Sardina* (sardine) empanadas are popular during *Cuaresma* (Lent).

Makes 18 to 20 small empanadas (3 1/2 inches in diameter)

Masa (Dough)
- 1/2 teaspoon kosher salt
- 2 1/2 ounces (5 tablespoons) buttermilk
- 1 cup all-purpose flour
- 4 tablespoons all-vegetable shortening (no trans fat)

Relleno (Stuffing)
- 1/3 cup finely diced yellow onion
- 2 teaspoons minced garlic
- 1 cup diced poblano pepper
- 1 tablespoon canola oil
- 1 cup roughly chopped cilantro leaves
- 1/2 teaspoon crumbled oregano
- Freshly ground black pepper

- 1 15-ounce can Latino sardines in spicy tomato sauce (or cooked tuna or other fish)
- 2 tablespoons freshly squeezed lime juice
- 6 heaping tablespoons bread crumbs

- 1 egg
- 1 teaspoon cold water

Adorno (Garnish)
- Sesame seeds

1. Dissolve the salt in the buttermilk. On a clean, dry surface, combine the flour and shortening with your fingers, working quickly so the shortening doesn't get too soft. The mixture should look coarse and mealy. Add the buttermilk mixture all at once and again work quickly with your fingers to mix the dough. Form a ball, wrap it in plastic, and let the dough rest at room temperature for 20 to 30 minutes.

2. In a hot skillet, sauté the onion, garlic, and poblano in the oil for 2 minutes. Add the cilantro and oregano, and season with black pepper. (The sardines are very salty, so don't add salt.) Let the mixture cool completely.

3. In a medium bowl, break the sardines into small chunks with a fork. Combine the sardines with the cooled vegetable mixture. Add the lime juice and bread crumbs, and mix well until pasty and moist but not runny. (You will have more stuffing than you need for this recipe. You can freeze the leftovers for later use or triple the dough recipe.)

4. Preheat the oven to 350°F.

5. On a clean, floured surface, roll the dough with a floured rolling pin until it's very thin and is stretched as far as it will stretch without breaking. Cut 3 1/2-inch circles with a cookie cutter. Place 1 heaping teaspoon of filling in the center of each circle. Fold each circle into a half-moon and seal the edges by pressing them with your fingers. Use a fork to form ridges around the edges. Make an egg wash by beating 1 egg with 1 teaspoon of cold water. With a pastry brush, varnish the empanadas with the egg wash. Sprinkle a pinch of sesame seeds on each empanada.

6. Bake the empanadas on a baking sheet lined with parchment paper or foil until the dough is cooked and medium brown all over (20 to 25 minutes). Turn the baking sheet around halfway through the baking time for even browning.

Recipe Variation

Empanadas *de Atún* (tuna-filled baked pastries): Follow the recipe above, but substitute the spicy sardines with seasoned grilled or canned tuna.

CALDO DE MARISCOS
Guatemalan Bouillabaise

A *Caldo* (soup) *de Mariscos* (seafood) is from the tropical city of Escuintla, called *ciudad de las palmeras* (city of palm trees), in south-central Guatemala. Every family adds its own distinctive touches to *caldo de mariscos*, and this is my version. Serve this soup with lime juice and hot sauce and a very cold beer—preferably Guatemalan beer.

Serves 1 to 2 people

1/3 cup roughly chopped shallots or onion

1/3 cup roughly chopped leek

1 teaspoon roughly chopped garlic

1/3 cup roughly choppped red bell pepper

2 bird's eye (Thai) chiles, stems removed

1/3 cup roughly chopped Roma tomato

1 1/2 tablespoons roughly chopped cilantro stems

1 1/2 tablespoons roughly chopped parsley stems

1 tablespoon canola oil

1/4 to 1/2 teaspoon ground achiote disolved in a little water

1 fresh bay leaf

3/4 teaspoon fresh thyme (or 1/4 teaspoon dried thyme)

1/8 teaspoon crumbled oregano

1 tablespoon canned crushed tomatoes

2 teaspoons fish sauce (or 2 to 3 anchovies mashed to a paste)

1/4 teaspoon kosher salt

Freshly ground black pepper

2 cups seafood stock

3 cherrystone clams, scrubbed

3 mussels, scrubbed and debearded

4 2-inch cubes sea bass

2 shrimp, peeled, deveined, tails on

3 to 4 squid rings

1 stone crab claw

2 teaspoons freshly squeezed lime juice

Adorno (Garnish)

Cilantro sprigs

Lime slices

1. Purée the first 8 ingredients in a blender or food processor.

2. Put the oil in a hot, medium-size heavy pot and add the purée, achiote liquid, and herbs, and fry until aromatic (about 2 minutes). Add the tomatoes and fish sauce and cook 1 minute. Season with salt and pepper.

3. Add the stock and cook until very hot (about 3 minutes). Add the clams and mussels, cover the pot, and cook 2 minutes. Add the rest of the seafood and cook until tender (2 to 3 minutes). Turn the seafood halfway through the cooking time to ensure even cooking. Taste and adjust seasonings, if needed.

4. Transfer the soup to a bowl and season it with the lime juice.

5. Serve the soup garnished with cilantro sprigs and lime slices.

Amalia's Note

Fish sauce is available in the ethnic or Asian section of most grocery stores in the United States.

LANGOSTINOS CON SALSA DE AJO Y CHILE
Roasted Prawns with Garlic and Bird's Eye Chile Sauce

A Bird's eye chile is a tiny, tasty, fiery chile that goes well with just about every recipe. It is a close substitute for Guatemala's signature chile, chiltepe. This is an easy dish that can be part of a main meal or an appetizer. Serve it with *Curtido con Rábanos* (spicy radish-cabbage slaw, page 263) and *Papas al Vapor con Mantequilla de Ajo, Limón y* Cilantro (steamed fingerling potatoes with garlic, lime, cilantro, and achiote butter, page 327).

Serves 4 to 6 people

3 garlic cloves, halved

3/4 tablespoon roughly chopped cilantro stems

2 bird's eye (Thai) chiles, stems removed

1 tablespoon freshly squeezed lime juice

1 tablespoon olive oil

3/4 teaspoon kosher salt

Freshly ground black pepper

12 prawns, peeled, deveined, tails on, butterflied, rinsed, patted dry

Adorno (Garnish)

3/4 cup minced, sautéed red bell pepper

Cilantro leaves

Cebollín (chives), sliced

1. Preheat the oven to 375°F. In a blender, purée the garlic, cilantro stems, chiles, lime juice, oil, salt, and pepper. Taste and adjust seasonings, if needed.

2. In a medium bowl, combine the puréed ingredients with the prawns, making sure the prawns are coated thickly with the sauce.

3. Distribute the prawns evenly on a baking sheet lined with parchment paper and roast them in the oven al dente (until the prawns look opaque, 5 to 7 minutes). Rotate the baking sheet halfway through the roasting time for even cooking.

4. Arrange the prawns attractively on a platter.

5. Garnish the prawns with bell pepper, cilantro, and chives.

COCINA DE DÍAS FESTIVOS
TRADITIONAL HOLIDAY CUISINE

*F*ood is an integral part of Guatemalan culture. Certain dishes are associated with certain religious events. Food plays an important role in the celebration of major holidays. Guatemalans know well what foods will be available at any given celebration, and they look forward to eating these dishes year after year. Culinary holiday traditions pass from generation to generation.

Growing up in Guatemala was an experience that left in me not only with fond family memories, but also with very vivid recollections of aromas and flavors. Although there are other foods associated with these holidays, this brief chapter containing only major holidays draws from my own experiences in Guatemala and my favorite foods. The recipes appear elsewhere in this book.

Semana Santa (Holy Week)

This is one of Guatemala's most important holidays. During Holy Week, symbolic, colorful, dramatic representations of Jesus's life are celebrated countrywide. This celebration is taken to the highest level in La Antigua. Following are dishes often eaten during Holy Week.

- *Bacalao a la Vizcaína* (Guatemalan cod Biscayne, page 241)
- *Pescado Envuelto en Huevo con* Salsa *de Tomate* (egg-battered fish with potatoes in tomato sauce, page 243)
- *Verduras Encurtidas* (vegetables marinated in aromatic herb sauce, page 279)
- Empanadas *de Sardina* (spicy sardine-stuffed baked pastries, page 245)
- *Molletes* (cream-stuffed buns with spiced panela sauce, page 349)

Virgen de la Asunción (Virgin of the Assumption)

This holiday takes place on August 15. It is a day to celebrate the patron saint of Guatemala City. Many of the foods eaten during this celebration are street foods, such as *chuchitos* (page 40), tostadas (page 111), and others in chapter 4 (page 105).

Fiesta de Todos los Santos (All Saints Day/Day of the Dead)

This religious holiday takes place on November 1. It is a unique and bizarre celebration of death. People bring food, play live music, and even dance in the cemeteries to honor their departed loved ones. Following are dishes often eaten for this feast.

- *Fiambre* (a 1-dish meal of marinated vegetables, meats, cold cuts, seafood, and cheeses, page 267)
- *Ayote en Dulce* (acorn squash in spiced *panela* sauce, page 348)

Día de Guadalupe (Day of the Virgin of Guadalupe)

This event occurs on December 12. It is an important religious holiday in Guatemala, Mexico, and other Latin American countries. It celebrates the appearance of the Virgin of Guadalupe to Juan Diego. Street vendors in improvised shacks gather around the streets and at the atrium of *Templo de Guadalupe* church to sell the traditional foods year after year. Following are dishes often eaten for this feast.

- *Buñuelos* (pastry puffs with spiced anise syrup, page 354)
- *Torrejas* (raisin-stuffed buns with spiced syrup, page 350)
- *Arroz con Leche* (Guatemalan rice pudding, page 92)
- *Garnachas* (tasty morsels topped with chicken and spicy cabbage slaw, page 120)

Noche Buena y Navidad (Christmas Eve and Christmas Day)

Christmas Eve (December 24) is more important than Christmas Day (December 25) in Guatemala. On Christmas Eve, Guatemalans await the birth of baby Jesus at midnight. Throughout the day of December 24, family and friends have short gatherings at their homes to eat and drink and to deliver presents, blessings, and best wishes to their relatives and close friends. Everyone returns home before midnight to spend this special time with their loved ones.

As soon as the clock marks midnight, everyone rushes to hug each other and say, *"Feliz Navidad!"* Neighborhoods erupt with joy as people light fireworks in the streets nonstop for about an hour. The fireworks create a loud, smelly environment, and a smoky haze lingers for hours afterward.

Guatemalans dine on any one or a combination of the following foods immediately after midnight. This is a very intimate time for family, during which peace and love reign. People exchange gifts and best wishes right after dinner. On Christmas Day, people continue celebrating by visiting other family and friends. Firecrackers start again at noon and are repeated again on New Year's Eve and New Year's Day.

- Tamales *Navideños* (Christmas tamales, page 48)
- Tamales *Negros* (sweet Christmas tamales with mole sauce, page 49)
- *Pavo Navideño* (Guatemalan holiday roasted turkey, page 211)
- *Ponche de Frutas* (fresh pineapple and dried fruits hot holiday punch, page 379)
- *Uvas, Manzanas y Nueces* (red grapes, Washington apples, and a variety of nuts in the shell): This is the only time of the year these items are purchased by almost every home in Guatemala City.

Fiestas Titulares y Celebraciones Patronales (State Fairs and Patron Saint Celebrations)

Each department and municipality in Guatemala has its own fair and patron saint celebration with unique local customs and traditional foods.

ENSALADAS, ESCABECHES Y ENCURTIDOS
SALADS AND MARINATED AND PICKLED VEGETABLES

THE GUATEMALAN COLD KITCHEN

Along with ancient traditions came ancient methods of preserving foods. People developed the methods I describe in this chapter—*escabeche, encurtido, salmuera,* and *vinagreta*—before refrigeration was invented. These recipes and techniques likely came to Guatemala and to Latin America from the ancient world and Old World via Spain, undergoing transformations along the way.

Escabeche is of Arab origin. In Guatemala *escabeche* is a technique that consists of sautéing onions, garlic, fresh herbs, and spices in olive oil and finishing them with good-quality vinegar. It is a quick, chunky pan sauce used to top fried fish or other seafood. The contrast between the vinegary sauce and the fried food is fantastically delicious.

Escabeche is also a technique used to pickle, or flavor and preserve, vegetables. Guatemalan-style pickles combine chile peppers and denser vegetables, such as carrots and cauliflower, with onions, garlic, and an array of herbs and spices. In contrast, *encurtidos* (also called *curtidos*) are vegetables or proteins quickly pickled in a sauce of vinegar, water, and spices. The main difference between *escabeches* and *encurtidos* is that *encurtidos* contain no oil. Also, in *encurtidos*, the vegetables are cooked separately and then combined with the vinegar sauce for pickling.

Escabeches and *encurtidos* play a large role in the Guatemalan diet. Both are used in street foods and in home cooking to quickly and easily inject flavor into foods. Both provide a healthy way of cooking foods instead of deep frying them or bathing them with heavier cream sauces. *Escabeches* and *encurtidos* are delicious, wholesome ways to eat vegetables. An *escabeche* can be a part of an entrée, a salad, a side dish, or a condiment. *Encurtidos* are used to make many dishes, including *fiambre*. The pickled vegetables are a major flavor component of this dish.

Salmuera, or marinating in vinegar, herbs, and spices, is another simple technique that quickly infuses a lot of flavor into foods. Some dishes require very little marinating time, and others require marinating for a few hours or overnight. Marinating time depends on the vegetable texture and the cuts used. The denser the texture and bigger the cut, the longer the marinating time required. Dishes that can be marinated within minutes are julienne cuts of lighter-textured vegetables, such as cabbage and onions.

Vinagreta is simply a *salmuera* containing oil. *Vinagreta* is used to marinate vegetables and meats, as in *Patitas a la Vinagreta* (pickled pig's feet with spicy cabbage-carrot slaw, page 273). *Vinagretas* are also used to dress salads.

Escabeches, encurtidos, salmueras, and *vinagretas* all deliver an equal amount of flavor. Fat-free flavoring agents such as orange, lime, lemon, vinegar, wine, and other alcohol can be used as a base for any of these techniques. The only recipes and techniques that require any oil are *escabeche* and *vinagreta.*

ABOUT *FIAMBRE*

Friends and families in Guatemala come together every year to prepare and eat *fiambre* on November 1, All Saints Day (Day of the Dead). *Fiambre* is an elaborate dish with anywhere between 30 and over 50 ingredients, depending on the maker. Preparation begins weeks before the cooking day, and often entire families take part. Guatemalans eat this heavy and substantial one-dish meal for their holiday lunch and after visiting and decorating the tombs of their loved ones. Some families take *fiambre*, drinks, and even live music to the cemetery and celebrate until the wee hours of the morning. The giant hand-made kites from Sumpango in Sacatepéquez, with related spirit tales, are also a tradition of the season.

Guatemala is home to several versions of *fiambre*. The dish can have different colors (white, green, or red), and it can be mildly sweet or savory depending on ingredients, seasonings, and condiments. Each family has developed a preferred style, and versions vary from region to region. But all share some of the same ingredients, and all are culinary masterpieces.

Fiambre is a dish born in Guatemala. The closest dish to *fiambre* is the Italian antipasto—but *fiambre* contains many more ingredients (including a variety of marinated vegetables) and is eaten only as an entrée on November 1. No other dish like *fiambre* exists elsewhere in Latin America, which is puzzling because many of its ingredients have ties to Spain and France. In Spain *fiambre* is the term used for "cold cuts," and the French word *charcuterie* is the term used to refer to foods such as hams, sausages, and cured meats. These ingredients play a big role in Guatemalan *fiambre*. (Coincidentally, Spaniards use the term *fiambre* as slang for "dead body," too.)

Fiambre makers usually get fresh ingredients at the larger *mercados abiertos* (open markets), cold cuts and cheeses at specialty shops, and jarred and canned items at the supermarket. *Fiambre* is not difficult to make; it just takes advance planning and plenty of helping hands. When Guatemalans make *fiambre*, they always make lots of it—for themselves, to share with friends and relatives, and even to sell. Good Guatemalan cooks become well known within their friends' social circles and develop followers, especially during the holidays.

I've had opportunities to make *fiambre* with different groups of people, and I've found it interesting to see the different approaches people use. During one of my visits to Guatemala close to All Saints Day, I had a chance to make *fiambre* with my cousins and aunts. We all gathered in the kitchen, and everyone had a task, a cutting board, and a knife. On another visit, I observed *fiambre* making at a close friend's home and tasted a sweet *fiambre* with fewer ingredients. On a subsequent visit, I made *fiambre* with my sister and a group of her girlfriends. We cooked almost everything from scratch, and we had more than 60 ingredients by the time we started assembling the *fiambre*. As we were dicing, slicing, chopping, and reminiscing about our childhoods, we had the time of our lives. This is what *fiambre* is all about in Guatemala—paying respects to the dead, sharing good memories, and spending quality time with family and close friends.

Pacaya Palm Flowers In Their Sheaths (page 11)

Curtido Crudo

CURTIDO
Herbed Pickled Cabbage Slaw

A *Curtido* can be a topping, a salad, or a side dish. *Curtidos* are used to top *pupusas*, tostadas, *mixtas*, Guatemalan tacos, and other foods. They can also serve as bases for other dishes. *Curtido* complements grilled or fried foods nicely because of its mild acidity and great flavor. A picture of this recipe paired with the dish Pupusas (cheese-filled corn masa cakes with herbed pickled cabbage slaw) is shown on page 28.

Makes 4 cups

3 cups green cabbage, shredded

1/2 cup thinly shredded carrots

1/2 cup julienned yellow onion

3 cups very hot water

3 tablespoons champagne vinegar or white wine vinegar

3/4 teaspoon crumbled oregano

1 Serrano pepper, thinly sliced (optional)

3/4 teaspoon kosher salt

1. Combine the cabbage, carrots, and onion with the hot water in a nonreactive bowl.

2. Add the rest of the ingredients and mix well to blend flavors. Let the *curtido* sit for 15 to 20 minutes in the refrigerator before serving. Taste and adjust seasonings, if needed.

Recipe Variations

Curtido Crudo (spicy lime cabbage slaw): In a bowl, thoroughly mix 3 cups shredded cabbage; 3 tablespoons freshly squeezed lime juice; 1/2 cup julienned carrots or red bell pepper; 1 thinly sliced Serrano, jalapeño, or other hot pepper of choice; and 3/4 teaspoon kosher salt. Taste and adjust seasonings, if needed.

Curtido con Rábanos (spicy radish-cabbage slaw): Follow the *Curtido Crudo* recipe, but substitute 1/2 cup chopped radishes for the carrots or red bell pepper and add 1 tablespoon chopped cilantro.

Amalia's Notes

Make *curtido* (except *curtido crudo*) the day before you plan to eat it for optimum flavor. Store it in the refrigerator in a jar with a tight lid. *Curtido* with vinegar keeps in the refrigerator up to 3 months. Discard the *curtido* after the vegetables start breaking down.

For a fresh and delicious salad, substitute the hot water with cold water. Combine all the raw ingredients, marinate, and then drain off the water, and serve alongside stews or grilled meats.

Marinated and pickled foods taste less salty when they're cold. Taste the *curtido* for seasoning at the temperature it will be when you serve it.

ENSALADA RUSA

Marinated Green Beans, Carrots, Potatoes, and Baby Peas in Light Aioli

Ensalada Rusa (Russian salad) originated in Russia and traveled across Europe, changing along the way. It probably came to Latin America through Spain. Many variations of this salad exist in Latin America. This is my version. It's inspired by my mom's delicious recipe. I really like it as a side for grilled meats or Chiles *Rellenos* (page 129).

Serves 4 to 6 people

1 cup julienned carrots
1 cup julienned green beans
1 cup russet potatoes cut into 1-inch cubes
1 cup frozen baby peas, thawed

Salmuera (Marinade)

2 ounces (1/4 cup) champagne vinegar or white wine vinegar
3 cups water
1/2 to 1 teaspoon minced garlic
1/2 teaspoon thyme
1/2 teaspoon crumbled oregano
1 bay leaf
1 teaspoon kosher salt
Freshly ground black pepper

1 cup thinly julienned red onion

Salsa (Light Aioli)

1/3 cup light mayonnaise
1 teaspoon Dijon mustard
1 teaspoon minced garlic
2 tablespoons finely chopped flat-leaf parsley
Kosher salt
Freshly ground black pepper

Adorno (Garnish)

2 hard-boiled eggs, chopped

1. Steam the vegetables (except peas) one by one until al dente. Let them cool.

2. Combine all the marinade ingredients in a bowl and mix them well with a whisk.

3. In a large bowl, combine the cooked vegetables with the marinade and the red onions. Place in the refrigerator overnight to let the flavors blend.

4. Combine all the aioli ingredients in a medium bowl and mix them well. Taste and adjust seasonings, if needed.

5. Drain the vegetables well in a colander and discard the marinade and bay leaf. Make sure the vegetables are almost dry before combining them with the aioli, or the aioli will not adhere to the vegetables. Mix the aioli and the vegetables gently with a soft spatula, using folding strokes to keep them whole. Taste and adjust seasonings, if needed.

6. Serve the salad garnished with hard-boiled eggs.

Amalia's Note

Marinated and pickled foods taste less salty when they're cold. Taste the *ensalada* for seasoning at the temperature it will be when you serve it.

FIAMBRE ROJO

Marinated Vegetables, Meats, Cold Cuts, Seafood, and Cheeses

Serves 6 to 8 people

Verduras (Vegetables)
- 2 1/2 cups shredded cabbage
- 2 cups julienned green beans
- 2 cups quartered cauliflower florets
- 2 cups julienned beets
- 2 cups julienned carrots
- 8 asparagus spears
- 2 ounces (1/4 cup) baby peas

Caldillo (Vinaigrette)
- 1/4 cup Guatemalan Sharp brand vinegar, champagne vinegar, or white wine vinegar
- 3/4 cup fat-free, low-sodium chicken stock
- 1/2 cup water from cooked vegetables
- 1 tablespoon Spanish capers
- 1/2 cup olive oil or to taste
- 1/2 tablespoon grated fresh ginger
- 1 tablespoon minced garlic cloves
- 3/4 teaspoon mustard seed
- 3/4 teaspoon black peppercorns
- 2 bay leaves
- 3/4 teaspoon thyme
- 1/2 teaspoon crumbled oregano
- 1 1/2 to 2 teaspoons sugar
- 2 teaspoons salt

- 1 cup finely chopped flat-leaf parsley leaves
- 1 cup thinly sliced red onion

Enlatados/Botes (Canned/Jarred Ingredients)
- 1/4 cup thinly sliced palmito (hearts of palm)
- 8 to 10 pickled baby onions
- 1 ounce (1/8 to 1/4 cup) thinly sliced baby pickles
- 10 Spanish olives stuffed with pimentos, sliced
- 1 tablespoon Spanish capers
- 1 ounce (1/8 to 1/4 cup) jarred roasted red bell pepper strips
- 4 pacaya flowers in brine

Pollo, Mariscos y Carnes Frías (Chicken, Seafood, and Cold Cuts)
- 1/2 cup shredded store-bought rotisserie chicken
- 1/2 cup ham strips
- 1/2 cup thinly sliced Spanish chorizo
- 1/2 cup Serrano ham strips
- 1/2 cup cooked Latino chorizo slices
- 1/2 cup cooked shrimp, tuna, or sardines (or other proteins)

Proteínas Vegetales (Vegetable Proteins)
- 1 ounce (1/8 to 1/4 cup) fava beans (optional)
- 1 ounce (1/8 to 1/4 cup) garbanzo beans (optional)

Quesos (Cheeses)
- 1 cup crumbled queso fresco (fresh Latino cheese)
- 1 ounce (1/8 to 1/4 cup) American or mild cheddar cheese cut into strips

Adorno (Garnish)

Leaf or butter lettuce

2-ounce jar baby corn

2 hard-boiled eggs, cut in wedges

3 radishes, cut into flowers

1 ounce (1/8 to 1/4 cup) thinly sliced yellow onion

1 ounce (1/8 to 1/4 cup) sliced sautéed mushrooms

2 ounces (1/8 to 1/4 cup) crumbled dried Cotija cheese

Chamborote chile (or manzano chile, or cut a Fresno chile into a flower)

Day 1:

1. Cook all the vegetables (except the beets) in 4 cups of salted boiling water. Cook them al dente one at a time in the same water, in the order listed, and reserve 1/2 cup of the water. Cook the beets separately, submerged in water, for 40 minutes. Peel the beets under cold running water, then julienne them. Combine all the vegetables except the asparagus and let them cool. Set the asparagus aside for use as a garnish.

2. Combine all the *caldillo* (vinaigrette) ingredients (except the chicken stock) in a blender and process until very creamy. Add the chicken stock and process again to combine. The *caldillo* will have a strong taste. This is necessary to marinate all the cooked vegetables.

3. In a large nonreactive bowl, combine all the cooked vegetables with the *caldillo* and the parsley and red onion. Let the vegetables marinate overnight. For even marinating, mix vegetables gently with a soft spatula occasionally. Taste the next day and adjust seasonings, if needed.

Day 2:

4. Open all the canned and jarred ingredients. Combine a little of each of the juices to make 1/4 to 1/3 cup. Add the juices to the marinated vegetables and mix well. Prepare all the animal and vegetable proteins and cheeses. Prepare all the garnishes. Put all the ingredients in individual bowls.

5. Assembly: In attractive salad plates or bowls, layer all ingredients starting with the lettuce, followed by some marinated vegetables, some canned/jarred ingredients, some chicken, some seafood, some cold cuts, some vegetable proteins, and some of the cheeses. Repeat these layers until you've used up all the ingredients. Make sure the last layer shows a little of every ingredient used.

6. Finish the servings with the garnishes. Start with the baby corn, then use the egg wedges, radishes, yellow onion, mushrooms, asparagus spears, the cheese, and the chile.

Amalia's Notes

Marinated and pickled foods taste less salty when they're cold. Taste the *fiambre* for seasoning at the temperature it will be when you serve it.

Fiambre rojo should look medium pink. It keeps for 3 days after assembly. Or you can freeze it in small portions.

What traditionally follows this meal is a fruit dessert such as *Ayote en Dulce* (acorn squash in spiced *panela* sauce, page 348) or *Jocotes en Dulce* (a fruit native to Guatemala cooked in spiced *panela* sauce).

For a tasty vegetarian *fiambre*, substitute vegetable stock for chicken stock, leave out all animal proteins, and increase the amount and variety of legumes. For *fiambre blanco* (white *fiambre*), omit the beets. For *fiambre verde* (green *fiambre*), substitute the beets and carrots with green vegetables.

ENSALADA DE AGUACATE, LECHUGA, TOMATE Y CEBOLLA ROJA

Avocado, Bibb Lettuce, Tomato, and Red Onion Salad with Red Wine Vinaigrette

A You can prepare this simple and delicious salad in minutes. It's perfect for a barbecue or to accompany your favorite meal. Add other lettuces or greens of your choice or top the salad with grilled chicken to make it into a satisfying and healthy meal.

Serves 4 to 6 people

Vinagreta de Vino Tinto (Red Wine Vinaigrette)

1 ounce (1/8 cup) red wine vinegar

3 ounces (3/8 cup) olive oil

1/4 teaspoon thyme

1/4 teaspoon crumbled oregano

1/2 teaspoon mustard seed

Kosher salt and freshly ground black pepper

4 to 5 Bibb lettuce heads, washed and spun dry

12 to 18 grape or cherry tomatoes (3 per serving), halved

3/4 cup thinly julienned red onion

3 ripe avocados, peeled, pitted, and cut in small cubes (or balls made with a melon baller)

1. Combine all the vinaigrette ingredients in a blender and process until creamy. Taste and adjust seasonings, if needed.

2. In a bowl, coat the lettuce lightly with the vinaigrette. Then distribute the lettuce among 4 to 6 plates and arrange it attractively.

3. Garnish the lettuce with the remaining ingredients in the order listed.

4. Drizzle a little vinaigrette on top of each salad and season with freshly ground black pepper.

CHILES *EN ESCABECHE*

Spicy Fresh Chile Peppers in Herbed Champagne Vinaigrette

A Chiles *en Escabeche* is a popular dish in Guatemala and other Latin American countries. I store batches of marinated peppers in canning jars and keep them in the refrigerator for weeks. The longer they sit in the sauce, the better they taste. Chiles *en Escabeche* is the perfect spicy complement for any dish.

Makes about 6 1/2 cups

1/2 cup olive oil

2 cups julienned carrots

2 cups quartered cauliflower florets

2 cups jalapeño strips, seeds and veins removed

2 cups julienned Vidalia or yellow onions

1 tablespoon minced garlic

1 teaspoon fresh thyme

1 teaspoon crumbled oregano

2 bay leaves

1 teaspoon kosher salt

Freshly ground black pepper

2 ounces (1/4 cup) champagne vinegar or white wine vinegar

1 3/4 cups water

1. In a large and deep skillet, heat the olive oil over medium heat. Add the carrots and cauliflower and sauté for 2 minutes. Add the jalapeño, onion, garlic, and herbs, and sauté until onion is translucent and the vegetables are al dente (3 to 4 minutes). Turn off the heat.

2. Season the mixture with salt and pepper and add the vinegar. Add the water and mix gently with a soft spatula. Let the vegetables marinate in the refrigerator overnight. Taste and adjust seasonings, if needed.

Amalia's Note

Marinated and pickled foods taste less salty when they're cold. Taste this dish for seasoning at the temperature it will be when you serve it.

PATITAS A LA VINAGRETA
Pickled Pig's Feet with Spicy Cabbage-Carrot Slaw

A *Patitas* (little feet) are a favorite dish among Guatemalans. Pig's feet are perfect for pickling. The mild acidity and seasonings contrast well with the richness and texture of the meat. This dish is easy to make and keeps in the refrigerator for days. The dish can have other ingredients than those mentioned here, such as pacaya flowers, cubed potatoes, and baby peas. It can be a salad or an appetizer. My sister's friend adds *patitas* to *fiambre*.

Serves 4 people as an appetizer

4 cups water
2 fresh pig's feet (cut by butcher into 6 pieces)
2 bay leaves
1 bunch green onions, trimmed
1/2 teaspoon kosher salt

2 cups shredded cabbage
1 cup julienned carrots
1 cup julienned green beans

Vinagreta (Vinaigrette)

2 ounces (1/4 cup) champagne vinegar or
    white wine vinegar
1/2 cup olive oil
1/2 teaspoon Dijon mustard
1 teaspoon minced garlic
1 teaspoon thyme
1 teaspoon crumbled oregano
1 bay leaf
1 teaspoon kosher salt
Freshly ground black pepper

1 cup julienned onions
1/2 cup very thinly julienned red bell peppers
1 Serrano pepper, thinly sliced

Adorno (Garnish)

3/4 cup finely chopped parsley leaves

1. In a medium pot, bring the water to a boil. Carefully add the pig's feet pieces, bay leaves, onions, and salt, and cook until tender (20 to 30 minutes). Discard the water, onions, and bay leaves. Let the pig's feet cool.

2. Steam the vegetables one by one until they are al dente. Let them cool.

3. In a blender, combine the vinaigrette ingredients and process until creamy. Taste and adjust seasonings, if needed.

4. In a large bowl, combine the cooked vegetables, pig's feet, vinaigrette, onion, bell peppers, and Serrano slices. Let the flavors blend in the refrigerator overnight. Mix the ingredients occasionally for even marinating. Taste and adjust seasonings, if needed.

5. Serve the dish garnished with parsley.

SALPICÓN

Beef Salad with Tomato, Mint, and Sour Orange

This scrumptious salad is ideal for entertaining. Traditionally *salpicón* is made with the beef from *Cocido de Res* (aromatic beef and vegetable soup, page 219) and served as a side dish along with the soup, rice, and warm corn tortillas. But you don't need to make the soup to cook the beef for this fantastic salad. It is easier to make it this way. Flank steak is a leaner and healthier alternative to the tougher and fattier cuts used in the traditional version of *salpicón*. In Guatemala *salpicón* is made with either sour orange juice or lime juice. A good substitute for sour orange juice is a combination of orange juice and lemon juice. For a flavor twist, add finely chopped or shredded radishes to this mixture.

Serves 4 to 6 people

1 pound flank steak
1/2 teaspoon salt
Freshly ground black pepper
2 to 3 teaspoons oil
1 1/4 cups fat-free, low-sodium beef stock
1/2 onion, halved
2 bay leaves

1/2 cup finely diced onions
1 cup finely diced vine-ripened tomatoes
2 tablespoons finely chopped mint leaves
2 tablespoons freshly squeezed orange juice
1 1/2 tablespoons freshly squeezed lemon juice
1/2 teaspoon kosher salt
Freshly ground black pepper
1/2 Serrano pepper, minced (optional)

Adorno (Garnish)
Leaf lettuce
Mint leaves (optional)
Grape tomatoes
Blue corn tortilla crunchies or triangles

1. Season the flank steak with salt and pepper. In a hot, medium-size, deep skillet, sear the meat on both sides in a little oil until medium brown (about 4 minutes per side). Add the stock, onion, and bay leaves, and bring to a quick boil. Lower the heat, cover, and braise until the meat fibers separate easily when pulled (about 1 1/2 hours). Check the meat during the cooking time and make sure the liquid stays at about 1 1/2 cups at all times. (Add 1/2 cup of stock or water at a time as needed). When the meat is done, transfer it to a cutting board and let it cool. Discard the onion and bay leaves. Pour the broth into a cup and freeze it for another use.

2. Cut the meat into 2-inch uniform chunks and chop them coarsely in a food processor. Chop the meat in batches, using the pulsing function for better control.

3. Combine the meat with the rest of the ingredients (except the garnishes). Taste and adjust seasonings, if needed.

4. Serve the salad garnished with lettuce, mint leaves (if using), grape tomatoes, and/or blue corn tortilla crunchies or triangles.

CURTIDO PARA ENCHILADAS

Pickled Slaw for Guatemalan Enchilada Lettuce Cups

 Use this *curtido* for Guatemalan Enchiladas (page 115) or as a side dish. The color is so vibrant that it will make any dish pop. This *curtido* keeps in the refrigerator for 2 weeks.

Makes about 4 3/4 cups

2 cups shredded cabbage

1 cup julienned green beans

1 cup julienned carrots

2 beets

Water

Salmuera (Marinade)

2 ounces (1/4 cup) champagne vinegar or white wine vinegar

3 cups water

1 yellow onion, julienned

3/4 to 1 teaspoon thyme

2 bay leaves

1 teaspoon kosher salt

Freshly ground black pepper

1. Steam the vegetables (except the beets) one by one until they're al dente. Combine them in a bowl and let them cool. Cook the beets separately in a saucepan with enough water to cover them completely. Cook the beets until they're tender (about 40 minutes). Transfer the saucepan to the sink. Drain the hot water and cool the beets under cold running water. With your bare hands, peel the beets by squeezing them gently while they're still submerged in the cold water. Julienne the beets and combine them with the rest of the vegetables.

2. In a nonreactive medium bowl, mix all the marinade ingredients. Combine the marinade with the vegetables and toss well. Refrigerate the mixture overnight. Taste and adjust seasonings, if needed. The longer the vegetables marinate, the deeper the flavor will be.

Amalia's Note

Marinated and pickled foods taste less salty when they're cold. Taste this dish for seasoning at the temperature it will be when you serve it.

CURTIDO DE PAPAYA VERDE

Green Papaya Slaw with Onion and Oregano Sauce

Green papaya salad is popular in Oriente, the eastern part of Guatemala, where my grandmother lived. This salad goes well with roast pork, grilled chicken, or any other grilled protein. In the United States, the best papayas for this recipe are the small Asian papayas available at Asian markets. At the time of purchase, make sure the peel is deep green and taut, without blisters. The papaya should feel hard, not mushy. When cut, it should be light green inside with white seeds.

Serves 4 to 6 people

3 cups julienned green papaya

Salmuera (Marinade)

2 ounces (1/4 cup) champagne vinegar or white wine vinegar

3 cups cold water

1 teaspoon crumbled oregano

1 bay leaf

1 cup julienned white onion

1 teaspoon kosher salt

Freshly ground black pepper

Adorno (Garnish)

Pickled papaya seeds

1. To prepare the papaya, peel it, cut it in half, scrape out the seeds and inner core with a rouded soupspoon. Reserve the seeds. Julienne the papaya and steam it in small batches until cooked al dente. Let the papaya cool.

2. Combine all the marinade ingredients in a non-reactive bowl. Marinate the seeds separately in a cup with a small amount of the same marinade. Add the steamed papaya to the rest of the marinade. Marinate the papaya and the seeds for 1 hour or longer.

3. Discard the marinade. Serve the papaya garnished with the seeds. Taste and adjust seasonings, if needed.

Amalia's Notes

Papaya can also be pickled raw with lime juice. Shred the papaya and season it with plenty of lime juice, salt, and pepper.

Marinated and pickled foods taste less salty when they're cold. Taste this dish for seasoning at the temperature it will be when you serve it.

VERDURAS ENCURTIDAS
Vegetables Marinated in Aromatic Herb Sauce

 Verduras encurtidas (pickled vegetables) is a super-easy dish that you can make days ahead. Serve it as a salad or a side dish.

Makes 4 3/4 cups

3/4 cup julienned green beans

3/4 cup julienned carrots

3/4 cup quartered cauliflower florets

3/4 cup quartered broccoli florets

3/4 cup julienned red bell pepper

Salmuera (Marinade)

2 ounces (1/4 cup) champagne vinegar or white wine vinegar

3 cups water

1 teaspoon crumbled oregano

1 teaspoon dried thyme

1 cup julienned yellow onion

1 teaspoon kosher salt

Freshly ground black pepper

1. Steam the vegetables one by one until al dente. Combine them in a bowl and let them cool.

2. In a nonreactive medium bowl, make the marinade. Combine the vegetables with the marinade and toss well. Refrigerate overnight to pickle the vegetables. The longer they marinate, the deeper their flavor will be.

3. Discard the marinade. Taste the vegetables and adjust seasonings, if needed.

Amalia's Notes

You can use other vegetables in this recipe. Choose hard or nonporous vegetables that hold well when cooked, such as cabbage.

Verduras encurtidas keeps in the refrigerator up to 3 months in a jar with a tight lid.

Marinated and pickled foods taste less salty when they're cold. Taste this dish for seasoning at the temperature it will be when you serve it.

ENSALADA DE REMOLACHA CON SAL DE MAR

Fresh Beets with Onion, Lime, and Sea Salt

A This is one of my favorite salads of all time. Guatemalan beets are very earthy and sweet. They taste good either raw or cooked. Beets can be cooked in the same way as whole potatoes, but they take a bit longer. Beets can also be roasted in the oven. Either method works for this salad, but roasting is better for retaining nutrients. For another delicious salad, use cucumbers instead of beets.

Makes about 2 3/4 cups

3 medium fresh whole beets, stalks removed, washed

Water

1/3 cup freshly squeezed lime juice (or champagne vinegar or white wine vinegar)

1/4 cup julienned yellow onion

Sea salt and freshly ground black pepper

1. Put the beets in a medium saucepan and fill the pan with water to cover the beets. Bring to a boil on the stovetop, then lower the heat and cook until the beets are tender (about 40 minutes). Transfer the saucepan to the sink and drain the hot water. Cool the beets under cold running water. With your bare hands, peel the beets by squeezing them gently while they're still submerged in the cold water. Transfer the beets to a cutting board.

2. Slice or dice the beets and transfer them to a medium bowl. Add the lime juice and onions and season with salt and pepper. Serve the beets immediately or keep them in the refrigerator until you're ready to eat them.

Amalia's Notes

Serve this dish as a side or as a topping for a salad.

To roast beets in the oven, first rinse them and pat them dry. Rub them with a little oil and place them on a baking sheet. Bake the beets at 400°F until they're soft, but not mushy (30 to 40 minutes).

ENSALADA DE TOMATE Y HUEVO
Beefsteak Tomato and Egg Salad with Garlic Vinaigrette

 This is a salad that my mom made often to accompany *Chuletas Migadas* (breaded marinated pork cutlets, page 204). When you're pressed for time and you need a quick, delicious salad, this is an easy family pleaser.

Serves 4 to 6 people

Vinagreta (Vinaigrette)

1 tablespoon champagne vinegar or white wine vinegar

3/4 teaspoon minced garlic

1/2 teaspoon Dijon mustard

3 tablespoons olive oil

1 1/2 tablespoons water

1/2 teaspoon kosher salt or sea salt

Freshly ground black pepper

2 beefsteak tomatoes, peeled and thinly sliced

2 hard-boiled eggs, sliced

2 tablespoons julienned red onion

Adorno (Garnish)

1 tablespoon finely chopped flat-leaf parsley leaves

1. In a blender, combine all the vinaigrette ingredients and process until creamy. Taste and adjust seasonings, if needed.

2. Arrange the tomatoes attractively on a round platter. Top them with a layer of eggs and onions. Drizzle the tomatoes, eggs, and onions with the vinaigrette.

3. Garnish the dish with parsley.

Amalia's Note

To peel the tomatoes, cut a small X with a paring knife at the bottom of each tomato to break the skin. Submerge the tomatoes in boiling water until the skin close to the X starts pulling back (about 1 1/2 minutes). Plunge the tomatoes immediately in icy water to keep them from cooking further. Peel and slice the tomatoes. Alternatively, you may julienne the peel, roast it in the oven until crispy (about 5 minutes), and use it as a garnish, too.

ACOMPAÑANTES | SIDES

SIMPLICITY AND FRESHNESS

Guatemalans enjoy cooking and eating the wide array of fresh fruits and vegetables available at the *mercados abiertos* (open markets). Many families go to the markets once a week, while others go once a day to get the freshest produce. Side dishes are chosen not only for nutritional value, but also for appropriate pairing with main dishes.

Guatemalan side dishes are usually simple, quick, and easy to prepare. Freshness and great natural flavor are more important than complexity. Vegetables and fruits are the stars of the Guatemalan side dish, as they are accessible, affordable, and of high quality. They are tree or vine-ripened, so they taste great and require little cooking or seasoning to enhance their flavor. Legumes are also common side dishes. They pack a lot of fiber and nutrition, are very satisfying, and can complement just about any dish. (See chapter 2, page 55.)

This chapter describes side dishes that you can easily adapt to the vegetables of your choice. By combining seasonal produce with various sauces (chapter 12, page 305) you can create many different and delicious recipes. Many of the recipes are vegetarian or gluten-free—or easily made so with quick substitutions, such as vegetable stock for chicken stock and vegetable proteins for animal proteins.

ARROZ GUATEMALTECO
Guatemalan Vegetable Rice

A Rice is a staple in Guatemalan kitchens because so many Guatemalan dishes are saucy. The rice absorbs delicious juices and flavors and provides a break from spicy dishes. Guatemalan rice can be made with all the vegetables in this recipe or with just a few. Many different versions of this recipe exist throughout Guatemala. The picture on the left shows a simplified version of the dish omitting bell peppers and peas. The picture on page 146 shows another version. A picture of this recipe paired with the Mayan stew Pepián Negro is shown on page 144.

Serves 4 to 6 people

1 cup long-grain white rice

1 tablespoon canola oil

3 1/2 tablespoons finely chopped yellow onion

1/2 teaspoon minced garlic

1/2 cup julienned red bell pepper

1/2 cup julienned carrots

1/2 cup finely chopped Roma tomato

Pinch of ground cloves

1/2 teaspoon kosher salt

Freshly ground black pepper

2 cups fat-free, low-sodium chicken stock

1/2 cup frozen baby peas, thawed

1. Sauté the rice in the oil for 1 minute. Add the onion and sauté 1 minute. Add the garlic and sauté 1 minute. Add the bell pepper, carrots, and tomatoes, and sauté 1 minute. Finally, add the cloves, salt, pepper, and stock, and stir well. Bring to a quick boil, lower the heat, and simmer covered until most of the liquid is absorbed (15 to 20 minutes).

2. Add the peas, turn off the heat, cover, and steam the peas with the residual heat. Fluff the rice and vegetables with a fork right before serving.

Recipe Variations

Arroz con Chipilín (rice with chipilín leaves): Follow the *Arroz Guatemalteco* recipe, but substitute 1/4 cup chopped fresh or frozen *chipilín* leaves for the carrots.

Arroz con Frijoles (rice with black beans): Follow the *Arroz Guatemalteco* recipe, but substitute black bean broth for the chicken stock and whole black beans for the carrots.

Amalia's Note

I don't rinse packaged, fortified rice because water washes away the added nutrients. Rinsing doesn't speed the process or do anything that cooking wouldn't do. This recipe makes delicious and fluffy rice in minutes. Rinse rice only if you are unsure of its source or its processing.

TORTITAS DE ESPINACA
Spinach Cakes with Red Bell Pepper Sauce

A *Tortitas de espinaca* (spinach cakes) is a recipe inspired by *envueltos de verduras* (vegetable fritters), a traditional side dish. This easy recipe is delicious and very nutritious. For a twist, substitute the spinach with cooked pacaya or izote flowers, kale, Swiss chard, green beans, or cauliflower florets.

Makes 8 cakes

3 tablespoons finely chopped onion

1 tablespoon canola oil

6 cups roughly chopped raw spinach leaves (1 1/2 cups cooked)

1 teaspoon kosher salt

Freshly ground black pepper to taste

Huevo Batido (Egg Batter)

2 eggs, separated

1/8 teaspoon kosher salt

1 teaspoon all-purpose flour

1 to 2 tablespoons canola oil

1 batch Salsa de Pimientos (red bell pepper sauce, page 330)

1. In a medium-hot skillet, sauté the onion in the oil until the onions are translucent (about 2 minutes). Add the spinach, season, and sauté until the spinach is almost wilted (about 2 minutes). Squeeze as much liquid as you can out of the spinach and set it aside.

2. Beat the egg whites until stiff peaks form. Add the yolks, salt, and flour. Beat 1 minute to make a soft batter. Add the spinach to the egg batter and mix well.

3. Add the remaining oil to a hot skillet. With a medium spoon, scoop the spinach batter and drop in the hot oil. Panfry until medium brown on both sides (about 1 1/2 minutes per side).

4. Serve the spinach cakes with *salsa de pimientos*.

GUACAMOL CHAPÍN
Guatemalan Guacamole

Guacamol is what Guatemalans call the delicious, simple avocado mash known in the United States as guacamole. The secret for a perfect *guacamol* is in the quality of the avocados. Guatemalan avocados are thicker-skinned, rounder, and darker than California avocados. The texture of a Guatemalan avocado is milky and buttery. Guatemalans often add them in chunks to soups and salads.

Makes about 1 3/4 cups

3 ripe avocados, mashed to a chunky texture

2 tablespoons freshly squeezed lime juice

1 tablespoon shredded onion

1/2 teaspoon crumbled oregano

1/2 teaspoon kosher salt

1. Combine all the ingredients in a bowl and mix them well. Taste and adjust seasonings, if needed.

Recipe Variation

Guacamol para Tostadas (guacamole for tostadas): Follow the *guacamol chapín* recipe, but omit the onion and oregano.

Amalia's Note

This basic avocado purée has multiple uses in the Guatemalan kitchen. The more lime you add, the longer it will last without turning black. Use it on *Mixtas y Shucos* (page 113), Tostadas *Guatemaltecas* (page 111), Tacos *Dorados con Guacamol Chapín* (page 117), as a side dish, and even as a sauce. To make a sauce, add herbs, chile peppers, water, and a little olive oil.

GÜICOYITOS CON MANTEQUILLA Y CEBOLLA

Steamed Baby Squash with Onion Butter

A*Güicoyitos* (baby squash) are delicious, tender, and juicy, and they cook very quickly. Guatemalan *güicoyitos* are bright green vegetables that resemble baby pumpkins. If they are not available at your local Latino store, a good substitute is *calabacitas*, an elongated baby squash from Mexico. *Calabacitas* have a similar texture and flavor. This is a quick recipe that you can modify easily by slicing and sautéing the squash in the onion butter instead.

Serves 4 to 6 people

3 cups *güicoyitos* or *calabacitas* (baby squash), washed, quartered lengthwise, then cut into 1-inch wedges

3/4 teaspoon kosher salt

White pepper to taste

3 tablespoons butter

2 1/2 tablespoons finely diced yellow onion

1. Steam the baby squash until it is cooked al dente (4 to 5 minutes). Season the squash with salt and white pepper and keep it warm.

2. Melt the butter over medium-low heat and cook the onion until it's translucent (about 2 minutes).

3. Transfer the baby squash to a serving platter and drizzle it with the onion butter. Mix carefully with a soft spatula.

TORTA DE GÜISQUIL
Chayote Squash Tortilla with Tomatoes and Onions

Güisquil (pronounced "WEE-skill") is chayote squash. It is available at many grocery stores in the United States. Chayote is a bright green, pear-shaped squash with thin, taut skin and juicy green flesh. When the squash is young, the seed is edible as is. When the squash is mature, the seed is encased in a rubbery membrane that must be removed. Wear gloves when you peel a chayote squash because it releases an invisible gluelike substance. This substance doesn't wash away with ordinary soap and water, and when it dries, it leaves a film on your palms that can only be removed with abrasive soap or a rough towel. Chayote makes delicious *Chilaquilas de Güisquil* (fresh cheese-stuffed chayote squash in egg batter with tomato sauce, page 31), or you can add it to soups or make it into desserts such as *Chancletas* (chayote squash au gratin with raisins, page 358). This is my Guatemalized version of the Spanish tortilla.

Serves 4 to 6 people

2 tablespoons finely diced yellow onion

1/2 cup finely diced Roma tomatoes

1 tablespoon canola oil

1 1/2 cups chayote squash, peeled, cored, and julienned

2 eggs, beaten and seasoned with 1/2 teaspoon kosher salt

Freshly ground black pepper

Adorno (Garnish)

2 teaspoons finely chopped flat-leaf parsley leaves

1. Preheat a broiler.

2. In a hot medium skillet with a heat-resistant handle, sauté the onions and tomatoes in the oil for 2 minutes. Add the squash and the eggs, and cook over low heat until the eggs are no longer runny (12 to 14 minutes). Do not stir.

3. Transfer the skillet to the broiler and broil until light brown (3 to 5 minutes). (Alternatively, invert the tortilla on a plate, slide it back into the skillet, and cook the other side over low heat for 2 minutes.)

4. Serve the *torta* garnished with parsley.

TORTITAS DE PAPA Y YUCA
Potato and Yuca Patties with Cheese and Honey

Yuca, also known as cassava or manioc, is a delicious tuber popular in Guatemala and throughout Latin America. People add yuca to soups, eat it as a snack, and mash it and make it into patties. Yuca is a good alternative to potatoes. Because of its high starch content, it is also processed into flour and made into tapioca. Yuca can be a bit gummy, and it has a stringy core that should be removed after cooking.

Makes 7 3-inch patties

2 cups cubed potatoes
1 cup cubed fresh or frozen (thawed) yuca

3 1/2 tablespoons finely chopped onion
2 tablespoons butter

1 egg, slightly beaten
1/2 cup crumbled Cotija cheese
2 tablespoons finely chopped parsley leaves
1/2 teaspoon kosher salt
Freshly ground white or black pepper
1/4 cup all-purpose flour

3 tablespoons canola oil

Adorno (Garnish)
Honey

1. Cook the potatoes in salted water until soft (10 to 15 minutes). Cook the yuca in the same water for 8 to 10 minutes. Remove the stringy inner core from the yuca and discard it. Mash the potatoes and then the yuca and combine them.

2. Sauté the onions in the butter until the onions are translucent (2 to 3 minutes). Set aside.

3. In a medium bowl, combine the mashed potatoes and yuca with the onion and butter, egg, cheese, parsley, and salt and pepper. Make uniform balls of dough with a cookie scoop and flatten them to form patties. To keep the mixture from sticking to your hands, coat them lightly with flour. Do not saturate the patties with flour.

4. Heat a medium skillet over medium heat. Add 1 tablespoon of oil to cover the bottom of the skillet lightly. Panfry the patties to a medium brown (2 to 3 minutes per side). Adjust the oil as needed as you continue frying all the patties.

5. Serve the *tortitas* warm with honey drizzled on top of them.

VERDURAS EN AMARILLO

Vegetable Medley in Tomato, Tomatillo, and Red Bell Pepper Sauce

Verduras en amarillo (vegetables in yellow sauce) takes its name from the bright yellow color of the sauce, which contains achiote. *Amarillo* is a delicious sauce that can taste different depending on the thickener used. It also makes a nice topping for potatoes or pan-seared chicken or beef.

Serves 4 to 6 people

1/2 cup cauliflower florets
1/2 cup julienned carrots
1/2 cup broccoli florets
1/2 cup cubed potatoes

Canola oil
Kosher salt and freshly ground black pepper

1 batch *Amarillo* (tomato, tomatillo, and red bell pepper sauce, page 329)

1. Steam all the vegetables al dente and set them aside.

2. When you're ready to serve the vegetables, quickly sauté them in a very light coating of oil and season them lightly with salt and pepper.

3. Drizzle some or all of the sauce on top of the vegetables.

ACELGA CON IGUAXTE

Swiss Chard Sauté with Spicy Tomato and Roasted Pumpkin Seed Sauce

A Guatemalans eat many greens, including wild greens native to Guatemala. This recipe works with many greens—including spinach, mustard greens, collard greens, and many others available at your local grocery store. *Iguaxte* ("ee-WASH-tay") is a simple, tasty Mayan sauce.

Serves 4 to 6 people

1 batch *Iguaxte* (spicy tomato and roasted pumpkin seed sauce, page 323)

6 to 8 cups fresh Swiss chard, washed, spun dry, and cut into 1-inch ribbons
Kosher salt and freshly ground black pepper

1. Add the Swiss chard to the same skillet in which you made the sauce. Over medium heat, wilt the chard slightly with folding strokes for about 1 minute. Turn off the heat and continue folding until the chard is well coated with the sauce. Season and taste.

2. Serve.

Amalia's Note

After washing and spinning the chard, stack 10 leaves at a time, roll them like a cigar, and slice them into ribbons.

PAPAS AL VAPOR CON MANTEQUILLA DE AJO, LIMÓN Y CILANTRO

Steamed Fingerling Potatoes with Garlic, Lime, Cilantro, and Achiote Butter

 Papas al vapor (steamed potatoes) can be combined with other vegetables to make the dish even more colorful. You can also use the seasoned butter for grilled seafood, beef, and chicken.

Serves 4 to 6 people

12 to 28 fingerling potatoes, halved lengthwise

1 batch *Mantequilla de Ajo, Limón y Cilantro* (garlic, lime, cilantro, and achiote butter, page 327)
Kosher salt and freshly ground black pepper

Adorno (Garnish)
1 tablespoon finely chopped flat-leaf parsely leaves

1. Steam the potatoes until they're cooked al dente (12 to 15 minutes). Test for doneness with a fork or the tip of a knife.

2. In a bowl, toss the steamed potatoes with 1 tablespoon or more of the seasoned butter. Use gentle folding strokes and a soft spatula to keep the potatoes from breaking. Season the potatoes and taste.

3. Serve the potatoes garnished with parsley.

Amalia's Note

Substitute the fingerling potatoes with other kinds of potatoes, carrot slices, broccoli or cauliflower florets, or any other seasonal vegetable you like.

ARROZ CON ESPÁRRAGOS
Rice with Asparagus and Cheese

Arroz con Espárragos is a delicious and simple recipe that you can make in minutes. My mom used to make it when we had guests for dinner. Asparagus is not native to Guatemala, so she used canned asparagus. This dish pairs well with saucy dishes, casseroles, and grilled meats. For a new twist, substitute the asparagus with cooked fresh corn—or use both.

Serves 4 to 6 people

1 cup long-grain white rice

1/2 tablespoon canola oil

1/4 teaspoon kosher salt

2 cups fat-free, low-sodium chicken stock

1 tablespoon butter

2 tablespoons Cotija cheese

Adorno (Garnish)

4 to 6 asparagus spears, trimmed, cooked al dente

1 tablespoon Cotija cheese

1. Sauté the rice in the oil for 1 minute. Add the salt and stock. Bring to a quick boil, lower the heat, and simmer covered until most of the liquid is absorbed (15 to 20 minutes).

2. While the rice is still hot, add the butter and cheese and mix well.

3. Serve the rice garnished with asparagus and cheese.

PURÉ DE PAPAS CON PEREJIL
Potato Purée with Olive Oil and Parsley

 Side dishes don't get any simpler than this. For a twist on this delicious recipe, add other herbs or sautéed shallots.

Serves 4 to 6 people

3 cups plain mashed potatoes

1 tablespoon olive oil

3 ounces (3/8 cup) hot fat-free, low-sodium chicken or vegetable stock

2 tablespoons finely chopped flat-leaf parsley leaves

Kosher salt and freshly ground black pepper

1 cup lightly mashed and chunky cooked potatoes

1. Combine the mashed potatoes with the oil, stock, parsley, and seasonings, and mix well to blend.

2. Add the chunky potatoes and incorporate them into the mashed potato mixture using folding strokes. Taste and adjust seasonings, if needed.

PAPITAS A LA MAGGI
Roasted Spicy Yukon Gold Potatoes with Maggi Sauce

Maggi sauce is a staple in many urban Guatemalan kitchens. It is also popular in other Latin American countries. It is a concentrated seasoning sauce with a high salt content. It is similar in looks and salt content to soy sauce, but it doesn't contain soy. Guatemalans use Maggi sauce to flavor scrambled eggs, rice, meats, soups, and even drinks. It has a unique taste and aroma and quickly injects flavor into any food. Maggi is a Swiss brand owned by Nestlé and is available at most Latino markets and grocery stores in the United States.

Serves 4 to 6 people

8 to 10 Yukon gold potatoes, scrubbed, quartered lengthwise

1 tablespoon canola oil

1 teaspoon cobán chile powder (or smoked piquín or árbol chile powder)

1 teaspoon kosher salt

Freshly ground black pepper

1 1/2 tablespoons Maggi sauce

Adorno (Garnish)

1 tablespoon green onions thinly sliced on the diagonal

1. Preheat the oven to 450°F.

2. Pat the potatoes dry with paper towels after cutting. In a bowl, mix the potatoes with the oil, chile powder, and seasonings using a rubber spatula. Make sure the potatoes are well saturated.

3. Lay the potatoes face up evenly spaced on a baking sheet lined with parchment paper or foil. Roast them until they're soft inside and brown and crispy outside (20 to 25 minutes). Rotate the baking sheet halfway through the baking time for even roasting.

4. Serve the potatoes drizzled with Maggi sauce and garnished with onions.

ZANAHORIAS Y GÜISQUIL SALTEADOS CON PICAMÁS

Spicy Carrots and Chayote Squash Sauté

A Picamás is a thick, spicy, flavorful green or red chile sauce from Guatemala. Guatemalans use it for *Elotes Locos* (Crazy Corn, page 125), *Mixtas y Shucos* (Guatemalan hot dogs, page 113), soups, sandwiches, and more. Picamás is available in Latino stores in the United States and online.

Serves 4 to 6 people

2 cups julienned carrots

1 tablespoon canola oil

2 cups julienned chayote squash

3 tablespoons finely diced onion

1/2 teaspoon minced garlic

2 teaspoons canola oil

1 tablespoon green Picamás (or hot pepper sauce of choice)

Kosher salt and freshly ground black pepper

Adorno (Garnish)

1/2 tablespoon *pimentón* (Spanish paprika) (optional)

1 tablespoon finely chopped flat-leaf parsley

1. In a hot skillet, sauté the carrots in 1/2 tablespoon of the oil for 2 minutes, season lightly with salt and pepper, and transfer them to a bowl. In the other 1/2 tablespoon of the oil, sauté the chayote squash for 2 minutes, season lightly with salt and pepper, and transfer to the same bowl.

2. Sauté the onion and garlic in 2 teaspoons of oil until the onion is translucent (about 1 minute). Add the Picamás sauce and mix well. Return the carrots and chayote squash to the skillet and sauté for 1 minute to combine all ingredients. Taste and adjust seasonings, if needed.

3. Serve the dish garnished with paprika (if using) and parsley.

Chiltepe Chile (page 6)

SALSAS, RECADOS, CHIRMOLES Y CHILITOS
SIMPLE, HEARTY, AND SPICY SAUCES AND SALSAS

Continued...

ACHIOTE: A Key Ingredient in Guatemalan Cooking

Achiote is widely used in Guatemalan cooking for adding color—not flavor or aroma—to dishes such as sauces, stews, soups, and more. It comes in small packages because a little goes a long way. The quantity used corresponds to the desired depth of color. A little achiote creates a yellow color, while more achiote creates deep orange.

Achiote is the seed of the pod of the achiote or annatto tree, which grows in Guatemala and elsewhere in the tropical Americas. In the United States, achiote is available in dried seeds, ground into a powder, and as a seasoned paste and liquid. Steeping the seeds in medium-hot oil releases their color quickly. The powder and paste work best when they are dissolved in liquid before adding them to foods such as sauces and stews to prevent clumping. The powder can also be used as a dry rub in conjuction with spices and herbs of choice. The seasoned paste can be broken into bits and also be used as a rub. Use the seasoned liquid as is straight from the bottle. The seeds and the powder are the best options for Guatemalan cooking, as the paste and liquid contain other flavors that may interfere with a recipe. Achiote can burn easily and become bitter.

In Guatemala, natural achiote paste without any additives is widely available at grocery stores. Sometimes the fresh seedpods are available at the *mercados abiertos* (open markets). Because Guatemalan fresh achiote paste contains no condiments or preservatives, once the package is opened, it can spoil quickly unless it is refrigerated. It can last in the refrigerator for a few months. Achiote freezes well and interestingly the paste doesn't harden. This is a good way to save it for a longer time.

GUATEMALAN ZEST

What is the difference between salsa, *recado*, *chirmol*, *sofrito*, and *chilito*? All are sauces with varying ingredients, textures, flavors, and preparation methods. All are zesty and delicious, easy to make, and can serve many purposes. But they do differ in some key ways. To point out the main differences, I'll discuss the sauces one by one, highlighting important characteristics and techniques.

In the United States, salsa means a cold, chunky mixture of cooked or uncooked ingredients. In Guatemala, a salsa is a sauce—generally a cooked one—served warm or at room temperature. In Guatemala, the techniques for making salsas vary. They include panfrying, simmering, simmering and then panfrying, pan roasting and then panfrying, and charring.

Recados are more elaborate sauces. They take a bit longer to make and contain more ingredients than salsas. The sauce of a *carne guisada* (beef stew) is a simpler *recado*. The hearty sauces of Mayan stews and tamales are more complex *recados*. The techniques for making *recados* may include pan roasting dried peppers, tomatoes, seeds, and spices; puréeing; panfrying; and simmering.

Chirmol is a quick and simple sauce that has multiple uses in Guatemalan cooking, such as topping eggs, tostadas, rolled crispy tacos, and so on. The technique for making *chirmol* involves panfrying chopped vegetables in a little oil. Another technique for making Chirmol is by grilling all or some of the ingredients to make a quick chunky sauce with raw onions and herbs of choice. Think of *chirmol* as a basic sauce that can be built into a bigger sauce by adding layers of other ingredients.

In Guatemala, *sofrito*, at its most basic level, can be a mixture of panfried onions and garlic and sometimes tomatoes. More elaborate *sofritos* can include other ingredients, such as fresh or dried chiles, spices, and more, depending on the purpose. *Sofrito* is the base of many Guatemalan sauces, such as *recados* and panfried *chirmol*, and of Guatemalan dishes such as beans, rice, soup, and stews.

The term *chilito* means "little chile." In the United States, a *chilito* would be called a salsa. A *chilito* is a simpler purée or lightly chunky sauce made of finely chopped ingredients. *Chilito* can be cooked or raw. An example of a raw *chilito* is chile de chiltepe, which is a combination of chiltepe chile, onions, herbs, lime juice, and salt.

Chirmol de Miltomate (page 312)

Chirmol (page 309)

CHIRMOL

Charred Tomato and Mint Salsa

 Chirmol de Tomate is so simple, yet so delicious. *Chirmol* is to Guatemalans what *chimichurri* is to Argentineans. *Chirmol* is always present with grilled meats. It is the delicious accompaniment to any Guatemalan *churrasco* (barbecue).

Makes about 1 1/4 cups

3 Roma tomatoes

2 tablespoons finely diced onion

1 tablespoon finely chopped mint

1 tablespoon finely chopped cilantro (optional)

2 teaspoons freshly squeezed lime juice

1/2 teaspoon minced bird's eye (Thai) chile (optional)

1/2 teaspoon kosher salt

1. Dry pan roast or grill the tomatoes until they're charred all over and soft (12 to 15 minutes). Chop them coarsely, but do not peel them.

2. Combine the tomatoes with the remaining ingredients. Taste and adjust seasonings, if needed.

 Amalia's Note

Use tomatillos instead of tomatoes—or use both—and follow the same steps.

CHIRMOL FRITO
Guatemalan *Sofrito*

Although this sauce is very simple, it tastes incredible on fried eggs, any grilled meat or chicken, rolled tacos, or tostadas. *Chirmol* is an integral part of Guatemalan cooking and forms the basis for many dishes. *Chirmol frito* is the cousin of *sofrito*, a mixture of oil, onions, garlic, peppers, tomatoes, and other ingredients that vary from country to country. *Sofrito* came to Latin America through Spain and was adapted to local tastes. *Sofrito* is to Latin Americans what mirepoix (a sautéed mixture of diced aromatic vegetables) is to the French.

Makes about 1/4 cup

2 teaspoons canola oil

2 1/2 tablespoons finely diced Roma tomatoes

1 tablespoon finely diced yellow onion

1 to 2 bird's eye (Thai) chiles (optional)

3 tablespoons water

1/4 teaspoon kosher salt

1. Put the oil in a hot skillet. Add the tomatoes, onion, chiles, water, and salt. Cook over medium heat until saucy and thick (about 3 minutes).

2. Taste and adjust seasoning, if needed.

Amalia's Note

Use this sauce as a basis for rice, soup, beans, and many other dishes. Also, build upon this sauce to complement other dishes. For example, you can add garlic, dried or fresh chile peppers, or dried or fresh herbs, such as oregano, thyme, bay leaves, cilantro, or parsley. Traditionally this sauce is chunky, but it can be puréed, too.

CHIRMOL DE MILTOMATE

Spicy Tomatillo Salsa

Miltomate (tomatillos) are native to Central America. They are widely used in Guatemalan cuisine. They have a papery husk that should be removed before cooking. Judge their freshness by their taut, bright green skin. Peel tomatillos under running water if the husks are hard to remove. This sauce is a good complement to grilled filet mignon and other meats. It can be a dipping sauce, too. A picture of this recipe is on page 308.

Makes 2/3 cup

8 small tomatillos, husked
1 Serrano pepper

1 1/2 tablespoons finely diced onion
1/2 tablespoon finely chopped flat-leaf parsley
1/2 tablespoon finely chopped cilantro
1 teaspoon freshly squeezed lime juice
1/2 teaspoon kosher salt

1. Dry pan roast or grill the tomatillos until they're charred and soft (about 8 minutes). Chop the tomatillos finely. Char the Serrano pepper and chop it finely.

2. Combine the tomatillos and Serrano pepper with the rest of the ingredients. Taste and adjust seasonings, if needed.

ADOBO
Guajillo, Achiote, and Tomatillo Sauce

A dobo, wet or dry, is popular in Latin America. Guatemalan adobo is a wet rub that enhances the flavor of proteins. In Guatemala *carne adobada* usually means pork marinated in this sauce and then grilled. However, adobo can be used with chicken or any other protein, too. Adobo is easy to make, and it gives proteins great flavor, color, and aroma. Adobos can be partly cooked or all raw.

Makes about 1 1/2 cups

1/2 cup roughly chopped tomatillos, husked

1 cup roughly chopped tomatoes

1 guaque (guajillo) chile, seeded, torn into small pieces

1 pasa (ancho) chile, seeded, torn into small pieces

1/4 cup water

1/3 cup chopped yellow onion

1 tablespoon minced garlic

1/4 teaspoon crumbled oregano

1 bay leaf

1/4 teaspoon ground cumin

1/8 teaspoon ground cloves

1/8 teaspoon ground *canela* (Ceylon cinnamon)

1/4 teaspoon ground achiote

1 tablespoon plus 1 teaspoon white wine vinegar

1 tablespoon canola oil

1 teaspoon kosher salt

Freshly ground black pepper

1. Cook the tomatillos, tomatoes, and chiles in the water until soft (about 5 minutes). Let cool.

2. Put the mixture with the remaining ingredients in a blender and purée to a fine consistency. The sauce should be thick and pasty so it will stick to the meat. Taste and adjust seasonings, if needed.

Amalia's Notes

The purée should be deep orange and tangy, with light to medium acidity. Marinate overnight for best results.

Use half of each of the chiles for a less spicy sauce, if desired.

MOLE
Chocolate and Chile Sauce

A This sauce varies from cook to cook and has many uses. Traditionally Guatemalans eat it with panfried sweet plantains. I use it not only for grilled plantains, but also for Tamales *Negros* (sweet Christmas tamales with mole sauce, page 49) or as a base for a chicken or pork stew. Mole can be made days in advance. It freezes well in ziplock freezer bags. You can thaw it quickly and easily by submerging the bag in cold water. Then transfer the sauce to a skillet to heat it through. Add water to bring the sauce back to the desired consistency, if needed. Savory mole (see instructions following this recipe) can also be used as a base for a stew or as a sauce to top pan-roasted chicken breasts or other protein of choice.

Makes about 1 1/2 cups

1 cup quartered Roma tomatoes (about 2 large tomatoes)

1/2 cup husked, quartered tomatillos (3 to 4 large tomatillos)

1 to 1 1/2 pasa (ancho) chiles, seeded

3 pitted prunes or 1 tablespoon raisins, soaked in very hot water

1 tablespoon ground pan-roasted pumpkin seeds

1 tablespoon ground pan-roasted sesame seeds

2 teaspoons canola oil

Sazón (Seasonings)

1/2 teaspoon ground *canela* (Ceylon cinnamon)

1/2 teaspoon ground allspice

1/8 teaspoon ground cloves

1 teaspoon sugar

1/8 teaspoon kosher salt

Freshly ground black pepper

1/4 to 1/3 cup Guatemalan chocolate

Para Espesar (Thickener)

1 to 2 tablespoons crumbled *champurradas* (or crumbled María cookies) (if needed)

1. Heat a skillet for 2 minutes over medium heat, then add the tomatoes and tomatillos. Dry pan roast until charred all over and mushy (about 8 minutes). Keep a close eye.

2. Separately, dry pan roast the chiles over medium heat (3 to 5 minutes). Keep a close eye on them, as they burn easily. Soak the roasted chiles in 1 cup of very hot water for 10 minutes.

3. Combine the roasted tomatoes and tomatillos with the soaked chiles and 1/4 cup of the soaking water, as well as the prunes or raisins, and purée in a blender to a fine consistency. The sauce should look smooth and velvety.

4. Dry pan roast the seeds over medium heat (3 to 5 minutes). Keep a close eye on them, as they burn easily. Grind the seeds in a coffee mill or a small food processor.

5. Heat the oil in a medium saucepan. Add the purée, the ground seeds, and the seasonings. Add the chocolate and cookie crumbs and let the chocolate melt gradually. Lower the heat and simmer the sauce for 5 minutes, stirring occasionally. The sauce should be a little thinner than spaghetti sauce and should look brown, smooth, and glossy. If it's too thick, add a little water. If it's too thin, cook it a little longer. Taste and adjust seasonings, if needed.

Recipe Variations

Mole para Pollo, Pavo, o Cerdo (savory mole for chicken, turkey, or pork): Start with the mole recipe above, but substitute all the sweet ingredients (prunes or raisins, sugar, chocolate, and cookie crumbs) for savory ingredients (1 small yellow onion cut into thick slices and 2 large peeled garlic cloves dry pan roasted as in step 2). Add 1/4 teaspoon crumbled oregano and 3/4 to 1 cup fat-free, low-sodium chicken stock during step 5. Thicken the sauce with 1 to 2 tablespoons of ground pan-toasted rice. (Instructions follow.) After simmering, taste and adjust the salt and pepper, if needed.

Pan toast rice in a dry skillet until medium brown. Stir the rice to allow for even browning. Keep a close eye on the rice, as it can burn easily. Grind the rice with a coffee mill or a small food processor and add it to the mole gradually.

Amalia's Notes

Guatemalan chocolate comes in different shapes and sizes (thin rounds, long thick tablets, and short thick tablets), depending on the brand. The chocolate is very hard and must be broken for measuring. To break the chocolate, put it in double ziplock bags, wrap it twice in a kitchen towel, and pound it with the smooth side of a metal meat mallet until the chocolate is almost powdery. Then transfer it to a measuring cup and measure the desired amount.

Champurradas are pieces of sweet and crunchy Guatemalan bread. They are about the size and thickness of chocolate-chip cookies.

María cookies are the Latino cousins of Marie biscuits from England. María cookies came to Latin America through Spain, where they are also very popular. María cookies are available in Latino stores and grocery stores in the United States.

RECADO PARA TAMALES COLORADOS
Roasted Ancho, Guajillo, Mulato, Tomato, and Pumpkin Seed Sauce

A Guatemalans use slightly varying ingredients and techniques to make this sauce. Some cooks prefer to simmer all the fresh ingredients in a little water instead of pan roasting them first. Pan roasting adds another layer of flavor. When my mom made tamales for Christmas, I used to watch her as she carefully pan roasted the sauce ingredients and strived to reach the right *sazón* (seasoning). This is my version of the sauce, which you can create easily at home. My sauce is a bit spicy and very flavorful. For a milder sauce, use 1/2 guajillo chile. You can use this sauce for Tamales *Colorados* (red chicken and pork tamales in banana leaves, page 47); for topping grilled meats, chicken, or pork; or as a base for a red *pepián* (stew). Traditionally this sauce is also used as a base for Tamales *Negros* (sweet Christmas tamales with mole sauce, page 49) with some variations. (See the instructions following this recipe.) This sauce freezes well in ziplock bags, so store any leftover sauce for later use.

Makes about 2 cups

1 cup quartered Roma tomatoes (about 2 large tomatoes)

1/2 cup husked, quartered tomatillos (3 to 4 large tomatillos)

1/2 cup chopped, seeded red bell pepper

1 small yellow onion, cut into thick slices

2 large garlic cloves, peeled

1 guaque (guajillo) chile, seeded

1/2 zambo (mulato) chile, seeded

1/2 pasa (ancho) chile, seeded

1 tablespoon ground pan-roasted pumpkin seeds

1 tablespoon ground pan-roasted sesame seeds

2 tablespoons canola oil

1 1/2 to 2 teaspoons ground achiote dissolved in a little water

Sazón (Seasonings)

1/4 to 1/2 teaspoons ground *canela* (Ceylon cinnamon)

Kosher salt and freshly ground black pepper

1. Heat a skillet for 2 minutes over medium heat, then add the vegetables. Dry pan roast them until they're charred all over and mushy (about 8 minutes). Keep a close eye.

2. Separately, dry pan roast the chiles over medium heat (3 to 5 minutes). Keep a close eye on them, as they burn easily. Soak the roasted chiles in 1 cup of very hot water for 10 minutes.

3. Dry pan roast the seeds over medium heat (3 to 5 minutes). Keep a close eye on them, as they burn easily. Grind the seeds with a coffee mill or a small food processor.

Recado Para Paches (page 320)

Recado Para Tamales Colorados (page 317)

318 | Amalia's Guatemalan Kitchen

4. Combine all the roasted vegetables with the soaked chiles and 1/4 cup of the soaking water and purée in a blender to a fine consistency. The sauce should look smooth and velvety.

5. Heat the oil in a medium saucepan and add the purée, achiote liquid, seeds, and seasonings. Lower the heat and simmer for 5 minutes. Taste and adjust seasonings, if needed. The sauce should be bright orange and should have the consistency of spaghetti sauce. If it's too thick, add a little chicken stock or water. If it's too thin, cook it a little longer.

Recipe Variation

Recado para Tamales *Negros* (roasted ancho, guajillo, mulato, tomato, pumpkin seed, and chocolate sauce): Follow the recipe above, but omit the achiote and convert the sauce from savory to sweet. Add only 1/2 teaspoon of salt and sweeten the sauce with 1/2 to 3/4 cup Guatemalan chocolate and 1 1/2 teaspoons sugar or to taste. Add 3 to 4 pitted prunes or 1 1/2 tablespoon raisins, soaked in very hot water, during step 4. The ending sauce should be dark brown, similar to the color of chocolate. To darken the sauce further, add either more chocolate or 1 to 2 tablespoons of browned instant corn masa flour. Brown the flour on a dry pan at medium-low heat until it's medium brown. Add the flour to the sauce gradually, making sure it doesn't clump in the sauce. (Or dissolve the flour in a little cold water first.) Traditionally this sauce is thickened with ground blackened plantain peel. If the sauce becomes too thick, add a little water.

Amalia's Note

Guatemalan chocolate comes in different shapes and sizes (thin rounds, long thick tablets, and short thick tablets), depending on the brand. The chocolate is very hard (and sweet) and must be broken for measuring. To break the chocolate, put it in double ziplock bags, wrap it twice in a kitchen towel, and pound it with the smooth side of a metal meat mallet until the chocolate is almost powdery. Then transfer it to a measuring cup and measure the desired amount.

RECADO PARA PACHES
Roasted Spiced Tomato and Dried Chile Sauce

A This sauce is one of the key ingredients for *Paches* (spicy potato and pork tamales, page 53). In Guatemala, there are many versions of this recipe from region to region. There are Guatemala City *paches* and Quetzaltenango *paches*. Some cooks prefer to simmer all the fresh ingredients in a little water instead of pan roasting them first. Pan roasting adds another layer of flavor. This is my version that you can create easily at home. My sauce is a bit spicy and very flavorful. For a milder sauce, use 1/2 guajillo chile. You can also use this sauce for topping grilled meats or chicken or as a base for *pepián* (stew). This sauce freezes well in ziplock bags, so store any leftover sauce for later use. A picture of this recipe is on page 318.

Makes about 2 cups

1 cup quartered Roma tomatoes (about 2 large tomatoes)

1/2 cup husked, quartered tomatillos (3 to 4 large tomatillos)

1/2 cup seeded, chopped red bell pepper

1 small yellow onion, cut into thick slices

2 large garlic cloves, peeled

1 guaque (guajillo) chile, seeded

1/2 zambo (mulato) chile, seeded

1 tablespoon ground roasted pumpkin seeds

1 tablespoon ground roasted sesame seeds

2 tablespoons canola oil

1 1/2 to 2 teaspoons ground achiote dissolved in a little water

Sazón (Seasonings)

1/2 teaspoon ground allspice

1/8 teaspoon ground cloves

Kosher salt and freshly ground black pepper

1. Heat a skillet for 2 minutes over medium heat and add the vegetables. Dry pan roast them until they're charred all over and mushy (about 8 minutes). Keep a close eye.

2. Separately, dry pan roast the chiles over medium heat (3 to 5 minutes). Keep a close eye on them, as they burn easily. Soak the roasted chiles in 1 cup of very hot water for 10 minutes.

3. Combine all the roasted vegetables with the soaked chiles and 1/4 cup the soaking water and purée in a blender to a fine consistency. The sauce should look smooth and velvety.

4. Dry pan roast the seeds over medium heat (3 to 5 minutes). Keep a close eye on them, as they burn easily. Grind the seeds with a coffee mill or a small food processor.

5. Heat the oil in a medium saucepan and add the purée, achiote liquid, seeds, and seasonings. Lower the heat and simmer for 5 minutes. Taste and adjust seasonings, if needed. The sauce should be bright orange and should have the consistency of spaghetti sauce. If it's too thick, add a little chicken stock or water. If it's too thin, cook it a little longer.

RECADO PARA CHUCHITOS
Tomato, Red Bell Pepper, and Guajillo Sauce

A *Recado para chuchitos* is the base sauce for the delicious small tamales called *Chuchitos* (see *Cazuela de Chuchitos*, page 40). Of all the tamale sauces, this is the easiest—and it is as scrumptious as the other ones. The sauce can be used as a base for a chicken, beef, or pork stew or as a side sauce for chips.

Makes about 2 cups

1 cup quartered Roma tomatoes (about 2 large tomatoes)

1/2 cup husked, quartered tomatillos (3 to 4 large tomatillos)

1 1/2 guaque (guajillo) chile, seeded

1/2 cup chopped, seeded red bell pepper

1 small yellow onion, cut into thick slices

2 large garlic cloves, peeled

1/2 cup fat-free, low-sodium chicken stock

2 tablespoons canola oil

1 1/2 to 2 teaspoons ground achiote dissolved in a little water

Kosher salt and freshly ground black pepper

1. Combine the first 7 ingredients in a medium saucepan and bring to a quick boil. Lower the heat and simmer, covered, until all the vegetables are soft (5 to 8 minutes). Purée in a blender to a fine consistency. The sauce should look smooth and velvety.

2. Heat the oil in a medium saucepan, then add the purée and achiote liquid and season with salt and pepper. Set the heat to low and simmer for 3 minutes. Taste and adjust seasonings, if needed. The sauce should be bright orange and should have the consistency of spaghetti sauce.

IGUAXTE

Spicy Tomato and Roasted Pumpkin Seed Sauce

 Iguaxte ("ee-WASH-tay") is a Mayan sauce with multiple uses. It can dress vegetables or serve as the base for a chicken braise or stew. Use it on pan-seared steaks or baked chicken breasts.

Makes about 1 1/2 cups

1 tablespoon canola oil

3 tablespoons finely diced yellow onion

1/2 cup finely diced red bell pepper

1 teaspoon minced garlic

1 cup finely diced Roma tomatoes

1 zambo (mulato) chile, seeded, torn into very small pieces

1/2 cup fat-free, low-sodium chicken stock

1 tablespoon ground roasted pumpkin seeds

3/4 teaspoon kosher salt

Freshly ground black pepper

1. Add the oil to a medium-hot skillet. Add the onion and bell pepper and sauté until the onion is translucent (about 2 minutes). Add the garlic and sauté 1 minute. Add the tomatoes, the chile pieces, and the stock, and continue cooking until all ingredients are soft (about 3 minutes longer).

2. Season with pumpkin seeds, salt, and pepper. Taste and adjust seasonings, if needed.

CHILITO

Bird's Eye Chile, Onion, Lime, and Olive Oil Sauce

A This is my favorite quick, spicy salsa. It's a condiment inspired by my sister's homestyle *chilito*, traditionally made with chiltepe chile. At home, my family likes to use this sauce daily to add spice to just about any dish I cook. You can use it on beans, fish, and even ceviche. Make the sauce in small batches. It keeps for a week in the refrigerator or longer when you use vinegar.

Makes about 1/2 cup

15 to 20 bird's eye (Thai) chiles

2 tablespoons chopped onion

2 tablespoons freshly squeezed lime juice (or 1 tablespoon white vinegar)

2 tablespoons water (or 3 to 4 tablespoons if using vinegar)

1 tablespoon olive oil

1/4 teaspoon kosher salt

1. Purée all ingredients in the blender.

2. Taste and adjust seasonings, if needed. Refrigerate the *chilito* until you're ready to use it.

Amalia's Note

For a chunky texture, chop all the ingredients by hand and combine them instead of puréeing. Add cilantro, parsley, or other herbs you like.

SALSA *PARA COCTEL*

Spicy Cocktail Sauce with Lime and Cilantro

 This cocktail sauce is great for *Coctel de Cangrejo y Aguacate* (spicy crab and avocado cocktail, page 237) or for oven-roasted fries.

Makes a little over 1 cup

3 garlic cloves

3/4 tablespoon roughly chopped cilantro stems

2 bird's eye (Thai) chiles

1 cup roughly chopped red bell peppers

4 tablespoons freshly squeezed lime juice

1/2 teaspoon kosher salt

Freshly ground black pepper

1. Combine all the ingredients in a blender and purée until smooth. Taste and adjust seasonings, if needed.

2. Use immediately or store in the refrigerator for later use. This sauce keeps for 2 days.

MANTEQUILLA DE AJO, LIMÓN Y CILANTRO

Garlic, Lime, Cilantro, and Achiote Butter

Elevate a steak to a 5-star status with this delicious compound butter. Place a quarter-size portion of the butter on grilled beef, pork, or chicken. Or use it to dress baked or steamed potatoes and grilled vegetables. The butter freezes well and keeps for weeks.

Makes a little over 1/2 cup

2 tablespoons butter
1/4 teaspoon ground achiote
2 tablespoons minced garlic

1 stick (1/2 cup) butter at room temperature

1/2 teaspoon cumin
2 tablespoons finely chopped cilantro
1 1/2 tablespoons freshly squeezed lime juice
1/4 teaspoon kosher salt
Freshly ground black pepper

1. Melt 2 tablespoons of butter in a small skillet. Add the achiote and dissolve. Add the garlic and cook until aromatic (about 1 1/2 minutes). Cool slightly.

2. In a medium bowl (or using a mixer with the paddle attachment), beat the 1/2 cup of butter with a sturdy spatula until it's creamy. While beating, gradually add the rest of the ingredients. Start with the melted butter mixture, and then add the cumin, cilantro, lime juice, and seasonings. Continue beating until the butter is light and fluffy (about 2 minutes). Taste and adjust seasonings, if needed.

3. Refrigerate or freeze the butter for later use.

SALSITA DE TOMATE CIRUELA
Quick Plum Tomato Sauce

A This delicious sauce is a staple in many Guatemalan homes, and its uses are endless. You can use it for tostadas, crispy rolled tacos, or fried or hard-boiled eggs. Build the sauce further by adding other ingredients, such as celery, herbs, spices, and chile peppers. Panfry the sauce in 1/2 tablespoon of canola oil for a twist in flavor. Or, make it very basic with just a few ingredients, such as tomatoes, water, onions, garlic, and a bay leaf.

Makes a little over 1 cup

1 cup roughly chopped Roma tomatoes
2 tablespoons chopped onion
2 garlic cloves
1/8 teaspoon thyme
1/8 teaspoon crumbled oregano
1/2 bay leaf
1/4 cup water

Sazón (Seasonings)
1/2 teaspoon white wine vinegar
1/4 teaspoon kosher salt

1. Cook the first 7 ingredients in a small saucepan and bring to a quick boil. Lower the heat, cover, and simmer for 5 to 8 minutes.

2. Purée all ingredients and season them with vinegar and salt. Return to the saucepan and heat through. Taste and adjust seasonings, if needed. Use the sauce immediately or save it in a jar for later. It lasts in the refrigerator for 1 week.

AMARILLO

Tomato, Tomatillo, and Red Bell Pepper Sauce

A Amarillo means "yellow." This sauce takes its name from the bright color of the achiote in it. *Amarillo* is a delicious sauce that can change slightly in flavor, depending on the thickener used. It makes a nice topping for potatoes or pan-seared chicken or beef.

Makes about 1 1/4 cups

1/2 cup fat-free, low-sodium chicken stock
1/3 cup roughly chopped yellow onion
1/3 cup roughly chopped red bell pepper
3 small garlic cloves
1/3 cup roughly chopped Roma tomatoes
1/3 cup husked, roughly chopped tomatillos
1 bay leaf

1 tablespoon canola oil
1/2 teaspoon ground achiote dissolved in a
　　little water
1/2 teaspoon kosher salt
Freshly ground black pepper

Para Espesar (Thickener)
1 tablespoon bread crumbs (or 1 tablespoon
　　all-purpose flour disolved in cold water or
　　1 corn tortilla broken into small pieces and
　　soaked in hot water and then puréed)

1. To make the sauce, combine the stock with the onion, bell pepper, garlic, tomatoes, tomatillos, and bay leaf in a medium saucepan, and bring to a quick boil. Reduce the heat and simmer, covered, until all vegetables are soft (5 to 8 minutes). Then purée with an immersion blender or regular blender.

2. Heat the oil in a medium saucepan and add the purée and achiote liquid and season with salt and pepper. Add the thickener and simmer for 3 minutes. Taste and adjust seasonings, if needed.

SALSA *DE* PIMIENTOS
Red Bell Pepper Sauce

 This multipurpose sauce can be used with grilled fish, beef, pork, or chicken, or it can be added to sautéed vegetables and pasta. You can also use it for dressing hard-boiled eggs or as a dipping sauce for corn chips or plantain chips.

Makes 1 1/3 cups

1/2 cup roughly chopped Roma tomato

1 cup roughly chopped seeded, deveined red bell peppers

1 guaque (guajillo) chile, seeded, torn into small pieces

1/2 cup water

1 tablespoon olive oil

1/3 cup finely diced onion

1 teaspoon minced garlic

1/8 teaspoon thyme

1 bay leaf

1/2 teaspoon kosher salt

Freshly ground black pepper

1. In a medium saucepan, combine the tomatoes, bell peppers, chile, and water, and bring to a quick boil. Lower the heat, cover, and simmer until tender (5 to 8 minutes).

2. Purée the cooked ingredients in a blender.

3. In the same saucepan, heat the oil and add the onion and garlic. Sauté until translucent (about 2 minutes). Add the thyme and bay leaf and purée. Season and taste.

CHIRMOL CRUDO

Salsa Fresca with Avocado, Mint, and Cilantro

 This fresh and delicious sauce is a good topping for grilled beef or sausages. It can also be an appetizer with plantain chips or corn chips. Or use it as base for a great seafood ceviche.

Makes a little over 1 cup

1/2 cup finely diced vine-ripened tomatoes

2 tablespoons finely diced yellow onion

1/2 cup finely diced avocado

1/2 teaspoon minced bird's eye (Thai) chiles

1/2 tablespoon finely chopped mint leaves

1/2 tablespoon finely chopped cilantro leaves

1 tablespoon freshly squeezed lime juice

1/2 teaspoon kosher salt

1. Combine all the ingredients in a bowl and mix well.

2. Taste and adjust seasonings, if needed.

CHIRMOL COBANERO

Spicy Pan-Roasted Tomato Sauce

A This sauce takes its name from the renowned Guatemalan chile native to the region of Cobán. This pepper has a unique flavor, and it's very spicy. Guatemalan home cooks use it in sauces, stews, and soups, and street vendors use it on fresh fruits along with lime and salt. You can use *chirmol cobanero* for grilled meats or chicken or as a snack with corn tortilla chips. For a twist in taste, simmer the vegetables instead of grilling them.

Makes about 1 cup

1 large Roma tomato

2 large tomatillos, husked

1 yellow onion slice (1/4 inch thick)

1/2 teaspoon cobán chile powder (or smoked piquín or árbol chile powder)

1/2 teaspoon kosher salt

1. Dry pan roast or grill the tomatoes, tomatillos, and onion until they are soft and charred all over.

2. Roughly chop the vegetables in a food processor, using the pulsing button for better control. Add the chile powder and salt. Taste and adjust seasonings, if needed.

 Amalia's Note

Peel the tomatillos under running water if the husks are hard to remove.

CHIRMOL MAYA
Grilled Tomatillo and Garlic Chile Sauce

 This sauce can be a topping for any grilled meat, chicken, fish, or sausage. For a flavor twist, add other fresh herbs and chopped raw onions to the cooked sauce.

Makes 1/2 cup

6 large tomatillos, husked

3 large garlic cloves, peeled

1 tablespoon finely chopped cilantro

1/2 teaspoon bird's eye (Thai) chile (or Serrano pepper)

2 teaspoons freshly squeezed lime juice

1/4 teaspoon kosher salt

1. Dry pan roast or grill the tomatillos and garlic until they're charred all over.

2. Process the tomatillos, garlic, cilantro, and chile in a food processor to whatever consistency you like. Season with lime juice and salt. Taste and adjust seasonings, if needed.

Amalia's Note

Peel the tomatillos under running water if the husks are hard to remove.

ALIOLI AL CILANTRO
Spicy Cilantro-Garlic Mayonnaise

*A*lioli (aioli) came to Latin America from Spain. The delicious garlic sauce is also popular in France, where it was traditionally made with just olive oil, garlic, and seasonings. (Egg yolks came later.) This version uses lime, chiles, and cilantro for a Guatemalan flair. The sauce can be used as a sandwich spread, for seafood, for grilled beef, or for dipping oven-roasted fries. It also can add great flavor to a potato or vegetable salad.

Makes 2/3 cup

2 large garlic cloves
1 bird's eye (Thai) chile
Kosher salt

2 tablespoons freshly squeezed lime juice
2 large egg yolks (use pasteurized eggs)
2 ounces (1/4 cup) olive oil
2 ounces (1/4 cup) canola oil

1 tablespoon finely chopped cilantro leaves
1/2 teaspoon kosher salt
Freshly ground black pepper

1. With a mortar and pestle, pound the garlic and chile to a paste with a little salt.

2. Add the lime juice and egg yolks and stir with the pestle in a circular motion until creamy. Continue stirring and add the oil little by little, making sure it is well incorporated into the egg mixture before adding more. The sauce should start looking like mayonnaise.

3. Continue adding oil slowly until all has been well incorporated into the sauce. This may take a few minutes. Continue stirring until a thick creamy sauce develops.

4. Transfer the sauce to a bowl. Add the cilantro and season with salt and pepper. Taste and adjust seasonings, if needed.

Amalia's Notes

Instead of a mortar and pestle, you can use a bowl and whisk and follow the same steps, except, put the garlic and chile in a zip lock bag and pound it gently with the smooth side of a meat mallet until pasty.

You can buy pasteurized eggs at grocery stores. Or you can quickly pasteurize large eggs at home by dipping them in boiling water for about 2 minutes and then immediately chilling them in icy water to stop the cooking process.

ADEREZO DE LIMÓN, AJO Y ACEITE DE OLIVA
Quick Lime, Garlic, and Olive Oil Dressing

A Guatemalans usually don't dress their salads and vegetables with heavy sauces or salad dressings. Often they will squeeze lime juice and sprinkle salt and pepper on a green salad—or use just oil and vinegar. This recipe offers a quick, delicious, and healthy way to dress your favorite salad. For a flavor twist, add other herbs and spices.

Makes about 1/4 cup

2 tablespoons freshly squeezed lime juice

2 large garlic cloves

1 tablespoon roughly chopped parsley

2 tablespoons olive oil

1/4 teaspoon kosher salt

Freshly ground black pepper

1. Combine all the ingredients in a blender. Process to make a smooth sauce. Taste and adjust seasonings, if needed.

2. Use the dressing immediately or refrigerate it for later use. It keeps in the refrigerator for 3 days.

CHIMICHURRI
Garlic, Parsley, and Oregano Sauce

Chimichurri is popular in Guatemala because there are many Uruguayan and Argentinean steakhouses in Guatemala City. *Chimichurri* can be either green or red, depending on the dominant ingredient. It varies from restaurant to restaurant, even within Argentina. *Chimichurri* is a delicious topping for grilled meats. It also makes a great marinade.

Makes about 1 1/4 cups

1 tablespoon red wine vinegar

3 tablespoons olive oil

3 garlic cloves

3 tablespoons roughly chopped flat-leaf parsley stems and leaves

1/2 teaspoon red chile flakes

1/2 teaspoon crumbled oregano

1 small bay leaf

2 tablespoons water

1/4 to 1/2 teaspoon kosher salt

Freshly ground black pepper

1. Combine all the ingredients in a blender or food processor to make a thick, smooth sauce. Taste and adjust seasonings, if needed.

2. Use immediately or refrigerate for later use. Bring to room temperature before using. *Chimichurri* keeps in the refrigerator for 1 week.

SALSA *DE* CHOCOLATE *OSCURO*
Guatemalan Dark Chocolate, Ancho, and Rum Sauce

A Salsa *de* chocolate is an easy, delectable sauce that can be the topping for many desserts found in the next chapter. It can also be the perfect pairing for fresh bananas or your favorite ice cream.

Makes about 1 cup

1 cup water

1/3 to 1/2 cup Guatemalan dark chocolate

1/4 cup unsweetened dark chocolate (86 percent cacao)

1 to 2 teaspoons ancho powder (optional)

1 1/2 to 2 tablespoons dark rum (optional)

1. In a small saucepan, bring the water to a quick boil. Add the Guatemalan sweet dark chocolate and dissolve it in the water by whisking it. Reduce the liquid by half.

2. Gradually add the unsweetened chocolate while continuing to whisk. Control the thickness by adding more or less of the unsweetened chocolate.

3. Whisk in the ancho powder and rum.

Amalia's Notes

Guatemalan chocolate comes in different shapes and sizes (thin rounds, long thick tablets, and short thick tablets), depending on the brand. The chocolate is very hard (and sweet) and must be broken for measuring. To break the chocolate, put it in double ziplock bags, wrap it twice in a kitchen towel, and pound it with the smooth side of a metal meat mallet until the chocolate is almost powdery. Then transfer it to a measuring cup and measure the desired amount.

You can purchase unsweetened dark chocolate bars (3.17 ounces) at grocery stores. Half the bar produces 1/4 cup chopped chocolate, the amount needed for this recipe.

PRINCIPIOS DULCES Ó FINALES FELICES
SWEET BEGINNINGS OR HAPPY ENDINGS

GUATEMALAN SWEET TOOTH

*g*uatemalans have a sweet tooth. Guatemalan cuisine includes a long list of sweet things, from light treats to more elaborate desserts. One area in which Guatemalans excel is *dulces típicos* (artisanal candy and confectionery) and chocolate. Every region of the country has its own specialties in candied fruits, fresh fruit desserts, seed-based brittles, marzipan, milk-based candies, coffee candies, raw sugarcane confections, empanadas, *panes* (sweet breads), other baked desserts, preserves, jellies, and more. Recipes pass from generation to generation and little changes over time.

Antigua is famous for its coffee, chocolate, and artisanal candies. A well-known family there has kept the tradition of making high-quality confections for more than a century. When sugarcane, wheat, milk, and coffee entered the scene during the era of European exploration,

ABOUT DULCE DE LECHE

In Guatemala dulce de leche is formed into elongated pieces about 3 inches by 1 inch called canillitas de leche (little milk legs) that have the texture of fudge. Canillitas, as most people call them, can be of two kinds: cinnamon brown and white. The darker canillitas are made the old-fashioned way with milk, canela, and caramelized sugar. The white canillitas are made with powdered and condensed milk that is not allowed to caramelize. Both types of canillitas come in elongated pieces, but the white ones are often piped out with a star-shaped tube and retain that shape. The brown ones look more rustic. Both are delicious and addictive.

The process of making traditional Guatemalan canillitas is long and labor intensive, as the milk mixture has to cook slowly for a long time to thicken, and it must be stirred often to keep it from sticking to the bottom of the pan and burning. One quick way to make dulce de leche is by using a combination of condensed and evaporated milk along with other ingredients (see page 366).

Depending where you are in Latin America, dulce de leche varies in texture, color, flavor, ingredients, type of milk (cow, goat, or other), and even in name. In Mexico dulce de leche is called cajeta, and in South America it is called manjar, manjar blanco, arequipe, doce de leite, and other names.

sweets flourished countrywide. Many recipes that entered the country with the Spanish colonists were adapted to local tastes. Like its cuisine, Guatemala's candy and dessert making is a blend of cultures, ingredients, and traditions that have been around for centuries. Guatemalan candy makers are proud of their products and their long traditions.

Rural religious celebrations and fairs are great places to observe and taste the sweet specialties of each region. Amatitlán, for example, is a touristy place where restaurants and street food reign. The colorful street huts display freshly made artisanal candies and other treats. In Quezaltepeque, my grandmother's town, artisans make *dulces de colación* (attractive hollow white figurines made of sugar painted with bright pink food coloring), and they also make the best *conserva de coco* (fresh coconut preserves) presented in blocks wrapped in waxed paper. In Esquipulas, home of the famous Shrine of the Black Christ, specialty candies, breads, treats, candles, and colorful hats abound in the streets.

Guatemala is a top exporter of high-quality cocoa beans and chocolate. Since Guatemala is the cradle of Mayan culture and of chocolate, chocolate houses are plentiful throughout the central region of the country. These range from mom-and-pop shops to factories. Guatemalans mostly consume their chocolate in drinks and sauces and rarely eat chocolate confections. As a result, the chocolate used for their recipes is minimally processed. Typically a cup of Guatemalan hot chocolate comes from freshly ground roasted cocoa beans, sugar, cinnamon, and sometimes vanilla. These ingredients are pressed into thin cakes and then dissolved in hot water.

Guatemalans also crave *helados de carreta* (artisanal ice cream sold by one-wheeled carts in the streets), fruit and cheese breads, cakes, and pastries. There are many European-style shops in Guatemala City that specialize in pastries adapted to local tastes. Small towns have great bakers that create some of the best *pan dulce* (sweet bread) I've ever tasted. There's also the everyday *pan francés* or French bread—which is not a baguette, but rather a long strip of delicious double rolls resembling bow ties. These rolls are crispy on the outside and doughy on the inside.

PANELA

During a recent trip to Esquipulas and Quezaltepeque, I visited a molienda. Moliendas are artisan sugarcane mills. While sugar processed commercially is one of the top industries in Guatemala, in some small towns, old-fashioned mills are still the way to process sugarcane and to make panela and other treats.

Drawing from my childhood memories of living with my grandmother and visiting moliendas then, during my visit, I noted that little had changed over time in that area. The rustic mill, the oxen, and the large cooking vessels were still there. Visiting a molienda is a cultural experience. The process of making panela from beginning to end is fun and exciting. Tastings are possible at just about every stage of the process.

Guarapo is freshly squeezed sugarcane juice that is delicious on the rocks. Cachaza is the head or foam that forms at about midpoint of cooking the juice. Orange tree leaves are used as spoons for tastings of cachaza. Miel is the syrup resembling molasses than can be used to top fruit or for cooking. Panela is the reduced miel that has been allowed to cool and harden in molds.

The flavor of panela is different from refined sugarcane, even though they come from the same source. Panela, like brown sugar, has a more complex flavor than refined white sugar. Panela is shaped differently and is popular in Latin America and in some Asian countries under different names, such as rapadura, raspadura, chancaca, papelón, piloncillo, panocha, atado, and dulce, to name a few.

EMPANADAS *DE LECHE*
Custard-Filled Pastries

A Sweet empanadas *de leche* are popular in Guatemala City year-round, especially during *Semana Santa* (Holy Week). They are totally different from other kinds of empanadas. Empanadas *de leche* are delicate and flavorful, with a delicious creamy core. The dough is colored with achiote, and this makes them bright orange. The filling is either a creamy custard made with eggs and milk or a mixture of *maizena* (cornstarch) and water flavored with sugar and *canela* (Ceylon cinnamon).

Makes 18 to 20 small empanadas (3 1/2 inches in diameter)

Masa (Dough)

1 cup cake flour

1/2 cup Bob's Red Mill stone-ground corn flour

1/8 cup sugar

1/2 teaspoon baking powder

1/2 teaspoon baking soda

1/8 teaspoon kosher salt

4 3/4 tablespoons vegetable shortening (no trans fat)

1 large egg

1/8 teaspoon vanilla extract

1 teaspoon ground achiote dissolved in 3 tablespoons cold water

Crema (Custard)

1 1/2 cups skim or 1 percent milk

1/4 stick *canela* (Ceylon cinnamon)

Rind of 1/2 orange

1 large egg yolk

1/4 teaspoon vanilla extract

1 tablespoon sugar

1 3/4 to 2 tablespoons cornstarch

1/8 teaspoon kosher salt

Extra cake flour

1/2 cup confectioners' sugar

1. In the bowl of a mixer, sift and combine the flours, the sugar, the baking powder and soda, and the salt. Add the shortening, and using the paddle attachment, mix it slowly to combine it with the dry ingredients until the mixture is coarse and mealy. Add the egg, vanilla, and achiote liquid. The dough is ready when it forms a soft ball in the center of the bowl (after about 2 minutes of mixing). Wrap the dough in plastic and let it rest in the refrigerator for 20 to 30 minutes.

2. While the dough is resting, make the custard. In a small saucepan, combine the milk, cinnamon, and orange rind, and simmer until aromatic, stirring occasionally (about 10 minutes). Keep a close eye on the mixture, as milk can scorch and boil over easily. Discard the cinnamon and rind and remove any remaining cinnamon pieces with a small strainer. Keep the heat on low.

3. In a small bowl whisk the egg yolk, vanilla, and sugar until well dissolved. Add the cornstarch and salt and whisk until very creamy. Temper the egg mixture with 1 tablespoon of the hot milk mixture, and whisk quickly. Add 2 more tablespoons gradually, and whisk until runny. Pour the egg mixture gradually into the hot milk while whisking quickly. Use a rubber spatula to scrape out every bit of egg mixture. Continue whisking the custard until it's thick and bubbly (2 to 3 minutes). Let the custard cool completely at room temperature.

4. Preheat the oven to 350°F.

5. On a clean, well-floured surface, roll the dough with a floured rolling pin. Roll slowly and carefully until the dough is stretched as thin and as wide as it will stretch without breaking. If the dough sticks to the rolling pin, sprinkle a light coating of sifted cake flour on the dough's surface. Cut 3 1/2-inch-diameter circles from the dough with a cookie cutter.

6. Put about 1/2 teaspoon of custard in the center of each circle. Fold each circle into a half-moon shape and seal the edges by pressing them carefully with your fingers. Do not over-stuff the empanadas, or the custard will leak out during baking. Use a fork to make ridges around the edges.

7. Bake the empanadas on a baking sheet lined with parchment paper or foil until the dough is cooked and looks matte (15 to 20 minutes). Turn the baking sheet around halfway through for even baking. Do not let the empanadas get brown.

8. Dust the baked empanadas with confectioners' sugar.

Amalia's Notes

You can also make the dough by hand. Simply mix all the ingredients on a clean surface or in a bowl.

Bob's Red Mill ground flours are available at most grocery stores in the United States.

Tempering is necessary to prevent the egg yolks from curdling when they hit the hot milk. Adding a little hot milk to the mixture first prepares it to thicken the milk more effectively.

POSTRE DE ATOL DE ELOTE
Fresh Corn Pudding

A Traditionally, *atol de elote* is a hot drink and a weekend favorite in Guatemala City. Street vendors selling *atol* gather at church atriums, *mercados abiertos* (open markets), at special celebrations, and even on the backs of pickup trucks with their large pots lined heavily with cloths to keep the drink hot. In Guatemala, *atol de elote* is made with *elote sazón*, which contains more starch than fresh corn and because of this cornstarch is not needed when making the hot drink. When you're using frozen corn, you need to add a bit of cornstarch to help thicken it and to give it puddinglike texture. This version of the drink makes a delicious hot or cold dessert.

Makes almost 2 cups

1 cup frozen fresh corn

1/2 cup cold water

2/3 cup skim or 1 percent milk

1/2 stick *canela* (Ceylon cinnamon)

1 tablespoon sugar

1/8 teaspoon kosher salt

1 1/2 tablespoons cornstarch dissolved in 2 tablespoons cold water

Adorno (Garnish)

Use any of the following:

Ground *canela* (Ceylon cinnamon)

Cooked corn kernels

Berries and mint

Chantilly rum cream

Salsa *de* Chocolate *Oscuro* (Guatemalan dark chocolate, ancho, and rum sauce, page 337)

1. In a blender, purée the corn, water, and milk to a fine consistency. Put a mesh sieve over a small saucepan and strain the corn mixture through the mesh into the saucepan. Add the cinnamon stick, sugar, and salt, and bring the mixture to a quick boil, stirring occasionally. Keep a close eye, as it can boil over easily. Simmer until aromatic (about 10 minutes).

2. Lower the heat and gradually add the cornstarch liquid, stirring constantly. Simmer uncovered until the mixture is thick and bubbly (2 to 3 minutes). Control the thickness of the dessert by addings more or less cornstarch. For a thinner, more drinklike *atol*, add half of the amount of cornstarch suggested in this recipe.

3. Serve immediately in cups with the garnish of your choice, or chill and serve cold.

Amalia's Notes

To make Chantilly rum cream: Whip 1/2 cup of heavy whipping cream (at room temperature) until firm peaks form (2 to 4 minutes). Add 2 teaspoons confectioners' sugar, 1/2 teaspoon vanilla extract, 1/2 teaspoon almond extract, and 1/2 tablespoon dark rum and whip to combine (about 1 minute).

AYOTE EN DULCE
Acorn Squash in Spiced *Panela* Sauce

Ayote en dulce is a favorite dessert eaten after *fiambre* (page 267) on All Saints' Day. In Guatemala it is made with a native mature *ayote* (squash), which is very hard on the outside and firm on the inside. This keeps the squash whole during cooking and afterward. In the United States, use acorn squash, pumpkin, butternut squash, or another squash with firm flesh. A young squash is too tender and will get mushy and fall apart during cooking. The *panela* sauce in this dessert is very flavorful, aromatic, and syrupy.

Serves 2 to 4 people

Dulce (Spiced *Panela* Sauce)

- 2 cups water
- 1/4 stick *canela* (Ceylon cinnamon)
- 1 star anise
- 2 cloves
- 3 allspice berries
- 3/4 to 1 cup *panela* (raw sugarcane), broken into small pieces

- 1 acorn squash, washed, cut into 12 pieces, peels and seeds included

1. In a medium saucepan, combine the water with the spices and *panela* and bring to a quick boil. Lower the heat and simmer covered until the mixture is aromatic and the *panela* has dissolved and become syrupy (about 20 to 30 minutes). Discard the spices (optional).

2. Add the squash peel side down and simmer uncovered until the squash is tender (about 20 to 30 minutes). The longer the squash sits in the sauce, the better it tastes, and the browner it becomes. This is the traditional way. Make this dish the day before for best results.

3. Serve the squash at room temperature or cold.

Amalia's Notes

This is traditionally a very sweet dessert. You can vary the sweetness by adding less *panela*. Be aware that if you use less *panela*, the sauce will be less syrupy.

Panela is very hard and must be broken for measuring. To break it, put it in double ziplock bags, wrap it twice in a kitchen towel, and pound it with the smooth side of a metal meat mallet until the *panela* is almost powdery. Then measure the desired amount.

MOLLETES
Cream-Stuffed Sweet Buns with Spiced *Panela* Sauce

A *Molletes* are popular during Holy Week and also at festivals, carnivals, and other street celebrations. Their sweet aroma inundates the space around them, and their inviting presentation lures people to buy them. Unlike the *panela* sauce in *Ayote en Dulce* (acorn squash in spiced panela sauce, page 348), this equally delicious panela sauce should be thin and not syrupy so that it can saturate the sweet buns. This is my version with a nontraditional garnish.

Serves 4 to 6 people

4 to 6 Latin sweet buns about 12 inches in diameter

Crema (Custard)
1 1/2 cups skim or 1 percent milk

1/4 to 1/2 stick *canela* (Ceylon cinnamon)

Rind of 1/2 orange

1 large egg yolk

1/4 teaspoon vanilla extract

1 tablespoon sugar

1 3/4 to 2 tablespoons cornstarch

1/8 teaspoon kosher salt

Dulce (Spiced *Panela* Sauce)
1 quart water

1 stick *canela* (Ceylon cinnamon)

2 star anise

4 cloves

4 allspice berries

8 ounces (1 cup) *panela* (raw sugarcane), broken into small pieces

Huevo Batido (Egg Batter)
2 large eggs, separated

1/8 teaspoon salt

1 tablespoon all-purpose flour

Canola oil

Adorno (Garnish)
Garnish each bun with your choice of:

Raspberries and mint, or

A sprinkle of rosicler (pink sugar) and one dried seedless prune (traditional garnish)

1. Slice off the sweet buns' tops. Scoop out the insides to hollow them. Save the tops and use the crumbs for another recipe.

2. Make the custard. In a small saucepan, combine the milk, cinnamon, and orange rind. Simmer until aromatic, stirring occasionally (about 10 minutes). Keep a close eye, as milk can scorch and boil over easily. Discard the cinnamon and orange rind and remove any remaining cinnamon pieces with a small strainer. Keep the heat on low.

3. In a small bowl, whisk the egg yolk, vanilla extract, and sugar until well dissolved. Add the cornstarch and salt and whisk until very creamy. Temper the egg mixture with 1 tablespoon of the hot milk and whisk quickly. Add 2 more tablespoons of milk gradually and whisk until runny. Pour the egg mixture gradually into the hot milk while whisking quickly. Use a rubber spatula to scrape out every bit of egg mixture. Continue whisking until thick and bubbly (2 to 3 minutes). Let the custard cool slightly.

4. Make the spiced *panela* sauce. Combine the water with the spices and *panela* and bring to a quick boil. Lower the heat and simmer until the mixture is aromatic and the *panela* has dissolved (about 15 minutes). Discard the spices.

5. Fill the buns with the cream and cover with the tops. Set aside.

6. Make the egg batter. Beat the egg whites to stiff peaks and gradually add the yolk, salt, and flour. Beat 1 minute to make a soft batter.

7. Heat a medium skillet and add 1 tablespoon of oil. Dip the first bun in the batter to coat it all over lightly, making sure the filling stays in. Carefully invert the bun holding the top with your finger and panfry top down first to seal the opening over medium heat to medium brown (about 2 minutes per side). Transfer to a platter lined with paper towels to absorb excess oil. Adjust the oil in the pan and repeat the procedure with the remaining buns. Pat each bun with extra paper towels to absorb as much oil as possible.

8. Immerse the buns side by side in the sauce and heat for 3 to 5 minutes or longer. The buns should be saturated with the sauce. Weigh them down by placing a plate slightly smaller than the saucepan on top.

9. Turn the heat off. Serve the buns garnished with raspberries and mint, or with a sprinkle of *rosicler* (pink sugar), one dried seedless prune, and some of the sauce.

Recipe Variation

Torrejas (raisin-stuffed buns with spiced syrup): Follow the *molletes* recipe, but slice the buns in half, spread soft butter flavored with cinnamon powder on each slice, and stuff each bun with 2 teaspoons of raisins. Close the bun, dip it in the egg batter, and follow steps 7 through 9. To make the sauce, follow step 4, but substitute the *panela* with sugar and add the rind of 1 lime and 1 tablespoon of rum (optional). Lastly, follow step 8. Garnish each bun with a sprinkle of *rosicler* (pink sugar), one dried seedless prune, and some of the sauce.

Amalia's Notes

Buy sweet buns at your local Latino bakery.

Tempering is necessary to prevent the egg yolks from curdling when they hit the hot milk. Adding a little hot milk to the mixture first prepares it to thicken the milk more effectively.

Another effective way to degrease the buns is to place them on a cooling rack, transfer them to the sink, and quickly run very hot water directly over the buns from the faucet as if you were rinsing them. Then pat each bun with extra paper towels to absorb as much water and oil as possible.

Panela is very hard and must be broken for measuring. To break it, put it in double zip-lock bags, wrap it twice in a kitchen towel, and pound it with the smooth side of a metal meat mallet until the *panela* is almost powdery. Then measure the desired amount.

Panela or piloncillo (page 11)

RELLENITOS

Plantain Dumplings Filled with Guatemalan Chocolate-Bean Purée

Rellenitos (stuffed little dumplings) are best when made with plantains that are ripe and yellow and not mushy. In Guatemala *rellenitos* are special treats. They are delicious and super-easy to make. Traditionally *rellenitos* are filled with sweet cinnamon beans or cream and shaped similar to eggs.

Makes 8 *rellenitos*

2 ripe unpeeled plantains (about 2 1/4 cups purée)
Water
3 tablespoons sugar

Relleno (Filling)

1 cup puréed canned black beans
1/2 teaspoon vanilla extract
1/4 cup Guatemalan chocolate
2 tablespoons sugar
1/8 teaspoon kosher salt

1 teaspoon ground *canela* (Ceylon cinnamon)
1 tablespoon sugar
1/2 cup all-purpose flour
1/3 cup canola oil

Adorno (Garnish)

Canela sugar (1 tablespoon sugar mixed with 1/2 teaspoon cinnamon)

1. Wash the plantains and cut them into 2-inch slices. Cook them in water with 3 tablespoons of sugar until soft (about 20 minutes). Cool slightly. Save 1/4 cup of the cooking water and discard the rest. Cover the plantains and keep them warm.

2. In a small skillet, combine all the filling ingredients, stirring constantly, until all ingredients are well blended and have formed a thick sauce (about 5 minutes). Let the filling cool.

3. Peel and mash the plantains. Add the cooking water, 1 teaspoon of cinnamon, and 1 tablespoon of sugar. Mix well to form a soft dough. Using an ice cream scoop, form 8 balls. Place the balls on a lightly floured surface. Using the back of a small skillet covered with plastic wrap, flatten each ball into a circle about 1/4 inch thick.

4. Put about 1 tablespoon of the chocolate purée in the center of each circle. Fold gently and carefully enclose the filling inside the dough. Shape the *rellenitos* to resemble eggs. Dust them with a little flour.

5. Add the oil to a hot skillet. Panfry the *rellenitos* over medium heat until golden brown (about 2 minutes per side). Transfer to a platter lined with paper towels to absorb excess oil.

6. Roll the *rellenitos* in cinnamon sugar and serve.

BUÑUELOS
Pastry Puffs with Spiced Anise Syrup

A Buñuelos are the Guatemalan cousins of French puffs made with *pâte à choux*. (*Pâte à choux* is a simple pastry dough used to make puffs, profiteroles, éclairs, French crullers, beignets, and more.) Guatemalan *buñuelos* are crisp on the outside, very puffy and light in texture, and almost hollow inside. They are a popular street food at religious celebrations, especially on Virgin of Guadalupe Day. Traditionally *buñuelos* are deep-fried. Baked *buñuelos* are just as delicious but healthier. This recipe offers both options. This pastry can also be used to make churros. *Buñuelos* and churros likely came to Latin America through Spain.

Makes 20 to 25 puffs

1 cup water
1 stick (1/2 cup) unsalted butter
1/2 teaspoon anise seed
1/4 teaspoon kosher salt
1/8 teaspoon baking soda
1 1/4 cups all-purpose flour, sifted

4 large eggs

Miel (Spiced Anise Syrup)
1 1/2 cups water
6 ounces (3/4 cup) sugar
1/2 teaspoon anise seed
1/2 stick *canela* (Ceylon cinnamon)
Rind of 1 lime
1 tablespoon freshly squeezed lime juice

1. Preheat the oven to 375°F. In a medium saucepan, combine the water, butter, anise seed, and salt, and bring to a quick boil. Turn the heat to low, add the baking soda and flour together, and beat vigorously with a wooden spoon to form a paste. Continue beating until the dough is uniformly mixed and doesn't stick to the edges of the pan.

2. Transfer the dough to the bowl of a mixer. With the paddle attachment, beat the dough on the lowest speed to cool it slightly (about 2 minutes). Increase the speed to medium, add 1 egg, and continue beating until the egg is well incorporated into the dough. Use a soft spatula to loosen the dough stuck to the sides of the bowl. Continue adding the eggs one at a time. Beat on high for 1 minute. The dough should hold the shape of balls and soft peaks.

3. Combine all the syrup ingredients in a small saucepan and bring to a quick boil. Lower the heat and simmer until aromatic (about 10 minutes). Strain.

4. Line a baking sheet with parchment paper. Scoop a teaspoon of dough and, with a finger, push the dough off the spoon onto the baking sheet. Bake the puffs until they're golden brown on the outside and hollow on the inside (15 to 20 minutes). Turn the baking sheet around half-way through for even baking. Serve immediately with the hot syrup.

Amalia's Notes

To deep-fry the puffs, heat 1 1/2 cups of canola oil in a small saucepan. Fry the dough over medium-low heat until the puffs are golden brown outside and puffy and hollow inside (6 to 7 minutes). Fry the puffs in small batches and use a wide, slotted spatula to turn them for even cooking. Transfer the puffs to a plate lined with paper towels to absorb excess oil. Serve the puffs with the hot syrup.

To make churros, put the dough in a pastry bag with a star tube and deep-fry in the same way as the puffs. (See above.) Squeeze out pastry pieces of 3 to 4 inches in length (or longer) into hot oil and fry them until they're medium brown and cooked (4 to 5 minutes). Sprinkle churros with a light coating of sugar as soon as they come out of the oil. If you wait to sprinkle the sugar, it will not stick.

DULCE DE DURAZNO Y CEREZAS
Fresh Peaches and Cherries in Syrup

Candied fruits in aromatic simple syrups are common throughout Guatemala. Any firm fruit can be candied in this way. Candied ripe mangoes are a popular dessert during *Cuaresma* (Lent). Pumpkin and squash are sometimes candied and then crystallized. After the fruit is candied, the sugar hardens on the outside of the fruit, and it changes the texture from soft to crunchy, juicy, and nearly translucent. Crystallization is an ancient method of preserving fruit. It came to Latin America from the Arabs through Spain. Crystallized fruit keeps for weeks in the refrigerator, as the sugar is a natural preservative. In Guatemala, freshly candied and crystallized fruits and artisanal candies are not kept refrigerated, as they are sold and consumed within a few days. Some candied fruit will become hard as a rock if kept unrefrigerated longer than a few days.

Serves 2 to 4 people

4 fresh peaches (or Anjou pears), preferably hard and unripe

2 1/2 cups water
1 cup sugar
4 cloves
1/2 stick *canela* (Ceylon cinnamon)
1 cup fresh cherries

1. Peel the peaches and make a cross-shaped cut touching the core all around each peach. Submerge the peaches in cold water to keep them from oxidizing (turning brown).

2. Combine the water, sugar, and spices, and bring to a quick boil. Lower the heat and simmer until aromatic (about 10 minutes).

3. Add the peaches and simmer, covered, until tender (15 to 20 minutes). Add the cherries and simmer uncovered until tender (3 to 5 minutes).

4. Serve at room temperature or cold.

CHANCLETAS
Stuffed Chayote Squash au Gratin with Raisins

A *Chancletas* is Spanish slang for "flip-flops." The name describes the shape of the chayote squash and this dessert. Chayote squash lends itself to many recipes, savory and sweet, as its delicate texture blends well with just about any flavor. In Guatemala *chancletas* are made with a different native squash that has starchy pulp and thick, dark green skin. This thick skin works well for encasing the prepared pulp, which is stuffed back inside and then gratinéed right before serving. Chayote squash contains more water and the skin is more delicate, but it's a good substitute.

Serves 4 people

2 chayote squashes, unpeeled and halved lengthwise

2 tablespoons melted butter
2 teaspoons brown sugar
1/8 teaspoon ground *canela* (Ceylon cinnamon)

4 tablespoons Maria cookie crumbs
1 tablespoon raisins
1 tablespoon sweet wine, such as moscato (or grand marnier)
1 tablespoon melted butter
1 egg yolk
1 tablespoon brown sugar
1/4 teaspoon ground *canela* (Ceylon cinnamon)
Pinch of ground cloves
Pinch of kosher salt

Adorno (Garnish)
2 tablespoons Maria cookie crumbs
1 tablespoon sliced almonds
1 tablespoon melted butter

1. Preheat oven to 350°F. Cook the chayote squash in lightly salted water and bring to a boil. Lower the heat, cover, and simmer until tender (12 to 15 minutes). Cool slightly. Remove the core and discard. Scoop out the pulp slowly and carefully with a teaspoon, leaving the peel intact. The skins should look similar to potato skins. Chop the pulp and set it aside.

2. Mix the melted butter with the brown sugar and ground cinnamon. Brush the skins with this mixture.

3. In a medium bowl, combine the pulp with the rest of the ingredients (except the garnish). Stuff the skins with this mixture. Top with the garnish and broil until the tops are medium brown (about 20 minutes).

Amalia's Notes

Chayote skins are edible.

Maria cookies are available at most grocery stores in the Latino aisle.

QUESADILLA
Guatemalan Cheese Bread

A This heavenly cheese bread is inspired by quesadilla de Zacapa, which is made with *mantequilla de costal* (artisan butter) and Zacapa cheese, both local specialties. Guatemalan dairy products are of very good quality—especially the ones from Zacapa. This is a hot, dry area in the eastern part of the country, close to my grandmother's hometown.

Makes 3 loaves

Baking spray (or nonstick baking spray
    with flour)
Flour
3 sticks unsalted butter at room temperature
1 1/2 cups sugar

8 large eggs
1 cup *crema* (Latino table cream)
1 cup finely crumbled Cotija cheese
3 1/2 cups rice flour

1. Coat 3 loaf pans with baking spray and flour. Preheat the oven to 350°F.

2. In the bowl of a mixer with the paddle attachment, cream the butter with the sugar until very smooth (4 to 5 minutes). Scrape the bottom and sides of the bowl with a soft spatula and beat until the sugar is well integrated with the butter and the mixture appears fluffy.

3. At medium speed, add the eggs one by one, making sure they are well integrated with the mixture before adding the next one. At low speed, gradually add the cream, cheese, and flour. Scrape the bottom and sides of the bowl occasionally and continue beating until all ingredients are fully incorporated, and the dough appears light and very fluffy.

4. Divide the dough equally among the pans. Bake until a knife inserted in the center comes out clean (35 to 40 minutes). Turn the pans around halfway through the baking time for even browning. Let the bread cool completely before taking it out of the pans.

Amalia's Note

During baking, the dough will rise slightly above the pans. Don't be concerned. The loaf will deflate to the top of the pan when it comes out of the oven. After you take the bread out of the pans and it has cooled, wrap it in plastic to keep it fresh.

MANJAR DE CAFÉ
Guatemalan Coffee Custard with Vanilla Beans, Raisins, and Berries

A This recipe is inspired by my grandmother's *manjar blanco,* a runny custard or *atol* (hot drink) that I used to enjoy during school breaks. Street vendors in Guatemala often offer this drink. They keep the drink hot in huge clay vessels lined with layers of cloth in a basket. Other popular drinks are rice with milk and *atol blanco.*

Serves 2 to 4 people

1 1/2 cups skim or 1 percent milk
1/4 stick *canela* (Ceylon cinnamon)
Rind of 1/2 orange
1/2 vanilla bean

2 tablespoons Guatemalan coffee essence
1/2 cup raisins

1 large egg yolk
1 tablespoon sugar
1/8 teaspoon kosher salt
1 1/2 tablespoons cornstarch

Adorno (Garnish)
Ground *canela* (Ceylon cinnamon)
Raspberries
Blackberries
Mint
Salsa de Chocolate *Oscuro* (Guatemalan dark chocolate, ancho, and rum sauce, page 337)

1. In a small saucepan, combine the milk, cinnamon, and orange rind. Slice the vanilla bean lengthwise and scrape the paste out with a knife. Add both the paste and the vanilla bean skin to the milk and simmer until aromatic, stirring occasionally (about 10 minutes). Keep a close eye, as milk can scorch and boil over easily. Discard the cinnamon, rind, and vanilla bean skin, and remove any remaining cinnamon pieces with a small strainer. Add the coffee essence and the raisins. Keep the heat on low.

2. In a small bowl whisk the egg yolk, sugar, and salt until well dissolved. Add the cornstarch and whisk until very creamy. Temper the egg mixture with 1 tablespoon of the hot milk and whisk quickly. Add 2 more tablespoons gradually and whisk until runny. Pour the egg mixture gradually into the hot milk while whisking quickly. Use a soft spatula to scrape out every bit of egg mixture. Continue whisking until thick and bubbly (2 to 3 minutes).

3. Pour the custard into attractive cups, cool slightly, and serve it garnished with cinnamon, berries, and mint.

Amalia's Notes

To make Guatemalan coffee essence: In a mug, combine 1 heaping tablespoon of freshly ground coffee beans with 2 tablespoons of water. Heat in the microwave for 30 seconds. Strain with a fine mesh sieve.

Tempering is necessary to prevent the egg yolks from curdling when they hit the hot milk. Adding a little hot milk to the mixture first prepares it to thicken the milk more effectively.

COCTEL DE FRUTAS
Fresh Tropical Fruit Cocktail

A This treat will please any crowd, from children to adults. There's no tastier or easier way to pack a ton of vitamins into a small cup. My mom made this dessert often when we had company. You can build it further by adding other seasonal fruits of your choice. This is my version adding other ingredients and fruits.

Serves 2 to 4 people

Jugo de Frutas (Fruit Juice)

1 cup freshly squeezed tangerine juice

1 tablespoon freshly squeezed lime juice

1 tablespoon sugar

1/2 teaspoon ground *canela* (Ceylon cinnamon) (optional)

1/4 cup dark rum or sweet wine (optional)

Cubos de Frutas (Fruit Cubes)

1 cup diced papaya (1/2-inch cubes)

1 cup diced pineapple (1/2-inch cubes)

1 cup diced kiwi (1/2-inch cubes)

Adorno (Garnish)

2 to 4 skewers (3 to 5 inches long)

Strawberries and blackberries

Mint sprigs

Edible flowers

1. Combine the tangerine and lime juice with the sugar and whisk well to dissolve. Add the cinnamon and rum (if using) and whisk to combine. Chill.

2. In a bowl, combine the fruit cubes. Chill.

3. Divide the fruit into 2 to 4 attractive cups and pour equal amounts of the juice on top of the fruit.

4. Skewer the strawberries and blackberries as desired and garnish the fruit cups with the skewers, mint sprigs, and/or edible flowers.

Amalia's Note

If you like, serve this dessert with berry coulis. Serve the coulis on the side or pour it into the cups after the juice but before the fruit cubes (similar to a tequila sunrise). To make berry coulis: Purée 1/2 cup blackberries, 2 teaspoons sugar, and 1 teaspoon lime juice, then strain the mixture.

BOCADO DE LA REINA
CON SALSA DE RON Y MANGO

Guatemalan Bread Pudding with Mango-Rum Coulis

A The term *bocado de la reina* means "queen's morsel"—an ironic name, since its main component is day-old bread! My mom used to make this treat to use up bread that wasn't eaten during the week. It takes very little time and effort to make. You can build it further with sauces and fruits. This is my quick version using store-bought muffins and bread.

8 portions

Baking spray and flour (or nonstick baking spray with flour)

4 *pan dulce* (Latin sweet buns about the size of muffins), torn into chunks

4 white dinner rolls, torn into chunks

1/2 cup skim milk

2 egg yolks, beaten

1 tablespoon dark rum (preferably Guatemalan rum)

1/2 teaspoon ground *canela* (Ceylon cinnamon)

1 teaspoon vanilla extract

1 1/2 tablespoons melted butter

2 tablespoons freshly squeezed orange juice

1 teaspoon finely chopped orange zest

1/2 teaspoon baking powder

2 egg whites

1 1/2 tablespoons sugar

1/2 cup raisins rolled in all-purpose flour

Mango-Rum Coulis

1 cup chunks of ripe mango

2 tablespoons sugar

1 teaspoon freshly squeezed lime juice

1/4 cup dark rum (preferably Guatemalan rum)

Adorno (Garnish)

Mango slices

Mint

1. Preheat the oven to 350°F. Coat 2 loaf pans with baking spray and flour.

2. To make the dough, combine the first 11 ingredients (except the baking spray and flour) in a medium bowl and mix well with a soft spatula.

3. Beat the egg whites to stiff peaks and add the sugar. Beat 2 minutes more.

4. Add the egg whites to the dough and combine quickly with folding strokes, mixing for about 2 minutes. Distribute the dough equally between the 2 pans. Sprinkle the raisins evenly over the dough, and with the tip of a paring knife, push them into the dough.

4. Bake until the tip of a knife comes out clean (25 to 30 minutes). Let cool for 10 to 15 minutes. Unmold from the pans and slice.

5. Combine all the coulis ingredients in a blender and purée them to a fine consistency. Transfer to a bottle and drizzle on each slice of bread pudding.

6. Garnish each serving with mango slices and mint.

Amalia's Note

Pan dulce and savory rolls (which can be used in place of dinner rolls) are available at Latino stores. The type of bread you use for this recipe, will affect the texture of the final dish. Crispy breads will produce a firmer bread pudding. Softer breads will produce a very moist and less firm bread pudding. Use the breads you prefer.

CREPAS DE CHOCOLATE OSCURO CON DULCE DE LECHE

Guatemalan Dark Chocolate Crepes with *Dulce de Leche*

A Crepes are not a traditional Guatemalan dessert, but they are popular in Guatemala City. Two Guatemalan ingredients, dark chocolate and *dulce de leche*, work deliciously with crepes in contrast with the berries and mint. *Canillitas de leche* (little milk legs) are the Guatemalan version of *dulce de leche* presented in a unique way. *Dulce de leche* is popular throughout Latin America, and every country has its own version and name for it. This is a quick and delicious way to make this dessert into a sauce rather than as the traditional Guatemalan fudge.

Makes 20 to 25 6-inch crepes

Dulce de Leche Rápido (Quick *Dulce de Leche*)

- 1 14-ounce can condensed milk
- 1 14-ounce can evaporated milk
- 1 stick *canela* (Ceylon cinnamon)
- 1 vanilla bean, split in half lengthwise (or 2 teaspoons vanilla extract)

Mezcla para Crepas (Crepe Mix)

- 1 1/2 cups dark chocolate milk
- 3 large eggs
- 2 1/2 ounces (5 tablespoons) water
- 2 tablespoons canola oil
- 1 1/4 cups all-purpose flour
- 1/4 teaspoon kosher salt
- High-heat cooking spray

Adorno (Garnish)

Salsa de Chocolate Oscuro (Guatemalan dark chocolate, ancho, and rum sauce, page 337)

Raspberries

Mint sprigs

1. Mix all the *dulce de leche* ingredients in a pan and cook them slowly over medium-low heat until the mixture is medium brown and thick, about 1 hour. During the cooking time, stir the mixture frequently to keep it from sticking to the pan. When the mixture is ready, let it cool.

2. To make dark chocolate milk: In a saucepan, combine 1 1/3 cups of skim milk with 1/2 cup of Guatemalan dark chocolate. Bring to a quick boil, lower the heat, and simmer uncovered until the chocolate is fully dissolved. Keep a close eye, as milk will foam and boil over. Chill before using.

3. Combine all the crepe mix ingredients in a blender in the order listed. Allow the batter to rest for 10 minutes to get rid off any air bubbles. (Alternatively, whisk all the ingredients in a bowl by hand.)

4. Heat a crepe pan or small nonstick skillet and keep it at medium-low heat. Spray it with cooking spray before about every third crepe. Pour about 2 tablespoons of the batter on the skillet to make uniform crepes and swirl the batter around quickly to fully coat the skillet with a thin layer. Cook each crepe until matte or until edges loosen (almost 1 1/2 minutes on one side and 1 minute on the other side). Crepes should be thin and flexible. It may take a couple of crepes to get the hang of it.

5. Fill the crepes with *dulce de leche* and roll them or make triangle shapes.

6. Serve the crepes garnished with chocolate sauce, raspberries, and mint sprigs.

Amalia's Note

Guatemalan chocolate comes in different shapes and sizes (thin rounds, long thick tablets, and short thick tablets), depending on the brand. The chocolate is very hard (and sweet) and must be broken for measuring. To break the chocolate, put it in double ziplock bags, wrap it twice in a kitchen towel, and pound it with the smooth side of a metal meat mallet until the chocolate is almost powdery. Then transfer it to a measuring cup and measure the desired amount.

BEBIDAS CON ESTILO
DRINKS WITH STYLE

WORLD-CLASS COFFEE

Guatemalan coffee is among the best in the world. In fact, Guatemala ranks within the world's top ten high-quality coffee producers. What makes the coffee so good? Coffee plants need just the right weather conditions, terrain, and rich soil in order to thrive. Guatemala has all these things. Coffee grows throughout the country, including Oriente (Esquipulas), but the best coffee in Guatemala comes from the highest elevations, such as in Cobán, Antigua, Fraijanes, Huehuetenango, and Atitlán.

During one of my routine trips to Guatemala, I stayed in Antigua (a UNESCO World Heritage Site). This city attracts people for several reasons. The charming colonial city has a small-town feel. You can walk to many places or take a *tuk-tuk* (very small motorized taxi). It is the former capital of the country, and it was partially destroyed by natural disasters. The ruins remain, as do a great deal of beautiful colonial buildings, convents, great shopping, cobblestone streets, and more. The city lies in Panchoy valley, which is surrounded by mountains and volcanoes. The weather in Antigua is almost perfect. This ancient city is home to many Americans and Europeans, who are drawn by the city's charm, mystique, traditions, and long history. It is one of my favorite places in the country. Antigua deserves to be called the cultural and culinary capital of Guatemala. It produces exquisite classic cuisine, coffee, chocolate, and *dulces típicos* (traditional handmade sweets). It has the only vineyard and winery in the country.

Antigua is famous for its high-quality coffee, which is the result of the local weather, altitude, volcanic soil, and traditional techniques. While visiting there, I had the opportunity to tour a coffee plantation and learn about the process of growing, roasting, and brewing coffee from beginning to end. I also enjoyed a tasting of the freshest and most delicious coffee ever while taking in the majestic view of the nearby Agua Volcano.

I learned many things during this tour. The coffee plant originated in Ethiopia. From there it spread to other parts of the world. Coffee came to Guatemala via the Spaniards. The coffee species that grows in Guatemala is the arabica plant. When the arabica plant is young, it is inserted (spliced) into the robusta coffee plant, whose roots are more disease-resistant. The arabica plant is delicate; splicing with the robusta plant strengthens it and allows it to grow properly. Growing and processing coffee takes several years. Yield varies for younger and older plants. Harvesting and processing are very labor intensive. The work is done almost entirely by hand. After witnessing all this, I realized that coffee drinkers around the world are fortunate to have high-quality coffees available at reasonable prices.

The characteristics by which a coffee's quality is judged resemble those of judging wines. Coffee connoisseurs consider a coffee's aroma, flavor, body, acidity, and aftertaste.

Guatemalans really enjoy *café con leche* (coffee with milk). The secret to a great cup of *café con leche* is in using fresh water, a high-quality coffee freshly roasted and ground, and hot milk. A common Guatemalan midafternoon snack is a cup of *café con leche* accompanied by *champurradas* or *pan dulce* (different types of sweet bread). Coffee can also be used as a base for sauces and desserts, or for gourmet drinks with French flair, such as *Café Flameado con Ron Oscuro* (Guatemalan spiced coffee flamed with dark rum, page 375).

MAYAN GOLD

acao ("ka-KAW" in Mayan), or cocoa beans were so precious to the ancient Mayas that the Mayas used them as currency and in their religious rituals. Cacao was not only an integral part of Mayan culture and religion, but it was also the food of kings and an offering for the gods. Cacao only grows in specific areas, so it was highly coveted. Cacao (cocoa beans) were well known to the classic Maya who may have learned about them from the Olmecs, who are believed to have had first contact with the plant and its cultivation. The Aztecs learned about cacao and its processing from the Mayas and readily adopted it. So did explorers from Europe. Chocolate is one of the many precious gifts the New World gave to the Old World. All the fine chocolate we enjoy today had humble beginnings in the tropical rain forests of southern Mexico, Central America, and the Amazon region of South America.

Chocolate has a very special place in Guatemalan hearts and cuisine. Artisanal chocolate producers, from rustic mom-and-pop shops to larger processors, are abundant throughout the country. Higher concentrations are in Antigua and Mixco (near Guatemala City), which is called *"La Tierra del* Chocolate" (the land of chocolate). Guatemalan chocolate is made with freshly ground roasted cocoa beans, *canela* (Ceylon cinnamon), sugar, and sometimes other flavorings. It is then pressed into tablets or thick rounds that must be dissolved in hot water or milk for cooking and eating. Cocoa powder, by contrast, is more processed and contains other ingredients. Cocoa powder tastes good when it's dissolved in hot milk, but it doesn't taste good in hot water. Because Guatemalan chocolate is so different from cocoa powder, there's a world of difference between Guatemalan hot chocolate and American hot cocoa, both in flavor and consistency. For this reason, cocoa is not a good substitute in Guatemalan cooking.

Once while traveling in Mixco, I visited with a family who had a tiny *tienda* (small neighborhood store), and on the counter there were piles of packaged chocolate boxes. I'd smelled the aromas of chocolate and cinnamon from blocks away. To my surprise, in the room next to the store, the family had an electric mill. They were about to make chocolate when I walked in. As I watched, they roasted the cocoa beans in a *comal* (clay griddle) right next to the mill, cooled it a little, combined it with *canela* and sugar, and passed it through the mill. In this humble environment with little equipment, the family was producing some of the best-tasting chocolate I'd ever had.

Hot chocolate is a special drink that is consumed at home and at special celebrations. Traditional Guatemalan hot chocolate is thick and foamy, much as it was when the ancient

Mayas drank it. The foam is achieved by beating the chocolate in a tall ceramic pitcher or deep pot with a *molinillo* (a special wooden beater or whisk). The foam can also be made by pouring the drink from one container to another while holding the pouring container up high. The latter technique was the one used by the classic Mayas, and the *molinillo* technique came later. The deep flavor and velvety texture of Guatemalan hot chocolate is best appreciated when it's made with hot water instead of hot milk. The perfect pairing for a cup of Guatemalan hot chocolate is a tamale, *champurradas*, or *pan dulce* (sweet bread).

In addition to drinks, you can also use chocolate in Mole (chocolate and chile sauce, page 315), in Tamales *Negros* (sweet Christmas tamales with mole sauce, page 41), in desserts such as *Crepas de Chocolate Oscuro con Dulce de Leche* (Guatemalan dark chocolate crepes with *dulce de leche*, page 366), and in sauces to top *Manjar de Café* (Guatemalan coffee custard with vanilla beans, raisins, and berries, page 360), fresh bananas, or *Postre de Atol de Elote* (fresh corn pudding, page 347).

CAFÉ FLAMEADO CON RON OSCURO
Guatemalan Spiced Coffee Flamed with Dark Rum

This recipe is inspired by the classic French *café brûlot*, which can be easily Guatemalized by substituting Guatemalan flavors. While at chef school, I practiced my flaming technique with this drink and with many other foods. Here I have adapted it for home cooking. The term *brûlot* means "burned," and this refers to the flaming or "burning" of the brandy used for this delicious drink. Traditionally *café brûlot* is made in a copper pot, but it can also be made in a stainless steel pot. The drink is not only delicious, but also entertaining. The Chantilly rum cream is not a part of the traditional recipe, but it works great with the drink and makes it a drink-dessert.

Serves 2 people

1 1/2 tablespoons sugar

Rind of 1/2 orange studded with 2 whole cloves

1 star anise

3 allspice berries

1/8 stick *canela* (Ceylon cinnamon)

1/4 cup dark rum (preferably Guatemalan rum)

2 cups freshly ground and brewed Guatemalan coffee

1 to 2 tablespoons Grand Marnier or Kahlúa

Adorno (Garnish)

Chantilly rum cream (optional)

Ground *canela* (Ceylon cinnamon)

1. In a stainless steel pot, melt the sugar over low heat, swirling the pot occasionally, to caramelize the sugar. This may take 5 to 8 minutes. Add the orange and coat it lightly with the caramelized sugar. Add the spices, allspice berries, and rum and set the mixture aflame using a long lighter or a match or tilting the pot slightly to expose the mixture to the flame of a gas burner. Soon after, add the coffee and stir well. Simmer for 3 minutes to infuse the coffee with flavor.

2. Distribute the Grand Marnier or Kahlúa between two cups and pour in the hot coffee, using a strainer to catch the orange rind and spices.

3. Garnish the drinks with Chantilly rum cream (page 377) and ground cinnamon, if you like.

CHOCOLATE

Guatemalan Hot Chocolate with Chantilly Rum Cream

Traditional Guatemalan hot chocolate is thick and foamy. The froth is achieved by stirring the chocolate in a deep ceramic pitcher or a deep pot with a *molinillo* (a special wooden whisk). The flavor and texture of Guatemalan chocolate are best appreciated when you make this recipe with hot water. This is the traditional method. However, children and some adults may prefer to make it with milk. Chantilly rum cream is not a traditional garnish, but it adds another layer of flavor and eye appeal to the drink.

Serves 2 people

6 to 8 ounces Guatemalan chocolate (3/4 to 1 cup of chocolate)

2 cups hot water or hot milk

Adorno (Garnish)

Chantilly rum cream (optional)

Ground *canela* (Ceylon cinnamon) (optional)

1. Combine the chocolate and hot water in a heat-resistant ceramic pitcher, deep pot, or saucepan. Whisk vigorously with a *molinillo* to dissolve the chocolate, holding the *molinillo* between your palms and rotating it back and forth quickly. Once the chocolate is dissolved, continue whisking until the mixture is thick and frothy (about 5 minutes). Alternatively, you can use a stainless steel whisk in place of a *molinillo*.

2. Serve the hot chocolate in cups, garnished with Chantilly rum cream and ground cinnamon.

Amalia's Notes

Guatemalan chocolate comes in different shapes and sizes (thin rounds, long thick tablets, and short thick tablets), depending on the brand. The chocolate is very hard (and sweet) and must be broken for measuring. To break the chocolate, put it in double ziplock bags, wrap it twice in a kitchen towel, and pound it with the smooth side of a metal meat mallet until the chocolate is almost powdery. Then transfer it to a measuring cup and measure the desired amount.

To make Chantilly rum cream: Whip 1/2 cup of heavy whipping cream (at room temperature) until firm peaks form (2 to 4 minutes). Add 2 teaspoons of confectioners' sugar, 1/2 teaspoon vanilla extract, 1/2 teaspoon almond extract, and 1/2 tablespoon dark rum, and whip to combine (about 1 minute).

PONCHE DE FRUTAS
Fresh Pineapple and Dried Fruits Hot Holiday Punch

A The aromas that permeate the kitchen when you're making *ponche de frutas* scream, "Christmas!" You can make this punch with just pineapple or with other fresh and dried fruits. Some adults like to spike it with Guatemalan *aguardiente* or rum. There's no more festive and scrumptious drink for entertaining guests or serving with Tamales *Navideños* (Christmas tamales, page 48) during the holidays. It keeps for days in the refrigerator.

Serves 4 to 6 people

Bolsita de Especias (Spice Sachet)

1/2 *canela* stick (Ceylon cinnamon)

1 star anise

6 allspice berries

6 cloves

6 black peppercorns

3 cups water

2 tablespoons sugar

1 cup finely chopped pineapple

1/4 cup diced apples

1/4 cup diced peaches

1/2 cup sliced dried fruits

2 tablespoons raisins

6 sliced dried pitted prunes

Guatemalan dark rum or Indita (Guatemalan sugarcane *aguardiente*) or other rum of choice (optional)

1. Enclose all the spices in a 4x4-inch piece of cheesecloth. Tie with kitchen twine, leaving a long string. Tie the string to the handle of a medium saucepan and place the sachet inside the pan.

2. Add the water and sugar to the pan and bring to a quick boil. Lower the heat, cover, and simmer until aromatic (about 10 minutes).

3. Add all the fresh and dried fruits and simmer for 20 to 30 minutes. Taste and adjust sweetness or spices, if needed.

4. Serve the punch in mugs with bits of fruit and some rum, if you like.

Amalia's Note

You can make this punch in a Crock-Pot. Simply combine all ingredients in the Crock-Pot and set it on high. When the punch is aromatic, adjust the heat to the lowest setting, and let it sit until you're ready to serve it. The punch tastes even better on day two.

PONCHE DE LECHE
Almond and Cinnamon Hot Punch

 This delicious hot punch is inspired by my grandmother's *ponche de leche* (milk punch). Sometimes she added diced baby squash to the hot mixture. This was often our after-school drink. For a delicious adult version, add a bit of rum.

Serves 2 people

1 1/2 cups skim milk
1/4 teaspoon almond extract
1/4 stick *canela* (Ceylon cinnamon)
3 teaspoons sugar
Pinch of kosher salt

1 egg, separated

Adorno (Garnish)
Dark rum (preferably Guatemalan rum)
Ground *canela* (Ceylon cinnamon)

1. In a medium saucepan, combine the milk, almond extract, cinnamon, sugar, and salt, and bring to a quick boil. Keep a close eye, as milk can scorch and boil over easily. Lower the heat and simmer until aromatic (about 10 minutes). Discard the cinnamon stick.

2. Beat the egg white until soft peaks form. Add the yolk and continue beating to combine. Temper the egg mixture with 1 tablespoon of the hot milk and whisk quickly. Add 2 more tablespoons gradually and whisk until runny. Pour the egg mixture gradually into the hot milk while whisking quickly. Use a soft spatula to scrape out every bit of egg mixture. Continue whisking until thick and bubbly (2 to 3 minutes). Turn off the heat.

3. Serve the punch in tall clear mugs. Add rum to taste and sprinkle the tops with ground cinnamon.

Amalia's Note

Tempering is necessary to prevent egg yolks from curdling when they hit hot milk. Adding a little hot milk to the mixture first prepares it to thicken the milk more effectively.

FRESCO DE PIÑA, MELÓN Y FRESA
Pineapple, Cantaloupe, and Strawberry Refresher

Guatemalans accompany everyday meals with refreshing and wholesome fresh fruit drinks or roasted seed-based drinks such as this one. Soda is something they have for special occasions; sodas could never take the place of a delicious *fresco*. This drink can be chilled and served alone or over ice. *Frescos* are best when the fruit is very ripe. Just about any fruit will work. You can freeze chunks of fresh fruits and use them as needed. You can turn *frescos* into *licuados* (smoothies) by blending the fruits with ice.

Makes 4 1/2 cups

1 cup pineapple chunks
1 cup cantaloupe chunks
1 cup hulled strawberries
3 cups cold water
3 to 4 tablespoons sugar
Ice

1. Combine the fruits, water, and sugar in a blender and purée to a fine consistency. If you like, pour the mixture through a wire or mesh colander to strain out the pulp.

2. Transfer the liquid to a pitcher and chill it. Taste and adjust sweetness, if needed. Serve in tall glasses filled with ice.

Amalia's Notes

You can make this drink with any number or type of fruits you like. You can also add fresh orange juice for another dimension of flavor. Adjust the amount of water and sugar according to the amount and type of fruits you use.

Fresh fruit drinks settle and need to be stirred before serving. Drinks containing ice should be sweeter to compensate for the dilution of melting ice.

HORCHATA DE PEPITA Y AJONJOLÍ

Rice, Cinnamon, and Roasted Pumpkin and Sesame Seed Drink

Horchata came to Latin America from Spain. It's popular in several Latin American countries with varying ingredients. This delicious *horchata* incorporates classic ingredients with Guatemalan ingredients. *Horchata* should be consumed within a day or two for optimum flavor.

Makes 1 quart

1/2 cup white rice soaked in 3 cups cold water for 7 hours or overnight

1/4 stick *canela* (Ceylon cinnamon)

2 tablespoons roasted sesame seeds

2 tablespoons roasted pumpkin seeds

1 teaspoon almond extract

4 tablespoons sugar or to taste

2 cups skim milk

Ice

1. In a blender, combine all the ingredients, except the milk and ice, and process to a fine consistency. Strain with a fine mesh colander.

2. In a pitcher, combine the rice mixture with the milk. Taste and chill.

3. Serve the *horchata* in tall glasses filled with ice.

Amalia's Note

Horchata settles and should be stirred before serving. Make the drink thinner by adding more water or milk. Drinks containing ice should be sweeter to compensate for the dilution of melting ice.

LIMONADA CON GENGIBRE, CHAN Y PANELA

Fresh Limeade with Fresh Ginger, Poppy Seeds, and *Panela*

Limonada (fresh limeade) is a very common *refresco* or *fresco* to accompany lunch or dinner. *Refrescos* or *frescos* are cold drinks made with fresh fruits or flavored powders. Traditionally this drink is made with just limeade and poppy seeds. The poppy seeds, fresh ginger, and *panela* elevate this drink to a gourmet level. During soaking, the seeds develop a gel-like film that you can feel on your tongue. Poppy seeds don't add flavor or aroma, but they do add eye appeal and a bit of nutrition.

Makes 1 quart

4 tablespoons *panela* (raw sugarcane) or sugar

1 cup cold water

1 cup freshly squeezed lime juice

2 cups ginger ale

1 1/2 tablespoons finely grated fresh ginger

2 tablespoons poppy seeds

1/2 cup thinly sliced limes

Ice

1. In a clear pitcher, dissolve the *panela* or sugar in the water. Add the rest of the ingredients (except ice) and stir well. Taste and chill.

2. Serve the *limonada* in tall glasses filled with ice.

Amalia's Notes

Fresh fruit drinks settle and need to be stirred before serving. Drinks containing ice should be sweeter than room-temperature drinks to compensate for the dilution of melting ice.

Panela is very hard and must be broken for measuring. To break it, put it in double zip-lock bags, wrap it twice in a kitchen towel, and pound it with the smooth side of a metal meat mallet until the *panela* is almost powdery. Then measure the desired amount.

Alternatively, to make orangeade, substitute the lime juice for 1 1/2 to 2 cups freshly squeezed orange juice.

FRESCO DE TAMARINDO
Tamarind and Raw Sugarcane Refresher

A Tamarind comes from a pod that must be peeled first to expose the gummy brown, sweet, highly acidic pulp. To make this drink, the pods must be soaked in water for a while to let them release the pulp on their own. When ready, the soaking water becomes cloudy, and the large seeds loosen and are easily visible. Alternatively, use sweetened tamarind concentrate or frozen tamarind pulp and dilute it with water. I like to sweeten the drink with *panela* for a flavor twist.

Makes 1 1/2 quarts

4 tablespoons *panela* (raw sugarcane) or sugar

4 cups plus 2 ounces cold water

1 14-ounce package frozen tamarind pulp, thawed

Ice

1. In a pitcher, dissolve the sugar in the water. Add the tamarind pulp. Taste and chill.

2. Serve the *tamarindo* in tall glasses filled with ice (optional).

Amalia's Notes

Fresh fruit drinks settle and need to be stirred before serving. Make the drink thinner by adding more water. Drinks containing ice should be sweeter than room-temperature drinks to compensate for the dilution of melting ice.

Tamarind pulp is available in the frozen aisle of grocery stores and Latino stores. Sweetened tamarind concentrate is available in Latino stores.

To make tamarind pulp: Buy 2 pounds of tamarind pods, peel them, and soak them in 2 cups of cold water at room temperature until the water is very cloudy and the pulp has come off the pods (4 to 5 hours). Strain the pulp and add water and sugar to taste.

Panela is very hard and must be broken for measuring. To break it, put it in double zip-lock bags, wrap it twice in a kitchen towel, and pound it with the smooth side of a metal meat mallet until the *panela* is almost powdery. Then measure the desired amount.

REFRESCO DE ROSA DE JAMAICA CON LIMÓN Y MENTA

Hibiscus, Lime, and Mint Refresher

A Hibiscus (*rosa de Jamaica* in Guatemala) is a dried flower similar in taste to cranberry. When you steep the flower as a tea, it infuses the water with a deep red winelike tint. Then it must be mixed with water and sweetened with plenty of sugar, as it is very acidic. In Guatemala *Jamaica* is a refreshing and delicious drink made with just water and sugar, but it can be mixed with limeade, mint, or soda for a new twist. The drink is popular in other Latin American countries, too. *Jamaica* is also available as a sweetened concentrate.

Makes 1 quart

2 cups water
1 cup hibiscus flowers
4 tablespoons sugar

2 cups cold water

8 lime slices
2 tablespoons mint leaves
2 teaspoons sugar
Ice

1. Combine the water with the hibiscus flowers and sugar in a medium saucepan and bring to a quick boil. Lower the heat and simmer uncovered for 5 minutes. Cool. Strain the liquid into a pitcher. Return the hibiscus flowers to the saucepan and add the cold water. Stir well and strain again into the pitcher. Taste and chill.

2. In a bowl, muddle the lime slices and mint leaves with the sugar, strain, and combine with the hibiscus tea. Serve in glasses filled with ice.

Amalia's Notes

Drinks containing ice should be sweeter than room-temperature drinks to compensate for the dilution of melting ice.

To muddle is to combine ingredients in the bottom of a glass to extract juices and flavors using a muddler—a large stick designed for this particular purpose. At home you can use a wooden spoon or any other sturdy stirring tool.

Sweetened concentrate *Jamaica* is available at Latino stores.

FRESCAVENA

Oats and Vanilla Cooler

A Frescavena is a refreshing and nutritious drink than anyone can make in minutes. In Latin America, flavored *frescavena* is a popular drink. It's packaged and labeled as FrescAvena. It is available at some Latino markets in the United States. This is my version inspired by the nostalgic drink.

Makes 2 cups

3/4 cup rolled oats

2 cups cold water

1/8 teaspoon vanilla extract

1/8 teaspoon almond extract

3 teaspoons sugar

Ice

1. Combine all ingredients (except ice) in a blender and purée to a fine consistency. If you like, strain out the oat pulp by passing the mixture through a wire or mesh colander.

2. Transfer the liquid to a pitcher and chill. Serve the *frescavena* in tall glasses filled with ice.

Amalia's Notes

Frescavena settles and needs to be stirred before serving. For a cremier drink, soak the oats in the water for a couple of hours or longer and use half water and half milk.

Drinks containing ice should be sweeter to compensate for the dilution of melting ice.

SANGRÍA *A LA AMALIA*
Red Wine and Citrus Punch

A Sangría came to Latin America from Spain and is popular in Guatemala City. Everyone has a unique recipe for making it. It ranges from a simple drink to an elaborate one with fruit bits and more. This quick and delicious crowd-pleasing version is perfect for a summer party. For a flavor twist, try it with other good quality red wines. Malbec and merlot will produce a hearty sangría, and zinfandel, a robust and spicy one.

Serves 2 to 4

2 cups Spanish Rioja
1/2 cup ginger ale
1 tablespoon Grand Marnier

1 orange, thinly sliced
1/2 lime, thinly sliced
1 tablespoon sugar

Adorno (Garnish)
1/4 cup green grapes, halved
1/4 cup ripe mangoes or peaches, peeled, diced small
1 orange slice, cut into half moons
2 lime slices
Mint sprigs

Ice

1. Combine the rioja with the ginger ale and Grand Marnier.

2. In a bowl, combine the orange and lime slices and sugar. Muddle with a muddler or use the back of a small sturdy plastic cup to release as much juice from the fruit as possible. While continuing to muddle, dissolve the sugar in the juice.

3. Pour the wine mixture into the bowl and stir well. Transfer to an attractive pitcher and chill. Keep the muddled fruit in the pitcher or strain.

4. Serve in tall glasses filled with ice and garnish.

Amalia's Note

To muddle is to combine ingredients in the bottom of a glass to extract juices and flavors using a muddler—a large stick designed for this particular purpose. At home you can use a wooden spoon or any other sturdy stirring tool.

EL BAR CHAPÍN
THE GUATEMALAN BAR

The Guatemalan home bar typically consists of basics such as *ron* (rum), *cerveza* (beer), whiskey, vodka, and vino (wine)—in the order of popularity. Rum is commonly used for *Cuba libre* (rum, Coke, and lime); beer is served with a wedge of lime and some salt; vodka is drunk straight or in screwdrivers; whiskey is served on the rocks, mixed with water, or mixed with sparkling water (highball). Sparkling water is also known as *agua mineral* (mineral water) in Guatemala.

Although wine drinking hasn't historically been part of the culture in Guatemala, it has become more popular in the past few years. New trends in winemaking, wine bars, and wine tasting in Antigua and Guatemala City indicate that Guatemalans are starting to become more enthusiastic and appreciative about wines. Guatemala now boasts its first winery in Antigua.

At bars, at restaurants, and at home, Guatemalans always accompany alcoholic drinks with *boquitas* (tapas). At a bar, the price of a drink usually includes a *boquita*—whether you request it or not. Depending on the bar and its location, these tasty treats may be anything from small bites to heartier snacks. This is probably a hospitality custom that Guatemalans adopted from the Spaniards and made their own. Chapter 4 (*Entradas, Boquitas y Chucherías*—appetizers, tapas, and street food, page 105) describes a variety of foods that serve well as *boquitas*.

At parties and special celebrations, such as weddings and quinceañeras (sweet fifteen gatherings), the glasses, alcohol, ice buckets,

TRADITIONAL FOOD-DRINK PAIRINGS

Guatemala's national drink is beer. At gatherings beer, rum, and whiskey are usually the drinks of choice. Some foods go best with beer, such as ceviche, barbecue, Mayan stews, open-faced tortilla sandwiches, soups, appetizers, tapas, and street food. At more formal celebrations, such as weddings, rum, whiskey, and wine may accompany the special meal.

sodas, and sparkling water are often sitting on the tables when guests arrive. It is customary for guests to prepare their own drinks right at their table. As ingredients run out, waiters replenish them. It is common practice to drink, dance, drink, eat, dance, drink, dance, and eat until the wee hours of the morning. Some celebrations last entire weekends as the main party spills into breakfast, lunch, and dinner for out-of-town guests.

The most popular Guatemalan alcohols are listed below. The perfect pairing for beer is the classic ceviche (page 225).

- Beers: Cerveza Gallo, Cerveza Cabro, Cerveza Monte Carlo, and Dorada draft and ice

- Rums: Ron Zacapa Centenario and Ron Botrán

- Sugarcane high-alcohol spirits: Indita Quezalteca, Venado, Indita-Rosa de Jamaica, Indita-Horchata, and other flavors

- Specialty drinks popular among the younger generation: Tikindia (Indita with Tiki soda); Indita (Indita with Coke); Indita Rosa de Jamaica in shots or mixed with sparkling water; Michelada (Guatemalan beer with prepared tomato juice); Campechano (Guatemalan white or aged rum with Coke or sparkling soda); Jaggershot (Jäggermeister shots); and Jaggerbomb (Jäggermeister with Red Bull).

INGREDIENT SOURCES

*B*efore shopping online, check your local grocery store. Many major chains carry a wide variety of Latin American products.

La Tiendita: Guatemalan Fine Handcrafts
Shop here for Guatemalan dark chocolate and Antigua coffee.
www.guatemalafinehandcrafts.com

Amigo Foods: Your Latin Food Store on the Internet
Shop here for Incaparina, chao mein, Ducal canned beans, pacaya flowers, jarred chiltepes, Picamás hot sauce, and more.
www.amigofoods.com

Goya Foods
Shop here for frozen products, tropical fruit pulp, rice, legumes, and more.
www.goya.com

La Tienda: The Best of Spain
Shop here for *bomba* or *calasparra* rice, saffron, olive oil, capers, olives, and more.
www.tienda.com

Melissa's: The Freshest Ideas in Produce
Shop here for banana leaves, chayote squash, dried chiles, Jamaica flowers (hibiscus), pumpkin seeds, *panela (piloncillo)*, jarred pimentos, and more.
www.melissas.com

Latin Merchant: Latin Food, Mexican Food, Spanish Food, South American Food, Creole Food, and Caribbean Food
Shop here for epazote, rice, yuca flour, instant corn masa flour, and more.
www.latinmerchant.com

Alibaba: Global Trade Starts Here
Shop here for many varieties of Guatemalan coffee, Maggi sauce, and more.
www.alibaba.com

Penzeys Spices
Shop here for chile peppers (dried and powdered), achiote, *canela* (Ceylon cinnamon), extracts, vanilla beans, and more.
www.penzeys.com

MEASUREMENT CONVERSIONS

U.S. DRY VOLUME MEASUREMENTS

1/16 teaspoon	Dash
1/8 teaspoon	a pinch
3 teaspoons	1 tablespoon
1/8 cup	2 tablespoons (1 standard coffee scoop)
1/4 cup	4 tablespoons
1/3 cup	5 tablespoons plus 1 teaspoon
1/2 cup	8 tablespoons
3/4 cup	12 tablespoons
1 cup	16 tablespoons
1 pound	16 ounces

U.S. LIQUID VOLUME MEASUREMENTS

8 fluid ounces	1 cup
1 pint	2 cups (16 fluid ounces)
1 quart	2 pints (4 cups)
1 gallon	4 quarts (16 cups)

U.S. TO METRIC CONVERSIONS

1/5 teaspoon	1 milliliter (1/1000 liter)
1 teaspoon	5 milliliters
1 tablespoon	15 milliliters
1 fluid ounce	30 milliliters
1/5 cup	50 milliliters
1 cup	240 milliliters
2 cups (1 pint)	470 milliliters
4 cups (1 quart)	.95 liter
4 quarts (1 galllon)	3.8 liters
1 ounce	28 grams
1 pound	454 grams

METRIC TO U.S. CONVERSIONS

1 milliliter	1/5 teaspoon
5 milliliters	1 teaspoon
15 milliliters	1 tablespoon
30 milliliters	1 fluid ounce
100 milliliters	3.4 fluid ounces
240 milliliters	1 cup
1 liter	34 fluid ounces
1 liter	4.2 cups
1 liter	2.1 pints
1 liter	1.06 quarts
1 liter	.26 gallon
1 gram	.035 ounce
100 grams	3.5 ounces
500 grams	1.10 pounds
1 kilogram	2.205 pounds
1 kilogram	35 ounces

OVEN TEMPERATURE CONVERSIONS

F	C	GAS MARK
275°F	140°C	gas mark 1 (cool)
300°F	150°C	gas mark 2
325°F	165°C	gas mark 3 (very moderate)
350°F	180°C	gas mark 4 (moderate)
375°F	190°C	gas mark 5
400°F	200°C	gas mark 6 (moderately hot)
425°F	220°C	gas mark 7 (hot)
450°F	230°C	gas mark 9
475°F	240°C	gas mark 10 (very hot)

ACKNOWLEDGMENTS

A cookbook is a team effort. I want to convey my sincere gratitude to everyone who supported and helped me in the creation of this book.

I thank my husband, Kenn, and son, Jens, for putting up with me while I tested recipes and made them try each one, and for being patient when I neglected the house to stay focused on my project.

I am very grateful to my in-laws, Judy and Bamse Damgaard, for their support of my work. My sincere thanks to my family in Guatemala, especially to my sister, Gilda, and her husband, Miguel Angel, and my nephews, Dany and Max, for their unconditional love and the time and effort they dedicated to me during my book journey. I am truly grateful to my mom for her support of my venture.

Many thanks to family and friends in Guatemala—especially my cousin Silvia and my friends Lotie and Lorena—who graciously invited me to their homes during holidays and celebrations. I fondly remember our fun cooking adventures, and I truly appreciate their hospitality and generosity in sharing their cooking secrets with me.

Thanks to the rest of the team that made this book possible, especially to my publisher, Beaver's Pond Press, for holding my hand throughout the project; to my photographer, Todd Buchanan, for being flexible and easy to work with; to my editor, Christine Zuchora-Walske, for helping me look good on paper; and to my designer, James Monroe, for being so gracious with every request I made.

Thank you, thank you all for helping me realize my dream.

Index

Page numbers in *italics* refer to photographs.

Work with Amalia

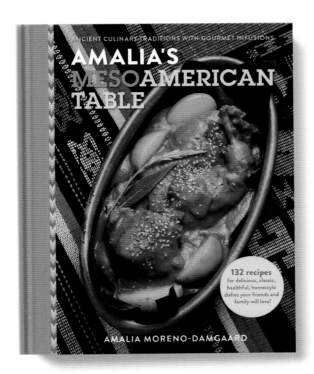

Amalia's Mesoamerican Table: *Ancient Culinary Traditions with Gourmet Infusions*

Amalia's most recent book is a Guatemala-centric sequel to *Amalia's Guatemalan Kitchen: Gourmet Cuisine with a Cultural Flair*, and aims to showcase the wide array of cuisines in the Central American region with close ties to Mexico, still relatively unknown to many. Mesoamerica offers naturally vegan, vegetarian, gluten-free foods, and more. But fully enjoying the dishes of this region isn't possible without understanding how the ancient cultures behind came to be. In *Amalia's Mesoamerican Table*, chef Amalia Moreno-Damgaard uses her signature blend of timeworn culinary traditions with modern infusions to create fresh and healthy recipes sure to entice home cooks and trained chefs alike.

Book Amalia for brand representation, product development, keynote speaking, cooking demonstrations, and other custom culinary experiences. For more information, visit AmaliaLLC.com or contact Amalia@AmaliaLLC.com

Connect with Amalia on:

@amaliamorenodamgaard

@AmaliaLatinGourmet

Amalia Moreno-Damgaard